CONTENTS

CW00675151

ROUTE MAP OF SPAIN inside front co*

ABOUT THIS BOOK 4 – 5

CATALUNYA, THE LEVANT & THE BALEARICS 6 – 39
Tour 1 The Catalan Pyrenees 8 – 13
Tour 2 The Costa Brava 14 – 18
Tour 3 Roman Relics & Golden Beaches 19 – 23
Tour 4 The Costa Blanca 24 – 29
Tour 5 Palm Forests & Rugged Peaks 30 – 33
Tour 6 The Magic of Mallorca 34 – 39

ANDALUCIA 40 – 77
Tour 7 Lunar Landscapes of the South 42 – 47
Tour 8 Spain's Moorish Legacy 48 – 53
Tour 9 The Sun Coast & Medieval Villages 54 – 59
Tour 10 The Great Mosque & Moorish Towns 60 – 65
Tour 11 The Trail of the New World Explorers 66 – 71
Tour 12 The White Towns of Andalucia 72 – 77

ARAGON, NAVARRA & LA RIOJA 78 – 95
Tour 13 The Ancient Kingdom of Aragon 80 – 85
Tour 14 Pyrenean Landscapes of Upper Aragon 86 – 90
Tour 15 Navarra & Wine Country 91 – 95

CENTRAL SPAIN & THE WEST 96 – 131
Tour 16 Art Treasures of Castilla-La Mancha 98 – 103
Tour 17 Traces of Don Quixote 104 – 108
Tour 18 Monuments & Mountains 109 – 113
Tour 19 The Route of the Royal Palaces 114 – 119
Tour 20 Remote Lands of the West 120 – 125
Tour 21 Historical Cities & Cathedrals 126 – 131

GREEN SPAIN 132 – 157
Tour 22 The World of Galicia 134 – 141
Tour 23 The Green Belt of Asturias 142 – 147
Tour 24 Landscapes of Cantabria 148 – 151
Tour 25 Exploring the Basque Country 152 – 157

PRACTICAL INFORMATION 158 – 165

INDEX AND ACKNOWLEDGEMENTS 166 – 168

ABOUT THIS BOOK

This book is not only a practical guide for the independent traveller, but is also invaluable for those who would like to know more about the country.

It is divided into 5 regions, each containing between 3 and 6 tours which start and finish in major towns and cities which we consider to be the best centres for exploration.

Each tour has details of the most interesting places to visit en route. Panels catering for special interests follow some of the main entries – for those whose interest is in history, wildlife or walking, and those who have children. There are also panels which highlight scenic stretches of road along the route and which give details of special events, crafts and customs. The route directions are accompanied by an easy-to-use map at the beginning of each tour, along with a simple chart showing how far it is from one town to the next in kilometres and miles. This can help you to decide where to take a break and stop overnight, for example. (All distances quoted are approximate.)

Before setting off it is advisable to check with the tourist information centre (addresses are given after the symbol $\boxed{i}$ at the end of town entries) at the start of the tour for recommendations on where to break your journey and for additional information on what to see and do, and when best to visit.

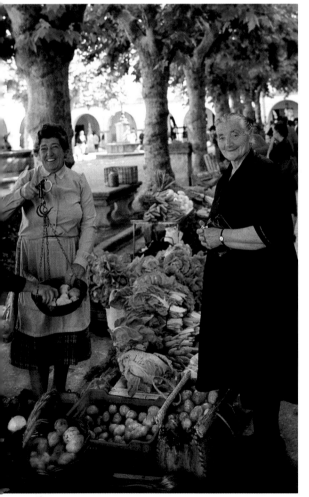

Customs Regulations

Visitors from EU countries can bring in items for their personal use without paying any duty. For cigarettes, cigars and tobacco, wines and spirits and perfume, maximum limits have been established. Customs duties are leviable on amounts exceeding their limits. Remember that wines, spirits and cigarettes are generally cheaper in Spain than in many countries.

Entry Regulations

You require a valid passport to enter Spain. Nationals of EU countries, the USA and Japan do not need a visa for stays of up to 90 days. It is always wise to check the current situation with your Spanish tourist office or consulate.

Emergency Telephone Numbers

Policia Nacional 091
Policia Municipal 092
These 24-hour numbers will not necessarily connect you with the nearest station but will get your message relayed. Describe the nature of the emergency (*urgencia*), your location and the services required.
Bomberos (Fire) 080
Medical Emergencies 061
Madrid: Ambulance Red Cross (Cruz Roja) 522 2222
Barcelona: Ambulance Red Cross (Cruz Roja) 300 2020

Health

Residents of EU countries are entitled to some free medical treatment if they produce form E111 or the relevant form from their country (obtain this before departure). However it is wise to buy a comprehensive travel insurance policy from a reputable company which provides full cover in case of accident or illness.

Currency

The peseta is available in the following denominations: notes – 1,000, 2,000, 5,000, 10,000; coins – 1, 5, 10, 25, 50, 100, 200, 500.

Credit Cards

Major credit cards are widely accepted. Cash can be obtained from banks and certain cash dispensers. Make a note of your credit card numbers and emergency telephone numbers in case of loss. Tell the company immediately if one of your cards is stolen or lost.

Banks

Savings banks, mostly offering exchange facilities, are called *cajas* (open: Monday to Thursday 8.30am–4.30pm, Friday 8.30am–2pm, Saturday (main branches only) 8.30am–1pm. June to September: Monday to Friday 8.30am–2pm, closed Saturday. Exchange facilities are available outside these hours at airports.

Time

Spain is two hours ahead of GMT in the summer and one hour ahead in the winter.

Post Offices

Post offices are generally open Mon to Sat 9am to 2pm. Mail can be sent addressed to you at Lista de Correos. Take personal identification when collecting. Post boxes are yellow and some have different sections for different destinations. *Sellos* (stamps) can be bought at *estancos* (tobacconists).

Telephones

International access codes are as follows: to call Spain from Australia, dial 00 11; Canada 011; New Zealand 00; UK 00; US 011. Country codes are: Australia 61; Canada 1; New Zealand 64; UK 44; US 1. Public phone booths are plentiful. They take 500, 200, 100, 50, 25, 10 and 5 peseta coins and some accept credit cards.

Public Holidays

1 January – Año Nuevo
6 January – Día de los Reyes (Epiphany)
Good Friday – Viernes Santo
1 May – Día del Trabajo (May Day)
15 August – Asunción
12 October – Día de la Hispanidad
1 November – Todos los Santos (All Saints' Day)
6 December – Constitucíon
8 December – Immaculada Concepción
25 December – Navidad (Christmas Day)

Route Directions

Throughout the book the following abbreviations are used for Spanish roads:
A – Autopista
C – Comarcal
N – Nacional

Electricity

220/225 volts AC and 110/125 in some bathrooms and older buildings. Spanish plugs have two round pins, so you will need an adaptor.

Seat Belts

Seat belts are compulsory for the driver and front-seat passenger. Middle- and rear-seat passengers must use seat belts if the vehicle is fitted with them.

Tourist Offices

Spanish National Tourist Offices:
Australia: 203 Castlereagh Street, Suite 21a, POBOXA-685, Sydney, NSW 2000.
Canada: 102 Bloor Street West, 14th Floor, Toronto.

UK: 57–8 St James's Street, London SW1A 1LD.
US: 665 Fifth Avenue, New York 10022; 8383 Wilshire Bvd, Suite 960, Beverly Hills, California 90211.

Embassies

Australia: Paseo de la Castellana 143, 28046 Madrid tel: 91 2798504.
Canada: Edificio Goya Calle Nuñez de Balboa 35, Madrid tel: 91 4314300.
UK: Calle de Fernando el Santo 16, Madrid 4 tel: 91 3190200.
US: Serrano 75, 28006 Madrid tel: 91 5774000.

Useful Words

The following words and phrases may be helpful.
English *Spanish*
hello *hola*
goodbye *adiós*
good morning *buenos días*
good afternoon *buenos tardes*
good evening and goodnight *buenas noches*
do you speak English? *¿habla usted inglés?*
yes/no *sí/no*
please *por favor*
excuse me, I don't understand *perdón, no entiendo*
could you please speak more slowly? *¿podría hablar más despacio, por favor?*
thank you (very much) *(muchas) gracias*
I am/my name is … *soy/me llamo*
what is your name? *¿como se llama usted?*
how are you? *¿como está?*
very well *muy bien*
where is … ? *¿dónde está …?*
open/closed *abierto/cerrado*
I would like … *me gustaría …*
do you have … ? *¿tiene … ?*
how much is … ? *¿cuánto es/vale/cuesta … ?*
1 to 10 *uno, dos, tres, cuatro, cinco, seis, siete, ocho, nueve, diez*

Drinking and Driving

The limit on drinking for drivers is 0.8g per 1,000cc. Drivers must submit to an alcohol test when requested by the authorities.

CATALUNYA, THE LEVANT & THE BALEARICS

This region has a variety of panoramas, but features like the long sweep of Mediterranean coastline and the common language bind it together. It includes three of Spain's best-known tourist areas – the Costa Brava, the Costa Blanca and Mallorca.

The capital of Catalunya is Barcelona, a thriving commercial centre. To the north are the eastern Pyrenees, which separate the Iberian peninsula from the rest of Europe. This is a sparsely populated area dominated by rugged mountains and green valleys irrigated by the rivers Ter, Llobegrat and Segre, together with tributaries of the Ebro. To the east, the rugged coastline of the Costa Brava features high cliffs, rocky coves and sandy beaches.

The Levant, including the Valencia region, famous for rice-growing, extends to the palm groves south of Alicante. The coast flattens out into long stretches of sandy beaches broken up by rocky promontories. This is the region of the *huertas*, fertile cultivated lands, irrigated by water from the Turia and Jacar rivers, that produce a rich harvest of oranges, lemons, olives vegetables and flowers. Inland, in the south lie desolate, lunar-like landscapes.

Opposite the Levant lies Mallorca, the largest of the Balearic Islands. Between the Sierra de Tramuntana in the west and the gentle slopes of the Sierra de Levante in the east is a plain of orchards, fields and wind mills. Known for the beauty of its coast, pinewoods and olive groves, the island is at its best in spring when the almond blossom is out.

Numerous invasions and occupations have shaped the culture. Phoenicians, Greeks, Carthaginian Romans and Moors have all played their part and left testimonies to their presence.

The official language is Catalá. Following periods of suppression it is again widely spoken in Catalunya and street names and place names are written in Catalá. A similar dialect is spoken in Valencia as a result of its conquest in the 13th century by King Jaime I of Catalunya. Mallorca has its own version known as Mallorquín.

Sunflowers throw back the light of the sun all over Spain

Tour 1

Scenery is the emphasis of this itinerary, which takes you into the heartland of the eastern Pyrenees. This provides wonderfully varied landscapes, from mighty mountain ranges to green valleys, rivers and lakes. Along the route are little Pyrenean towns and castles dating back to medieval or even Roman times, along with churches built in the typical Catalan Romanesque style. A highlight is undoubtedly the visit to Spain's most sacred sanctuary in the spectacular setting of the great Montserrat massif.

Tour 2

The once desolate Costa Brava (wild coast) has long since become one of Spain's most popular holiday areas. Parts are still very attractive, however, with picturesque little fishing villages set in sandy coves surrounded by pine-clad hills. The drive offers stretches of stunning beauty, as steep cliffs drop sharply into the sea. The vivid blues and greens of the Mediterranean and purple shades of the mountains,

coupled with the fragrance of the pines, are a part of its attraction. Visits to ancient Greek and Roman ruins, inland towns and a beautiful old monastery provide cultural interest.

Tour 3

The first part of the journey takes you down the Costa Dorada (golden coast), named for its splendid sandy beaches. The route passes through attractive scenery, where stretches of twisting hair-pin bends give way to more relaxed driving through rolling hills and valleys. Along the way there are picturesque resorts, old towns and one of Spain's greatest Roman cities. Travelling inland along part of the old Cistercian Route, the tour visits three beautiful monasteries in lovely surroundings.

Tour 4

The route begins with Valencia and continues along part of the Costa Blanca (white coast), known for its beaches of fine white sand, holiday resorts and mild winter climate. Dramatic rock formations provide impressive landscapes along the route.

The coast of Mallorca near the charming mountain village of Deia

Inland is a sharp contrast in scenery and interest, with several fascinating old towns.

Tour 5

A visit to a unique palm forest is followed by a drive down Spain's southeastern coast, where the Costa Blanca leads to the Costa Calida (warm coast). The tour combines wild, rugged mountain scenery inland with beautiful stretches of coastal road. The area of the Mar Menor, with its large saltwater lagoon and new tourist development, is an interesting part of the country.

Tour 6

There are two Mallorcas: that of mass tourism, and the Mallorca of fine mountain scenery, almond trees and olive groves. This tour visits some of its best features: monasteries, Roman remains, spectacular caves and picturesque fishing villages. There are beautiful stretches of coastline, with rocky coves and sandy beaches, the essence of this very Mediterranean island.

The Catalan
Pyrenees

Barcelona is the capital of Catalunya and Spain's second city and principal port. Its medieval past lives on in the old Barri Gòtic, while the elegance of the 19th century, shown in the Plaça Reial, contrasts with the unique flamboyance of Gaudí-designed buildings.

2/3 DAYS • 536KM • 332 MILES

ITINERARY

BARCELONA	▷ Montserrat (50km-31m)
MONTSERRAT	▷ Cardona (52km-32m)
CARDONA	▷ Solsona (20km-12m)
SOLSONA	▷ La Seu d'Urgell (76km-47m)
LA SEU D'URGELL	▷ Puigcerdà (48km-30m)
PUIGCERDÀ	▷ Ribes de Freser (49km-30m)
RIBES DE FRESER	▷ Ripoll (14km-9m)
RIPOLL	▷ Sant Joan de les Abadesses (10km-6m)
SANT JOAN DE LES ABADESSES	▷ Camprodon (14km-9m)
CAMPRODON	▷ Olot (30km-19m)
OLOT	▷ Vic (64km-40m)
VIC	▷ Santa Fé del Montseny
SANTA FÉ DEL MONTSENY	▷ Barcelona (65km-40m)

[i] *Gran Via de les Corts
Catalanes 658*

▶ *From Barcelona, take the A2
towards Lleida/Lérida. Leave
at junction 22 near Martorell
for the NII, travelling northwest, and after a few kilometres turn right on to the
C1411 towards Manresa. At
Monistrol village follow the
road up the mountain to the
monastery car park.*

❶ Montserrat, Barcelona
Set among wild rock formations
and jagged peaks is the
Monestir de Montserrat, which
contains Catalunya's most
sacred sanctuary. Vast numbers
of pilgrims gather each year to
venerate the Black Virgin,
patron of Catalunya, who is
kept here. The origins of the

RECOMMENDED WALKS

Montserrat has several short
walks in stunning scenery to
places such as Sant Miquel and
Sant Joan.

---

*The monastery of Montserrat,
spectacularly set high up in the
Montserrat mountains*

monastery, one of Spain's major
tourist attractions, centre on the
legend of the miracle-working
statue of the Virgin, supposedly
found in a cave near by in 880.
A chapel dedicated to her was
erected, and in 976 monks of
the Benedictine order founded
a monastery that steadily grew
in size and importance.

The church was rebuilt by
Philip II, who greatly favoured
the place. The monastery was

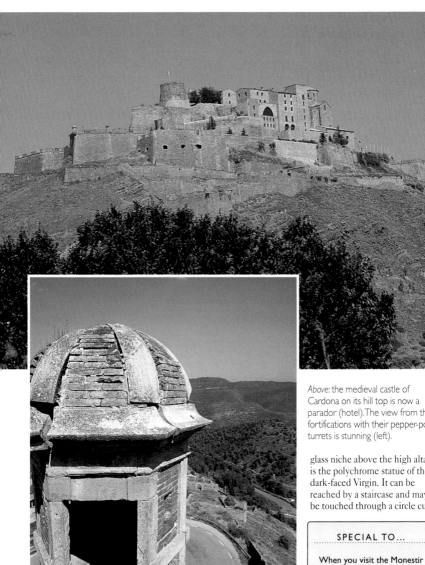

Above: the medieval castle of Cardona on its hill top is now a parador (hotel). The view from the fortifications with their pepper-pot turrets is stunning (left).

glass niche above the high altar is the polychrome statue of the dark-faced Virgin. It can be reached by a staircase and may be touched through a circle cut

SPECIAL TO...
....

When you visit the Monestir de Montserrat, it is worth making the effort to hear the Escolania. This is one of the oldest boys' choirs in Europe, dating back to the 13th century. The boys are brought up in the monastery and receive a religious education. The singing is dedicated to the Virgin of Montserrat. The choir performs daily at 1pm and sometimes at 6.45pm (except for July and Christmas).

fortified by the Catalans during the Peninsular Wars, but in 1812 it was sacked by the French, with the result that most of the present structure is from the 19th century, with some parts completed only after World War II. Before entering the monastery, stop for a moment on the observation platform to have a look at the dramatic surroundings. The most important part of the building is the Basilíca, built between 1560 and 1592 in the Renaissance style, and restored in the last century. The interior is a vast dark area lit by a mass of tiny lights. In a

FOR HISTORY BUFFS

The legend of the Black Madonna of Montserrat runs very deep in Spain. Her image was supposedly brought from Barcelona in AD50 by St Peter and hidden in a cave. The statue was found later by shepherds, who decided to transport it to Manresa. Upon reaching the site where the monastery now stands, the Lady appeared reluctant to proceed further. A chapel was erected in her honour, and this developed into the monastery. From Montserrat a short trip down the mountain by funicular, followed by a half-hour walk beneath the cliff brings you to the Santa Cova (sacred cave) where the statue is said to have been discovered.

in the glass. The library contains an impressive collection of books, and there are several museums.

A short ride by funicular takes you on an awe-inspiring journey to the Sant Joan ridge, where an observation terrace affords spectacular views of the great Montserrat massif.

> Rejoin C1411 and continue north to Manresa. Turn left on to the C1410 and continue northwest to Cardona.

2 Cardona, Barcelona

A final turn in the road reveals the magnificent sight of the old medieval castle of Cardona. Rising from a great brown rock cone, it looms over the little village below. The castle is made up of a group of buildings that were constructed between the 10th and 19th centuries. It once served to protect the salt mines of the Cardona family. In the castle you can visit the church and crypt, which have been well preserved. The views from here are magnificent.

> Continue on the C1410 for 20km (12 miles) to Solsona.

3 Solsona, Lleida/Lérida

Solsona is a picturesque little town with quaint streets, old houses and the remnants of medieval ramparts. There are ruins of a 12th- to 13th-century castle at the top of the hill. Near the bridge is the cathedral. Erected in the 12th century and rebuilt between the 14th and 15th centuries, it shows a combination of Romanesque and Gothic styles. The Diocesan Museum in the Palau Episcopal has a good collection of paintings, frescos and fine altar-fronts, while the exhibits in the salt museum are fashioned out of blocks of salt from Cardona.

> Follow the C1410 west. At Bassella take the C1313 north to La Seu d'Urgell (Seo de Urgel).

4 La Seu d'Urgell, Lleida/Lérida

Serving as a natural gateway to the tiny republic of Andorra, La Seu d'Urgell lies in a typical Pyrenean valley, surrounded by high wooded mountains. It is the centre of a bishopric and has a fine Romanesque cathedral dating back to the 12th century, with later additions. The Diocesan Museum has an interesting display of religious art. Other buildings of note are the 11th-century Romanesque Chapel of Sant Miguel and the 15th-century Casa de la Ciutat, built in Gothic style.

> [i] Avenida Valira

> Continue east on the N260 to Puigcerdá.

5 Puigcerdà, Girona/Gerona

Puigcerdà has a cosmopolitan atmosphere typical of border towns. It is attractively situated on a hilltop overlooking the Cerdanya, a district that is split between Spain and France. A bridge connects the town to Bourg-Madame in France. The main buildings of interest are the 15th-century Ajuntament, the 13th-century church of Sant

FOR CHILDREN

Children are likely to enjoy a delightful train journey in the little yellow train (le petit train jaune). This departs daily from La Tor de Querol or Bourg-Madame, which is within walking distance of Puigcerdà, and chugs through the Cerdanya region to the old walled town of Vilafranca de Conflent, in France. The train is something out of a fairy-tale and is popular with children.

Doménec and the church of Santa Maria, which is also 13th century. The town is a pleasant place to explore, with its lively main square, busy little streets and pretty houses with balconies. The boating lake to the north is a favourite resort, both in summer and winter. You can take a short side trip to Llívia, about 5km (3 miles) northeast. This little medieval town is a Spanish enclave within France and has a small museum displaying items from its pharmacy, apparently one of the earliest in Europe.

> [i] Querol

> Take the N152 east for 49km (30 miles) to Ribes de Freser.

BACK TO NATURE

The National Park of Cadí Moixero is home to many species of plants and animals. You might well spot red deer and roe deer, or a golden eagle soaring above you. The chamois lives here, venturing down the lower slopes only in winter. The area has an enormous variety of plants, which include rare species of buttercups, poppies and countless others. Trees, too, flourish here; you will see magnificent oaks and beeches, silver fir, maple trees and pine forests.

6 Ribes de Freser,
Girona/Gerona

This popular resort lies on the River Freser in an attractive setting of green forests. It is the starting point for a funicular ride up to Núria. The journey takes about 45 minutes and passes through mountains and pine forests. The Núria Sanctuary is a famous pilgrimage centre and the place is also a popular winter sports resort.

ⓘ *Plaça de l'Ajuntament 3*

▶ *Continue south for 14km (9 miles) on the N152 to Ripoll.*

7 Ripoll, Girona/Gerona

Although the town is essentially industrial, stop here to visit the Benedictine Monestir de Santa María which stands in the square. Founded in the 9th century, it was subsequently destroyed – first by an earthquake, then by fire – and later restored. It has a richly carved Romanesque door and a cloister with a fine collection of capitals depicting religious scenes.

ⓘ Plaça Abat Oliba

▶ *Take the C151 northeast to Sant Joan de les Abadesses (San Juan de las Abadesas).*

8 Sant Joan de les Abadesses, Girona/Gerona

As you arrive you will see the lovely 12th-century bridge over the River Ter. In the centre of the town stands the magnificent Abbey of Sant Joan. It was founded in the 9th century and belonged originally to the Benedictines. During the course of time it suffered severe damage and had to be rebuilt several times. The impressive Romanesque church and the magnificent Gothic cloister are fine examples of the architecture of these periods. In the central apse above the high altar is a beautiful 13th-century carving in wood of the Descent from the Cross.

ⓘ *Rambla Comte Guifré 15*

▶ *Take the C151 north for 14km (9 miles) to Camprodon.*

9 Camprodon,
Girona/Gerona

Camprodon lies in the heart of the Pyrenees, surrounded by mountains and woods. Attractive houses with red-tiled roofs and balconies look down on narrow, winding streets and squares. A familiar sight is the lovely 16th-century arched bridge that spans the river. Buildings of special interest include the Romanesque Monestir de Sant Pere (St Peter's), the parish church and the Ajuntament (town hall). Many Spanish families come to Camprodon in the summer to enjoy the healthy mountain air and good walking in beautiful surroundings.

ⓘ *Plaça d'Espanya*

▶ *Return south, join the C153 and continue southeast to Olot.*

10 Olot, Girona/Gerona

Olot is famed for the painted and carved figures that are used for the Nativity performances. The town is primarily industrial, but has several museums worth visiting. These include the Museum of Modern Art (a collection of 19th- and 20th-century paintings by Catalan artists), the Museu de la Casa Trinxeria (mainly furniture and interiors of the 17th to 19th

centuries), a modest museum with items of religious art from the 18th-century Iglesia de Sant Esteve and the Museu Garrotxa, which has a display of local fossils.

The town is in a volcanic region and evidence of old craters still remain, although they are mostly covered by vegetation. A detour of some 7km (4 miles) east along the C150 will take you to the black basalt village of Castellfollit de la Roca, which is perched on a clifftop looking over the River Fluvià.

ⓘ *Mulleres 53*

▶ *Take the C152, turning right on to the C153 south for 64km (40 miles) to Vic (Vich).*

> **RECOMMENDED WALKS**
>
> There is a lovely walk from Olot that takes you through the magnificent Fageda d'en Jordà beech forest to the large crater of the Volcà de Santa Margarida (Santa Margarita volcano). Another route from Olot follows the River Fluvià down the Vall d'En Bas, passing through several charming villages.

11 Vic, Girona/Gerona

The old episcopal town of Vic lies at the confluence of the rivers Méder and Gurri. Its two main attractions are the Plaça Major (main square) and the cathedral, which is situated on the edge of town. Founded in the 11th century and restored in the 18th, it features a handsome Romanesque bell-tower. Inside, look out for the richly ornate 15th-century marble altar and the elegant cloister, which is graced by a splendid monument to Jaime Balmes, counsellor to Pope Pius IX. The adjoining Museu Episcopal has an impressive collection of Romanesque art, works from the Gothic period and Roman relics.

The heart of the old town is the large and lively Plaça Major,

Wall paintings by Sert of the Stations of the Cross in the 18th century cathedral at Vic

which is lined with arcades and handsome buildings. This central square is surrounded by an area of narrow streets, winding alleys and little hidden squares. Amongst them you will find the Casa Consistorial (town hall), a fine building of Gothic origin, with more recent additions. Near by are the remains of a Roman temple dating back to the 2nd or 3rd century AD, and medieval walls.

> ℹ️ *Ciutat I*

> ▶ *Take the N152 south. At Tona take unclassified roads southeast to Santa Fé del Montseny.*

12 Santa Fe del Montseny

The Sierra del Montseny is a magnificent range of mountains luxuriantly covered by green forests. There are several routes through the Sierra that you could take on your homeward journey, all passing through attractive country. The suggested drive takes you through some exceptionally beautiful scenery to the Ermita de Santa Fe del Montseny, which stands at an altitude of 1,100m (3,610 feet) and offers wonderful views of the area. The tiny village here provides an excellent base for mountaineering in the area, or for those who want to walk.

> ▶ *Continue southeast and then return to Barcelona on the A7.*

The Costa
Brava

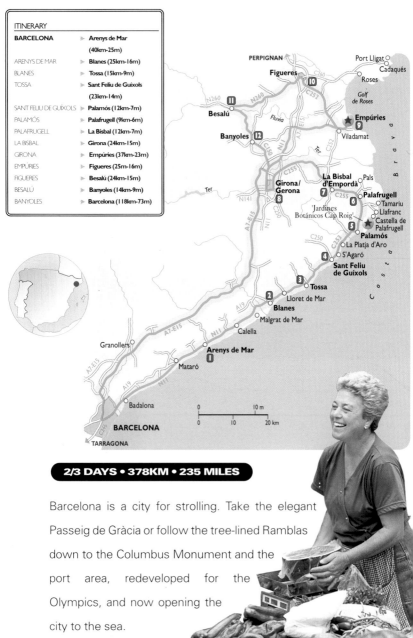

ITINERARY

BARCELONA	▶	**Arenys de Mar** (40km-25m)
ARENYS DE MAR	▶	**Blanes** (25km-16m)
BLANES	▶	**Tossa** (15km-9m)
TOSSA	▶	**Sant Feliu de Guíxols** (23km-14m)
SANT FELIU DE GUÍXOLS	▶	**Palamós** (12km-7m)
PALAMÓS	▶	**Palafrugell** (9km-6m)
PALAFRUGELL	▶	**La Bisbal** (12km-7m)
LA BISBAL	▶	**Girona** (24km-15m)
GIRONA	▶	**Empúries** (37km-23m)
EMPÚRIES	▶	**Figueres** (25km-16m)
FIGUERES	▶	**Besalú** (24km-15m)
BESALÚ	▶	**Banyoles** (14km-9m)
BANYOLES	▶	**Barcelona** (118km-73m)

2/3 DAYS • 378KM • 235 MILES

Barcelona is a city for strolling. Take the elegant Passeig de Gràcia or follow the tree-lined Ramblas down to the Columbus Monument and the port area, redeveloped for the Olympics, and now opening the city to the sea.

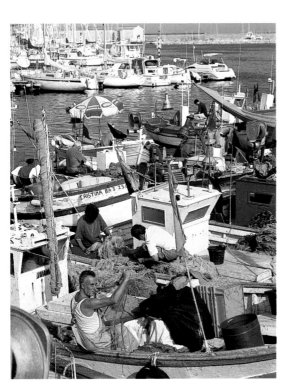

Despite the yachts and the holiday-makers, fishermen still ply their trade from Arenys de Mar

fountain in the main square. Further up, the Church of Santa Maria looks down on the roof-tops. A climb up to the top of the Sa Palomera southwest of the harbour provides a good view of the sandy bay of Blanes.

i *Plaça Catalunya*

▶ *Follow the road through Lloret de Mar to Tossa*

3 Tossa, Girona/Gerona
Tossa was called 'The Blue Paradise' by the French artist, Marc Chagall, who produced many paintings of the town in the 1930s. Some of his works are exhibited in the Museu de la Vila Vela, along with other paintings and a mosaic from the Roman settlement here. This is located in the old town, with its narrow streets and medieval houses contained within massive walls, and turrets from the 12th century. There is a splendid view from the light-house, which is situated on the highest point of the town.

i *Avenida Pelegrí 25, Ed Terminal*

---

i *Gran Vía de les Corts Catalanes 658*

▶ *Leave Barcelona from the Plaça Glòries Catalanes and take the A19 coast road east. Turn right at Badalona and join the NII through Mataró to Arenys de Mar.*

1 Arenys de Mar,
Girona/Gerona
The main attractions in Arenys are its pretty little port and its reputation for excellent seafood. The fishing harbour is fun to explore and is full of activity when the catch comes in. The large marina is now an interna-tional regatta centre.

The Church of Santa María (begun in 1584 by the French) is worth a visit to see the mag-nificent 18th-century retable (decorated panels above the altar) by the artist Pablo Costa.

Arenys has a long tradi-tion of white bobbin lace-making and although this is

gradually dying out, you may still see some of the local women, known as *puntaires*, sitting out on their doorsteps practising their ancient skills.

▶ *Continue on the NII coastal road. At Malgrat branch off northeast to Blanes.*

2 Blanes, Girona/Gerona
Blanes is a popular resort in an attractive setting. After explor-ing the harbour you can stroll along the promenade to the old town which has a lovely Gothic

> **BACK TO NATURE**
> ....
> Just beyond the harbour of Blanes is the Botanical Garden of Marimurtra (sea and myrtle), where you will find hundreds of species of plants, largely from the Mediterranean area. The garden is beautifully laid out on an original design by the German Karl Faust.

> **SCENIC ROUTES**
> ....
> The stretch between Tossa and Sant Feliu is particularly beauti-ful. Its tortuous bends take you high over mountain tops and down among the pine forests, with magnificent views of cliffs. The stretch between Besalú and Banyoles on the C150 also offers some splendid mountain scenery.

▶ *Continue northeast to Sant Feliu de Guíxols.*

4 Sant Feliu de Guíxols,
Girona/Gerona
This large, cheerful town is considered to be the capital of the Costa Brava. Its busy port and lack of a good, sandy beach

gives it a different ambience to some of its neighbours. The 11th-century Porta Ferrada (iron gate) and the adjoining church are the remains of a Benedictine monastery.

The Ermita de Sant Elm, on the outskirts of town, offers a splendid view of the coast.

[i] *Plaça Monestir 54*

▶ *Take the C253 to Palamós.*

5 Palamós, Girona/Gerona
Palamós's main attractions are its beautiful setting in a wide

curved bay and its lively port and yacht harbour. A major fishing centre, it is one of the most important towns in the region. Colourful fish auctions take place in a hall called the Lonja.

In the old part of the town is the 14th-century Gothic Church of Santa María amidst the original narrow streets.

[i] *Passeig del Mar s/n*

▶ *Take the C255 inland for 9km (6 miles) to Palafrugell.*

6 Palafrugell,
Girona/Gerona
Palafrugell is a busy commercial and shopping town. A few remains of Moorish walls can be seen and there is the little Gothic Church of San Martín. This is a good spot for a detour to some of the Costa's most delightful resorts. A short drive

through pine woods leads to Tamariu and another road takes you to the resorts of Castell de Palafrugell and Llafranc. There is a stunning view of the bays from the lighthouse below the Ermita de Sant Sebastián poised on the hill.

[i] *Carrilet 2*

▶ *Continue northwest on the C255 for 12km (7 miles) to La Bisbal d'Empordà.*

FOR CHILDREN

Children might enjoy a visit to the Museum of Underwater Archaeology, in the village of Pals, north of Palafrugell.

BACK TO NATURE

To the south of Castell de Palafrugell lies the lovely Jardí Botànic de Cap Roig (Botanical Garden), which features rare plants and Mediterranean shrubs and offers splendid views of the rocky bays.

The Costa Brava

The River Onar runs through the city of Girona

brown and yellow. While here, visit the large 14th-century Romanesque castle, once the seat of the ruling Bishops of La Bisbal d'Empordà, the parish church and the old bridge.

ⓘ *Plaça del Castell*

▶ *Continue west to Girona.*

8 Girona, Girona/Gerona
Founded by the Iberians, Girona was occupied by the Romans, the Moors, and retaken by Charlemagne in 785, later to form part of the kingdom of Catalunya and Aragon. The River Onar separates the new town from the old, which is located on the east bank and best explored on foot.

The old town is a step right back into the Middle Ages. You find yourself among dark, secretive streets, picturesque houses and hidden squares. The cathedral appears unexpectedly, rising majestically from a flight of steps. This impressive building, one of the finest cathedrals in Catalunya, dates back to the 14th century. The huge 12th-century embroidered 'Tapestry of the Creation' is a unique exhibit among many treasures in the museum. The adjoining 12th-century cloister is noted for its carved capitals. Other historic buildings are the former Iglesia Colegiata de Sant Feliu, with its tall tower, the old Episcopal Palace which is now the Art Museum and the 12th-century Banys Arabs (Arab Baths). Interesting by day, the floodlit old town is magical by night.

Pleasant areas in the new town are the Plaça de la Independencia, surrounded by attractive arcades, and the Parque de la Dehesa.

ⓘ *Rambla de la Llibertat 1*

▶ *Take the NII north and after 21km (13 miles) make a right turn to Empúries*

FOR HISTORY BUFFS

The name 'City of a Thousand Sieges' may be something of an exaggeration, but Girona did spend long periods under siege over the years. In that of 1809 a large force of Napoleon's troops was kept at bay for some six months by the citizens of the town, including a battalion of women and a few English volunteers.

The remains of the Roman town at Empúries, overlooking Roses Bay

9 Empúries, Girona/Gerona
This impressive archaeological site is one of the most important in Spain and has both Greek and Roman ruins. It was originally founded by the Greeks in the 6th century BC and known as 'Emporion' which means market. The place flourished and produced coins which were used in the region. In the 2nd century BC the Romans arrived to fight the Carthaginians, and built on to the existing town. Some of the most valuable pieces that have been excavated from the site can be seen in the Archaeological Museum in Barcelona. Empúries (Ampurias) became a bishopric under the Visigoths, but was destroyed during the conflicts with the Moors. The museum

RECOMMENDED WALKS

One very attractive walk is along the 'Avinguda de Mar', a cliff path that links the two pretty little resorts of Calella de Palafrugell and Llafranc .The route has beautiful views over each of the bays in turn.

7 La Bisbal d'Empordà, Girona/Gerona
La Bisbal dEmpordà is renowned for ceramics and has an Escola de Ceràmica (School of Ceramics). The tradition goes back to the Middle Ages, and contemporary work has been influenced by the designs of the Arabs, French and Italians. The pottery is to be seen all over the town and is recognisable by its dominant colours of green,

The fortifications on the medieval bridge, gateway to Besalú

has a collection of archaeological finds from the area, along with reconstructions of Greek and Roman life.

A detour northeast to the coast takes you to the delightful whitewashed village of Cadaqués and nearby Portlligat, where Salvador Dalí lived for many years.

▶ *Return to Viladamat and then take the C252 northwest to Figueres (Figueras).*

10 Figueres, Girona/Gerona
Figueres is a major town of the Empurdà region. Buildings of historical interest include the 14th-century Church of Sant Pere, with a fine Romanesque tower, and the Castell de Sant Fernand, an impressive 18th-century fortress. The exhibits in the Museu l'Empordà, on the town's tree-lined Rambla, include items from Empúries.

FOR CHILDREN

The Toy Museum in Figueres has a large collection of dolls from different countries and periods of history.

The real interest in Figueres, however, is the great Salvador Dalí, surrealist artist and eccentric, who was born here in 1904. The Museu Dalí (Dalí Museum) is a feature of the town with its distinctive glass domes. Here you can see some of Dalí's works presented in the most exciting and imaginative way. Whatever your feelings about his work, you should not miss this museum.

[i] *Plaça del Sol*

▶ *Take the C260 southwest for 24km (15 miles) to Besalú.*

11 Besalú, Girona/Gerona
A splendid old fortified bridge over the River Fluvià serves as the main entrance to the ancient town of Besalú. Once capital of the Garrotxa region, the town is a medieval treasure, with its narrow streets and old houses. Handsome buildings surround the Plaça Major, which is lined with attractive doorways. The massive Monestir de Sant Pere and the churches of Sant Vicenç and Santa Maria, are all from the 12th century.

[i] *Plaça Llibertat*

▶ *Take the C150 southeast to Banyoles (Bañolas).*

12 Banyoles, Girona/Gerona
The lakeside town of Banyoles is a popular summer resort. The lake has a good beach, offering facilities for bathing and watersports. On the Plaça del Font (Fountain Square) is the Museu Arqueologic which displays antiquities from the area. In the 10th-century Church of Sant Esteve (St Stephen), later rebuilt in the classical style, is a 15th-century retable, the work of the stone mason, Joan Antigo.

[i] *Passeig Indústria 25*

▶ *Continue on the C150, then join the A7 back to Barcelona.*

SPECIAL TO...

The sardana is an important part of Catalan folklore. The dance's origins are not clear, but it is thought to have roots in the Cerdanya region. It is danced all over Catalunya, at weekends or on festival days. Anyone may take part (but do try to learn some of the steps before joining in). The participants join hands and dance in a constantly moving circle to the accompaniment of the local *cobla* (band).

Roman Relics &
Golden Beaches

Barcelona's hills, Monjuïc and Tibidabo, are great places for entertainment. Museums, from modern art to archaeology, and the Olympic Stadium are on Montjuïc with the old fishermen's quarters below, now rejuvenated. Tibidabo has a funfair and stunning panoramic views. Between lies the amazing Gaudí creation of Parc Güell.

2/3 DAYS • 597KM • 373 MILES

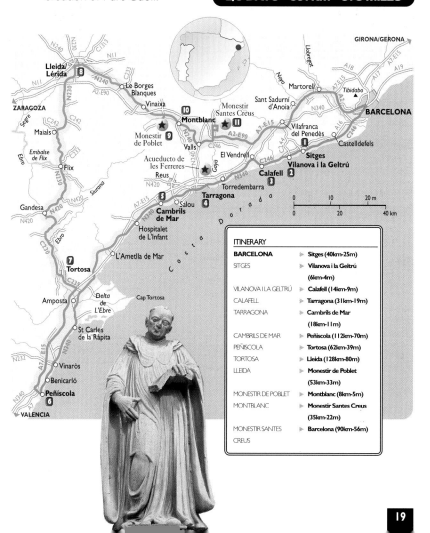

ITINERARY

BARCELONA	▶ **Sitges (40km-25m)**
SITGES	▶ **Vilanova i la Geltrú (6km-4m)**
VILANOVA I LA GELTRÚ	▶ **Calafell (14km-9m)**
CALAFELL	▶ **Tarragona (31km-19m)**
TARRAGONA	▶ **Cambrils de Mar (18km-11m)**
CAMBRILS DE MAR	▶ **Peñiscola (112km-70m)**
PEÑISCOLA	▶ **Tortosa (62km-39m)**
TORTOSA	▶ **Lleida (128km-80m)**
LLEIDA	▶ **Monestir de Poblet (53km-33m)**
MONESTIR DE POBLET	▶ **Montblanc (8km-5m)**
MONTBLANC	▶ **Monestir Santes Creus (35km-22m)**
MONESTIR SANTES CREUS	▶ **Barcelona (90km-56m)**

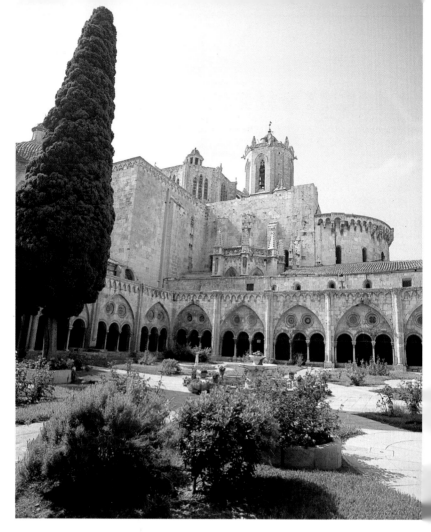

The cathedral at Tarragona, built over a period of time in a mixture of Romanesque and Gothic styles.

i Gran Via de les Corts Catalanes 658

▶ Leave Barcelona from the Plaça Espanya and take the C246 southwest to Sitges.

SPECIAL TO...

Penedès, southwest of Barcelona, is a major wine area, with production ranging from sparkling wines (*cavas*) to fine wines and liqueurs. It is known for its wines of high alcoholic content. On your return to Barcelona you might go via Vilafranca del Penedès and visit the Royal Palace and the wine museum which presents a history of wine.

❶ Sitges, Barcelona

Sitges is a traditional resort that lured Spanish families long before it became an international tourist centre. As well as its splendid sandy beach and shallow waters, Sitges is a picturesque little town with great charm. The local church, with its rose-coloured façade, adds to the picture. The Cap Ferrat Museum, once home of the painter Santiago Rusinyol (1861–1931), houses a collection of his paintings, together with works by El Greco, Picasso, Utrillo and others.

i Passeig Vilafranca

▶ Take a minor road southwest for 6km (4 miles) to Vilanova i la Geltrú (Vilanueva y Geltrú).

FOR CHILDREN

In Sitges, the museum in Casa Llopis displays the Lola Anglada Collection, an exhibition of European dolls from the 17th to 19th centuries.

❷ Vilanova i la Geltrú, Barcelona

This is an industrial town and a resort, with a fine sandy beach and picturesque fishing harbour. It has three museums of interest: the Casa Papiol, or Museu Romantic, which is devoted to life in the early

1800s; the Museu Balaguer, with a collection of antiquities and paintings; and the restored mansion, Castell de la Geltrú, where there are religious relics and ceramics from Catalunya.

i Parc de la Florida

▶ *Continue down the C246 coast road to Calafell.*

2 Calafell, Barcelona
The small fishing village of Calafell is another favourite summer resort with a long sandy beach, suitable for a quiet stop and a look at the Romanesque parish church and the ruins of the 12th-century castle.

▶ *Continue on the C246 to El Vendrell and join the N340 to Tarragona.*

4 Tarragona, Tarragona
The route passes through El Vendrell, the birthplace of the famous Spanish cellist, Pablo Casals (1876–1973).

A lovely Roman town, Tarragona was founded by Publius Cornelius Scipio during the Second Punic War of 218 BC. A stroll along the attractive tree-

The well-preserved Roman Aqueduct near Tarragona

lined Rambla Nova leads to the observation platform 'Balcó del Mediterrani', which offers a sweeping view of the coast. Below is the harbour and the Parc del Miracle, where you can see the remnants of a 2nd- or 3rd-century BC Roman amphitheatre, once the venue for combats between man and beast. The Museu Arqueologic has mosaics, ceramics and antiquities from the region. A climb from the centre of town takes you to the cathedral, which was built between the 12th and 14th centuries. It shows a harmonious blending of Romanesque and Gothic styles, with a fine façade and lovely rose window in the centre. The Passeig Arqueologic is a pleasant shaded walk along the foot of the massive city ramparts, which extend for some 1,000m (1,094 yards) and up to 10m (33 feet) in parts.

The Museu Paleo-Cristians, on the outskirts of the town, has a fine display of

Statue of Pablo Casals, the cellist, in his home town of El Vendrell

tombs, mosaics and jewellery. Adjoining it is an old Christian cemetery dating back to the 3rd century.

i Fortuny 4 Bajos

▶ *Continue on the N340 south to Cambrils de Mar.*

5 Cambrils de Mar, Tarragona
Cambrils de Mar is a picturesque little port with a maritime tradition. The harbour is dominated by an ancient church tower, originally a Roman defence fortification.

RECOMMENDED WALKS

Leave Tarragona from the Rambla Nova and drive 4km (2½ miles) north to the Roman Aqueduct, the Aqüeducte de les Ferreres (El Pont del Dimoni or Devil's Bridge). A pleasant walk of about 30 minutes takes you through a lovely area of pines to the base. Part of the structure has long disappeared but two tiers of arches still stand and are an impressive sight.

Roman Relics & Golden Beaches

The port becomes a hive of activity when the fishing fleet comes in, and has a reputation for good eating.

▶ *Continue south down the coastal road (N340) for 112km (70 miles) to Peñiscola.*

6 Peñiscola, Castellón
This is a veritable jewel of a place, rising like a fortress from a rocky peninsula that juts out to sea. The town was taken from the Moors in 1233 by King Jaime I. Its main feature is the castle, an impressive structure built by the Knights Templars. Later, the deposed antipope, Benedict XIII (Pope Luna), took refuge in the castle and spent his last years here until his death in 1422. The castle offers magnificent views of the coastline. Within the surrounding walls is the old town, a labyrinth of tiny winding streets – strictly for pedestrians only.

▶ *Drive inland to join the A7 north, turning off after 46km (29 miles) on the C235 to Tortosa.*

7 Tortosa, Tarragona
The episcopal town of Tortosa holds a commanding position over the delta of the River Ebro. The cathedral was begun in 1347 and built over a long

FOR HISTORY BUFFS

During the Spanish Civil War (1936–9), Tortosa was the scene of an important battle. On 24 July 1938, the Republicans, who were in control of Catalunya at the time, made an attack on the Nationalist forces who were advancing to Valencia. They crossed the River Ebro but were unable to advance further and had to remain in trenches until their ultimate defeat. The victory of the Nationalists is commemorated by a monument rising from the river.

period of time. The naves are 14th-century Gothic, while the façade and the chapel to the Mare de Deu de la Cinta (the Virgin), patron saint of the city, are baroque. Other buildings of note are the 14th-century Palau Episcopal and the Colegio de Sant Lluis, which was founded in 1544 by Emperor Charles V for converts from the Moorish faith, and has an elegant courtyard with some fine decoration. Many splendid old palaces from the 15th and 16th centuries can be seen, as well as remains of the city walls.

⬚ *Calle de la Rosa 10*

▶ *Take the N230 north to Gandesa, then turn right on to the N420 before turning left back on to the N230 to Lleida.*

8 Lleida, Lleida/Lérida
Originally an Iberian settlement, Lleida came under the Romans in the 2nd century BC and was the scene of numerous battles and sieges over the years. It was the birthplace of Enrique Granados (1867–1916), famed for his classical guitar compositions.

Enclosed within the city walls is the Seu Vella (old cathedral), which is dominated by a tall 14th-century octagonal tower. Built between the 12th

The ancient town of Tortosa is now a fascinating blend of old and new.

and 15th centuries, it shows the transition from Romanesque to Gothic. During the 18th century the cathedral was used as a garrison and has been undergoing restoration for some years. It has a fine Gothic cloister, noted for its tall, graceful arches.

Lleida also has the Seu Nova (new cathedral), which was built in the 18th century in neo-classical style, and was the first of its kind in Catalunya. A fine collection of 15th- and 16th-century tapestries is displayed in the museum. The 13th-century town hall, known as the Palau de la Paería, is noted for its fine façade and

SCENIC ROUTES

The drive from Barcelona down the eastern coast of Spain has some particularly scenic sections. After Castelldefels the C246 runs along the coast to Sitges, offering splendid sea views. Be prepared for countless curves and bends in the road. There are attractive stretches before Calafell, between Torredembarra and Tarragona; after Salou, on the N340; and between Tortosa and Lleida (N230).

⑩ Montblanc, Tarragona

Montblanc is an impressive sight, with its massive medieval ramparts and towers and narrow entrance gates. Overlooking the town is the Church of Santa María begun in the 14th century and never fully completed.

▶ *Continue on the N240 southeast to Valls. Turn left on to the C246, then left again on a minor road, crossing the A2 to Santes Creus.*

⑪ Monestir Santes Creus, Tarragona

The Santes Creus monastery, rises grandly over the forest around it. It is a fine example of the Cistercian style and is, like Poblet, amongst Catalunya's most important monasteries.

Founded in 1157, the monastery was occupied by Cistercian monks from France. It long enjoyed the favour of the Kings of Aragon but, like Poblet, it suffered damage during the wars of the 19th century, and is also under restoration. The church is 12th-century Romanesque and contains the royal tombs of former kings of Catalunya including that of Pedro III.

▶ *Return south to the A2 and join the A7 back to Barcelona, 90km (56 miles).*

BACK TO NATURE

The delta of the River Ebro attracts huge numbers of birds, both migrants from northern areas and residents, so the Parc Natural del Delta de L'Ebro, west of Tortosa was created to protect them. Among the many species that can be seen are plovers, avocets, black-winged stilts and red-crested pochards. Flamingos gather on the Salinas marshes although their presence and numbers are rather unpredictable. Other inhabitants include otters, the stripeless tree frog and terrapins.

---

attractive courtyard. Other places to visit are the churches of Sant Llorenç and Sant Martín, the 15th-century hospital of Santa María, and the Diocesan Museum in the Seminario.

Lleida makes an excellent centre for any number of excursions in to the Pyrenees.

ℹ *Avinguda de Madrid 36*

▶ *Take the N240 southeast towards Tarragona. Shortly after going under the A2 (motorway) turn right to the Monestir de Poblet.*

❾ Monestir de Poblet, Tarragona

Tucked away on the lower slopes of the Prades Mountains is the Monastery of Santa María de Poblet, founded in 1149 by Ramón Berenguer IV as a token of thanks to God for the regaining of Catalunya from the Moors. The following year 12 Cistercian monks, sent from Fontfroide (near Narbonne in France), began building the monastery which is a fine example of Cistercian art. The monks benefited from the patronage of the Aragon kings, for whom the monastery became a favourite stopping place for royal journeys. The lovely Gothic cloister and adjoining chapter house contain a number of abbots' tombstones in the pavement.

▶ *Rejoin the N240 and continue for 8km (5 miles) to Montblanc.*

The Costa
Blanca

ITINERARY

VALENCIA	▶ Sagunto (27km-17m)
SAGUNTO	▶ L'Albufera (55km-34m)
L'ALBUFERA	▶ Cullera (22km-14m)
CULLERA	▶ Gandia (27km-17m)
GANDÍA	▶ Denia (33km-21m)
DENIA	▶ Xabia (10km-6m)
XABIA	▶ Calpe (30km-19m)
CALPE	▶ Benidorm (22km-14m)
BENIDORM	▶ Guadalest (25km-16m)
GUADALEST	▶ Alcoi (36km-22m)
ALCOI	▶ Xátiva (49km-30m)
XÁTIVA	▶ Valencia (60km-37m)

Valencia, Spain's third city **2/3 DAYS • 396KM • 247 MILES**
and a busy port, is graced with many fine buildings such as the
Catedral (1262–1482), a mixture of Romanesque, Gothic and
baroque styles, La Lonja, built in 1483 as the Silk Exchange, and
the Inglesia de Santa Catalina with its hexagonal belfry.

ℹ️ *Calle de la Paz 48*

▶ *From Valencia, take the N340 north to Sagunto.*

🏁 Sagunto, Valencia

The original Saguntum was founded by the Iberians but was later allied to Rome. The town was attacked by the great Carthaginian general, Hannibal, in 218 BC. Abandoned by Rome, the citizens resisted for several months until the city finally fell to the enemy, sparking off the Second Punic War. Five years later the Romans recaptured the town and rebuilt it. Later, it was under Moorish occupation.

On one side of the Plaza Mayor (main square) stands the 14th-century Gothic Iglesia de Santa María, which has an 18th-century gilded altar with a fine cross in mother-of-pearl. From the road up the hillside, you can see stone arches over some of the streets, which once framed the old gates leading to various

parts of the town. The route will take you past the Teatro Romano (Roman Theatre). Dating back to the end of the 2nd century AD, it has a diameter of 50m (165 feet), with a capacity for some 6,000 spectators. A small museum alongside completes the visit.

The road winds its way up to the Castillo de Sagunto, from which there are sweeping views of the coast and the town below. The remains of the old fortress spread over the hillside and show evidence of Iberian, Carthaginian and Roman occupation, while the walls are mainly from the Moorish period.

ℹ️ *Plaza Cronista Chabret*

▶ *Return south on the N340 for 6km (4 miles). Join the A7 heading southwest around Valencia. After 20km (12 miles) turn left off the A7 and join the coastal road to El Saler and L'Albufera.*

Moorish walls surround the medieval castle spread over the hill at Sagunto but earlier it was a strongpoint for Iberians, Carthaginians and Romans too.

BACK TO NATURE

The large freshwater lagoon of L'Albufera is a nature park of great ecological importance, and is a paradise for birdwatchers. Among the species of birds that use this as their breeding ground are red-crested pochards, purple herons, black-winged stilts and numerous warblers. Little egrets are often seen feeding in the water and, in the autumn, thousands of wildfowl, lapwings and golden plover arrive to spend the winter. The arrival of these migratory birds can be watched from the village of El Palmar, on the lagoon,. The flight of the ducks is a famous sight in L'Albufera.

2 L'Albufera, Valencia

A short drive south beyond Valencia's El Saler beach will bring you to L'Albufera, Spain's largest lagoon (the name derives from the Arabic for 'small sea'). The lagoon is surrounded by rice fields and separated from the sea by a sand bar known as La Dehesa. Three channels carry fresh water into the sea.

▶ Continue to Cullera.

3 Cullera, Valencia

The effects of tourism have taken their toll on Cullera, like many other places, once a tiny fishing village and now characterised by high-rise blocks. The place still retains some of its old charm, however, and it is worth

going up the hill to the Ermita de Nuestra Señora del Castillo, which contains a venerated image of the Virgen del Castillo, patron saint of the town. Near by are the ruins of an old castle and a splendid view of the coast and surrounding rice fields.

ℹ Calter del Riu, 42

▶ Join the N332 and travel south for 27km (17 miles) to Gandía.

4 Gandía, Valencia

Gandía was formerly the seat of a dukedom given to the Borja family in 1485 by Ferdinand Catholic. Of major interest is the Palacio de los Duques (Ducal Palace), a handsome

Fishing boats gather in the harbour at Gandia, the town from where the Borjas set out for Italy

SCENIC ROUTES

The coastal road from Gandia to Denia is very pleasant, with long sandy beaches broken up by dramatic rock formations. There are many areas of lush vegetation with palm forests, orange groves and beautiful oleander and cypress trees. The road south of Xabia to Benidorm, the route to Guadalest, inland on the C3313, and the section from Alcoi to Xátiva on the N340 are particularly scenic.

Renaissance building notable as the birthplace and residence of Francisco Borja (1510–72), who became the 4th Duke of Gandía. He was the superior of the Jesuit Order, and was canonised as Saint Francis Borja in 1671. The building has seen considerable alterations since the 16th century and is now a Jesuit college. The state apartments are richly decorated and the patio is attractively adorned with coats of arms. The flooring is laid out to represent the four elements of the Creation and bordered by lovely ceramic tiles.

Close to the Palace are the 18th-century Ayuntamiento (town hall) and the Iglesia de Santa María, which is a good example showing the transition from Gothic to Renaissance architecture.

[i] *Marqés de Campo*

▷ *Continue on the N332 south. At Ondara take a left turn to Denia.*

5 Denia, Alicante
The original Denia is thought to have been colonised by the Greeks before the 8th century BC and known as Hemeroskopeion. Under the Romans it became Dianium, after the temple of Diana. It flourished as a port during the time of the Moors (715–1253), and at one time it controlled the island of Mallorca. Today it is principally a seaside resort and port.

The town is crowned by the remains of the old fortress, which provides a fine view of the surroundings. The area around the fishing port is fun to explore. Take a look at the small 18th-century Iglesia de Santa María and the 17th-century Ayuntamiento.

The Sierra del Montgo towers over the southern end of the town, rising to a height of 753m (2,470 feet). The climb to the top is arduous, but the views from the summit are superb. On a clear day you can see the outline of Ibiza, more than 100km (65 miles) away to the east.

[i] *Plaza del Oculista Duigues, 9*

▷ *Take the regional road down the coast for 10km (6 miles) to Xábia (Jávea).*

FOR CHILDREN

Between Ondara and Oliva, just off the N332, is a Safari Park, which has an amusement park and a host of attractions as well as the animals.

---

6 Xábia (Jávea), Alicante
The small fishing port of Xábia spreads along a wide bay between two prominent pine-covered rock masses, which descend sharply to the sea. The attractive setting, combined with a lively yacht marina and fine sandy beaches, make it an appealing little resort. In spring the place is filled with the scent of lemon and orange blossom. It has a late Gothic church shaped like a ship's hull.

At one end of the resort is the great rock of Cabo de la Nao, with some caves in its steep cliff face. Opposite is the tiny island of Portichol. Visit the lighthouse on Cabo de San Antonio for a good view of the coast towards Xábia and Cabo de la Nao.

[i] *Plaza Almirante Bastareche, 24*

▷ *Return westwards to the N332 and continue south for 30km (19 miles) to Calpe.*

7 Calpe, Alicante
Your approach to Calpe is heralded by the magnificent sight of the Peñón de Ifach – a famous landmark of the Costa Blanca – rising majestically from the sea. Nestling beneath this great volcanic mass is Calpe, whose dramatic setting features among its main attractions.

It is another in the long line of popular resorts to be found down this coast, with a fine

---

RECOMMENDED WALKS

The fit and energetic should enjoy a walk up a good path to the summit of the Peñón de Ifach (about 1 1/2 hours), from where there is a panoramic view of the Costa Blanca.

The Peñón de Ifach towers over the resort of Calpe. This landmark rock is 1,089 feet (332m) high sandy beach and busy fishing harbour. In the old part of town is a small Gothic-Mudejar church and a 16th-century tower, all that remains of the fortified walls.

ℹ️ *Avenida Ejércitos Españoles 66*

▶ *Continue along the N332 for 22km (14 miles) to Benidorm.*

8 Benidorm, Alicante
Benidorm is the Costa Blanca's most famous resort, attracting multitudes of visitors each year. The place has changed beyond recognition since the days when it was a sleepy little fishing village. It is now an international fun city, crammed with bars, shops and nightspots that provide non-stop entertainment, which holds particular appeal for the younger set. Tall hotels and apartment blocks dominate the skyline all along the bays.

Whatever your thoughts about Benidorm in season, its setting is dramatic, with its two splendid bays of golden sands and high-rise blocks silhouetted against the high mountains. Steer clear of the tourist area and explore the old fishing quarters, which have narrow streets and a pretty church with a blue dome. A rather elegant look-out terrace near by offers a sweeping view of the bay and the little island of Plumbaria. If you have time, take a boat-trip to the island and enjoy a swim.

ℹ️ *Avenida Martinez Alejos 16*

▶ *Take the C3318 north past Polop, then turn left on to the C3313 to Guadalest.*

FOR CHILDREN

In Benidorm is a recreation park called Aqualandia, located in the park north of town, where the children can slide down water chutes and enjoy a range of other amusements.

9 Guadalest, Alicante
A drive through some spectacular scenery will bring you to the dramatic sight of Guadalest, a tiny village with a Moorish castle, perched on top of a lofty mountain crag. Most of the village was destroyed by an earthquake, but you can clamber up to the fortress, known as the Costa Blanca's 'eagle's nest' for its impregnable position and superb views over the surrounding landscapes.

▶ *Continue on the C3313 west for 36km (22 miles) to Alcoy o Alcoi.*

10 Alcoy o Alcoi, Alicante
The town of Alcoy lies in a setting of olive groves and vineyards against a backdrop of the Sierra de Montcabre, presenting an attractive picture as you approach it. Alcoy is famous for its *peladillas*, a very popular sweet in Spain, made of sugar-coated almonds. The town has

The ruins of the Moorish castle at Guadalest in an impregnable position on a crag above the village

two fine churches, the Iglesia de Santa María and the Iglesia de Santo Sepulcro, which has attractive tile decorations. The Museo Arqueológico (Archaeological Museum) houses an extensive collection of Iberian pottery and Greek tablets found in the area.

i Centro de Iniciativas Turísticas, Avenida Puente San Jorge

SPECIAL TO...

The festival of the Moors and Christians is celebrated all over Spain, but is especially colourful in Alcoy where it takes place between 22 and 24 April, and centres on St George's Day, 23 April. For three days an image of St George (to whom the village had appealed for help in times of need) is carried through the streets and around the walls of a great cardboard castle. Mock battles are fought between the Moors and the Christians, inevitably ending in victory for the Christians. This is all accompanied by bell-ringing, fireworks and jollity.

▷ *Take the N340 north to Xátiva (Játiva).*

⑪ Xátiva, Valencia

The ramparts of Xátiva are apparent from some distance, rising from twin peaks. Set among olive groves and vineyards, Xátiva is an attractive little town of fountains and trim trees, with a number of interesting monuments. Some fine old palaces and fountains can be seen on and around Moncada Street, which is a very picturesque area. The Colegiata (Collegiate Church) is an excellent example of the 16th-century Renaissance style and the municipal hospital opposite has a fine 16th-century Plateresque façade.

FOR HISTORY BUFFS

A short detour of about 8km (5 miles) on a minor road southwest of Xátiva takes you to the small village of Canals. The castle here is famed as the birthplace of Alonso Borja. The Borja family came to Canals from Aragón in the 14th century and Alonso, who was born here in 1378, later became Pope Calixtus III. His nephew, Rodrigo Borja(1431–1503), or Borgia as the name was written in Italian, became Pope Alexander, notorious for his scandalous behaviour and father of Lucretia and Cesare Borgia.

Allow time for a visit to the Museo Municipal, which has an extensive collection of antiquities, including the Pila de los Moros, a Moorish basin from the 11th century with, unusually for a Muslim artwork, decorations of human figures.

There are good views from the cypress-planted Calvary and the Ermita de San Feliu (hermitage of St Felix). A further climb up the hill takes you to El Castillo, a 16th-century castle built on Iberian and Roman foundations, from which there is a magnificent view of the surrounding countryside.

i Alameda Jaime I, 35

▷ *Return to Valencia on the N430.*

SPECIAL TO...

Those with an interest in musical bands should make a point of visiting Liria, a short distance northwest of Valencia. Known as the 'City of Music', it has an international reputation for its bands of musicians. It is said great rivalry exists between the bands, who jealously guard their own territory.

RECOMMENDED WALKS

Many of the antiquities displayed in the museum in Alcoi were found in the nearby Sierra Sereta. A steep climb of about half an hour will take you to the top, where there are magnificent views of the surrounding mountainous landscapes.

Palm Forests &
Rugged Peaks

Alicante, one of the gateways for the Costa Blanca, has much to see. In the old town, the Town Hall with its two impressive towers is near the 17th-century cathedral and ornate Inglesia de Santa María. The harbour and Explanada de España are worth seeing and the Castillo de Santa Barbara offers fine views.

ITINERARY		
ALICANTE	▶	**Alicante (24km-15m)**
ELX	▶	**Orihuela (33km-21m)**
ORIHUELA	▶	**Murcia (24km-15m)**
MURCIA	▶	**Alhama de Murcia**
		(32km-20m)
ALHAMA DE MURCIA	▶	**Aledo (21km-13m)**
ALEDO	▶	**Totana (9km-6m)**
TOTANA	▶	**Lorca (20km-12m)**
LORCA	▶	**Aguilas (39km-24m)**
AGUILAS	▶	**Marazzón (46km-29m)**
MARAZZÓN	▶	**Cartagena (39km-24m)**
CARTAGENA	▶	**La Unión (17km-7m)**
LA UNIÓN	▶	**Alicante (98km-61m)**

6/7 DAYS • 576KM • 356½ MILES

The Explanada de España, with wavy multi-coloured pavings, extends along the seafront at Alicante. *Left:* the harbour

which are thought to be at least 150 years old and have seven stems that grow out from the main trunk. The dates are cut in winter from the female palms, while some of the male trees are bound to bleach the fronds. These are then sold for Palm Sunday processions.

i Parque Municipal

> SPECIAL TO...
>
> The Misteri d'Elx (Mystery of Elche) is a play about the Assumption of the Virgin. It takes place on the Feast of the Assumption in the Basílica of Santa María, with spectacular performances on 14 and 15 August. The actors are local and the music medieval.

i Explanada de España 2

▷ *Take the N340 southwest for 24km (15 miles) to Elche/Elx.*

❶ **Elche o Elx,** Alicante
The main attraction here is the unique palm forest, but Elche has a rather Moorish look, with its whitewashed houses, flat roofs and palms. There is an excellent view over the town and palm grove from the tower of the 17th-century baroque Santa María Basílica. The Palacio de Altimira near by was built in the 1400s as lodgings for the kings of Spain. In the

Museo Arqueológico there is a copy of the Lady of Elche sculpture, thought to be 4th or 3rd century BC, found in the vicinity and now in the Archaeological Museum of Madrid.

The Palmeral de Europe (Palm Forest of Europe), the largest date palm grove in Europe, lies to the east of the town and was originally planted by the Moors. Many of the palms reach a height of 25m (82 feet). In the Huerto del Cura (Priest's Orchard) you can see the impressive trees of the 'Palmera Imperial' species,

The Renaissance belfry of the Cathedral at Murcia

▶ *Continue on the N340 for 33km (21 miles) to Orihuela.*

2 Orihuela, Alicante
Orihuela lies on the banks of the River Segura, which provides irrigation for the surrounding orange and lemon groves. The Cerro de Oro (Hill of Gold) rises in the background. The name of the town is thought to be derived from the Roman Aurariola. The town suffered severe damage from an earthquake in 1829. Among the few old buildings to survive are the El Salvador cathedral, built in the 14th and 15th centuries, with fine Gothic vaulting; the late-Gothic Santiago Church,

---

SCENIC ROUTES

Particularly attractive stretches include the approach to Elx and on to Orihuela through a palm and orange grove; the Leyva Valley, between Alhama de Murcia and Aledo, high up in the mountains of the Sierra de España; Puerto de Mazarrón to Cartagena; and La Unión back to San Javier both on the N332 west of the large saltwater lagoon of the Mar Menor.

---

and the Santo Domingo College, former home of the University of Orihuela, founded in the 16th century.

ℹ *Francisco Díaz 25*

▶ *Continue for 24km (15 miles) on the N340 south-west to Murcia.*

3 Murcia, Murcia
Capital of its province, Murcia spreads along both sides of the Río Segura, in the heart of the *huerta* (a fertile, irrigated region). Murcia is the seat of a bishopric and a university town. The cathedral, built in the 14th century with later Renaissance and baroque additions, features an impressive façade and a splendid 18th-century belfry. Inside are lavish Renaissance decorations in the Capilla de los Junterones and the rich late-Gothic of the Chapel of los Velez. There is a good view of the town and surroundings from the belfry.
Museums in Murcia include the Museo Internacional del Traje Folklórico, which has costumes from all over Spain.

ℹ *Alejandro Sequer 4*

▶ *Take the N340 southwest to Alhama de Murcia.*

FOR HISTORY BUFFS

Just south of Murcia is the Santuario de la Fuensanta, a pilgrimage centre overlooking the *huerta*. Consecrated at the end of the 17th century, it has a fine façade, crowned with two towers.

---

4 Alhama de Murcia, Murcia
On the way to Alhama de Murcia, stop at Alcantarilla, 9km (6 miles) out of Murcia, to visit the Museo de la Huerta (Irrigation Museum). Amongst the exhibits is a huge old water-wheel called a *noria*, which the Moors used for irrigation.

Continue through orange and lemon groves, then by corn-fields to a large, craggy rock topped by the tower of an old Moorish fort. Below lies the ancient spa town of Alhama de Murcia, which is known for its warm, medicinal sulphur springs, and still has traces of Roman occupation.

▶ *Continue along the N340. At Totana take a right turn and drive to Aledo.*

5 Aledo, Murcia
At the southern end of the Sierra de España is the small medieval town of Aledo, famous for its old castle, which was held for a long period by the Knights of the Calavatra (1085–1160) during the Moorish occupation.

BACK TO NATURE

The natural park of the Sierra de España is Murcia's largest nature reserve with rugged mountains and high peaks. Among its inhabitants are wild sheep (moufflon), wild cats, boar and foxes; eagles, owls and partridges are some of the birds to be seen here. .

▶ *Return on the same road to Totana, 9km (6 miles).*

6 Totana, Murcia
Totana was a town of some importance under the Romans. The 16th-century Iglesia de Santiago (St James) has a fine 17th-century baroque portal and Mudejar coffered ceiling. Some 7km (4 miles) away, is the Ermita de Santa Eulalia, the town's patron saint, famed for its Mudejar roof and 16th-century murals.

▶ *Take the N340 south to Lorca.*

7 Lorca, Murcia
At the entrance to the Valley of El Guadalentín lies the town of Lorca, an important agricultural centre. The town was a bish-

opric under the Visigoths, called Ilurco by the Romans, and Lurka by the Moors. Above the town are the remains of the old Moorish castle, built between the 13th and 15th centuries, and the medieval churches of Santa María, San Juan and San Pedro.

Further down the hill is the Iglesia de San Patricio, with a Renaissance tower and baroque doorway, and the elegant Ayuntamiento.

ⓘ *López Gisbert 12, Palacio Guevara*

▶ *Take the N302 and the N332 southeast to Aguilas.*

8 Aguilas, Murcia
The seaside town of Aguilas dates back to the 17th century and is comparatively unchanged. Its two most impressive buildings are the Mudejar-style Ayuntamiento and the Iglesia de San José. A climb up to the Castillo de San Juan de las Aguilas on top of the hill provides a fine view of the bay and distant mountains.

▶ *Take the N332 northeast for 46km (29 miles) to Mazarrón.*

9 Mazarrón, Murcia
The main features in the small inland town of Mazarrón are the Castillo de los Vélez, with the remains of an old watch tower, and the Iglesia de San Andrés, which has a fine 16th-century Mudejar coffered ceiling.

A short drive leads down to Puerto de Mazarrón, which lies in a splendid bay.

ⓘ *Avenida Doctor Meca 47*

▶ *Continue on the N332 northeast to Cartagena.*

RECOMMENDED
WALKS

The Sierra de Espuña offers many lovely walks in pine forests and mountain terrain.

🔟 Cartagena, Murcia
Cartagena is Spain's major naval base and a big commercial port. Founded by the Carthaginians in the 3rd century BC, it became the region's capital under the Romans. It declined under the Moors but rose to importance during the 16th century. Worth visiting are the Iglesia de Santa María la Vieja, the Roman Torre Ciega (literally, blind tower) and the Ayuntamiento. On the main quay of the port is the world's first submarine, launched by Isaac Peral in 1888.

ⓘ *Plaza Ayuntamiento*

▶ *Take the N332 east to La Unión.*

⓫ La Unión, Murcia
La Unión emerged as an important centre for lead mining a century ago. The Mercado (market) and the Casa del Piñon are two examples of early 20th century architecture, making full use of wrought-iron, The August festival of the 'Cante de las Minas' (mining songs) is held in the market place.

East is the modern resort of La Manga del Mar Menor with golf, tennis and watersports.

▶ *Return to Alicante on the northeast coast road (N332).*

The ornate doorway of the Church of San Patricio, Lorca, is a fine example of baroque carving

The Magic of
Mallorca

Although for many it is just a gateway to beach resorts, Palma has charm and it is well worth exploring its historic buildings – the Gothic Cathedral with its landmark spire, the Ajuntament, and La Lonja, the former Exchange, as well as the lively Passeig de Borne, crammed with shops and bars. West of Palma, the 14th century Castell de Bellver, built on a hill by Mallorcan kings and now a museum, has fine views of Palma Bay from its commanding position.

ITINERARY

PALMA	▶ **Port D'Andratx**
	(33km–21m)
PORT D'ANDRATX	▶ **Valldemossa (43km–27m)**
VALLDEMOSSA	▶ **Deià (10km–6m)**
DEIÀ	▶ **Port de Sóller (14km–9m)**
PORT DE SÓLLER	▶ **Monestir de Lluc**
	(37km–23m)
MONESTIR DE LLUC	▶ **Pollença (21km–13m)**
POLLENÇA	▶ **Alcúdia (15km–9m)**
ALCÚDIA	▶ **Coves d'Arta (45km–28m)**
COVES D'ARTÀ	▶ **Manacor (29km–18m)**
MANACOR	▶ **Porto Cristo (13km–8m)**
PORTO CRISTO	▶ **Coves del Drac (2km–1m)**
COVES DEL DRAC	▶ **Felanitx (29km–18m)**
FELANITX	▶ **Santanyi (16km–10m)**
SANTANYI	▶ **Palma (51km–32m)**

3 DAYS • 358KM • 223 MILES

Fishing boat with floats in the harbour at Port Andratx

SCENIC ROUTES

The road along the magnificent Serra de Tramuntana, across the northwest of the island, is outstanding. The corniche from Andratx to Sóller is one of the most beautiful drives in Mallorca. There are spectacular views of the coast from look-out posts such as the Mirador Ricardo Roca and Ses Animes, and around Banyalbufar.

authoress George Sand. The Reial Cartouxa (Royal Carthusian Monastery) where they stayed is the main feature of the village. After the monks were expelled in 1835 the place served as lodgings for travellers. The apartments, or rather cells, where the couple stayed are furnished in the style of the period, and include the piano on which the great master composed some of his best-known works. In the cloister is a very old pharmacy. First

Terrace at Valldemossa monastery where Chopin stayed

i Plaça Major 3

▷ From Palma take the C719 southwest to Port d'Andratx.

❶ Port d'Andratx, Mallorca
From a tiny fishing village, Port d'Andratx has become one of Mallorca's most prominent yachting centres, and sailing vessels of all shapes and sizes are moored in the harbour. The town is set in an attractive bay surrounded by hills and has a pleasant seafront promenade lined with bars and restaurants. The yachting set provides an international atmosphere during the season.

▷ Take the C710 and branch off to the right to Valldemossa.

❷ Valldemossa, Mallorca
To many, the name of Valldemossa conjures up visions of Chopin, music and romance. The Polish composer Frédéric Chopin spent the winter of 1838 to 1839 here with the French

FOR CHILDREN

There are a number of amuse-ment parks near Palma. At Costa d'en Blanes, north of Palma Nova, Marineland has spectacular shows of perform-ing dolphins and sea lions, an aquarium of sharks, a mini zoo, train rides and much more. In Magaluf, south of Palma Nova, are two special attractions, Aquapark and El Dorado, a re-created Wild West town, with gun fights and stage shows.

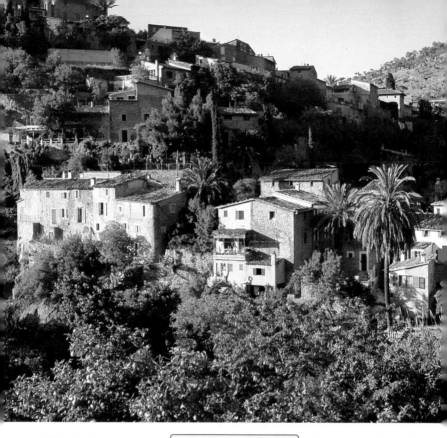

established by the monks as early as 1723, it looks much the same as it must have done then. Take a look, too, at the small museum in the monks' library.

▶ *Rejoin the C710 for 10km (6 miles) to Deià (Deyà).*

8 Deià, Mallorca

Deià has long been a favourite haunt for writers and artists, such as the poet and writer Robert Graves who spent some time here after World War II. The village consists of a delightful cluster of red houses on top of a hill, idyllically set among almond trees and groves of oranges, lemons and olives. Behind the parish church is the cemetery where Graves is buried. There is a wonderful view from here of the surrounding mountains and rocky coves below. A somewhat precipitous climb down the hill takes you to the sea.

▶ *Continue on the C710. Take a left turn to Port de Sóller.*

RECOMMENDED WALKS

Mallorca has so many attractive areas for walking that you can more or less make a choice anywhere along the route. The Sierra de Tramuntana in the northwest of the island offers countless hikes in magnificent scenery. Booklets can be obtained from the local tourist office.

4 Port de Sóller, Mallorca

The route from Deià passes through the small hamlet of Lluc Alcari, where Pablo Picasso lived for a time. The picturesque old fishing port of Port de Sóller is now a popular tourist spot. It has an attractive harbour, framed by the pine-covered hills of the Sierra de Tramuntana and an excellent sandy beach. The Santuario de Santa Catalina, by the old fishing quarter, provides a fine view of the resort. Five

The mellow village houses of the mountain village of Deia set amongst olive groves and almonds

kilometres (3 miles) inland is Sóller town, linked to Port de Sóller by a narrow-gauge railway or by road, where the Convent de Sant Francesc (St Francis) is worth a visit, along with the handicrafts centre in the local museum.

i Passeig es Través

▶ *Rejoin the C710 and branch off left to the Monestir de Lluc.*

5 Monestir de Lluc, Mallorca

Situated on one of the highest points of the island is Mallorca's principal monastery and pilgrimage centre. The entrance is lined with houses and doorways, which once provided shelter for pilgrims who arrived here to venerate the Virgin of Lluc, patron saint of the island. Inside the monastery is a

Back in the town, other places worth a visit are the Gothic chapel of Roser Vell, which has a fine altarpiece, the church of Montision (both 18th century), and the baroque-style Convent de Sant Domènech. There is a Roman bridge just outside town.

Port de Pollença, some 6km (4 miles) away, is an attractive little fishing port set in a wide bay framed by the dramatic silhouette of the Sierra de Sant Vincenc (San Vincente mountains). It is a very popular, fast-developing resort and yachting centre.

If you have time, continue northeast into the Formentor peninsula, one of the most scenic parts of the island. A drive to the lighthouse at the end of Cap de Formentor offers magnificent views of this superb coastline.

▷ *From Port de Pollença take the coast road for 15km (9 miles) to Alcúdia.*

RECOMMENDED
WALKS

A pleasant stroll can be taken in Port de Pollença along the seafront promenade, which starts from the end of town and follows the sea, well shaded by trees and lined with attractive residential villas and gardens.

7 Alcúdia, Mallorca
The little medieval town of Alcúdia is encircled by some impressive old ramparts dating back to the 14th century. Inside are small narrow streets and handsome mansions, mainly from the 16th and 17th centuries. The town had quite a sizeable Roman population and the local museum has exhibits of Roman times as well as prehistoric artefacts. A colourful market takes place on Tuesdays and Sundays just outside the old city walls.

wooden statue of the Virgin encrusted with jewels. There is also a 17th-century church, and a small museum with a collection of paintings, ceramics and religious items. Mass is celebrated each day, when you can hear the stirring singing of the famous boys choir of Lluc.

▷ *Continue on the C710 for 21km (13 miles) to Pollença (Pollensa).*

6 Pollença, Mallorca
Pollença's crowning glory is the Calvari (Calvary), which stands at the top of an impressive flight of 365 steps. Those who make it to the top will find a little white 18th-century chapel with an old crucifix and a good view over the bays of Alcúdia, Pollença and even as far as Cap de Formentor. On Good Friday there is a service in the chapel followed by a torchlit procession down the steps.

Steps lead up through the village of Pollença to the Calvary standing some 35m (115 feet) high, overlooking the sea. They consist of a vast number of caverns and are noted for the extraordinary, sometimes grotesque shapes of the stalactites and stalagmites.

Artà itself features some attractive mansions, churches and the Almudain, a medieval fortress containing a sanctuary. Near by, the Ermita de Betlem (Sanctuary of Betlem) stands high on a hill with a fine view of the bay of Alcúdia.

▷ *Take the C715 southwest for 29km (18 miles) to Manacor.*

9 Manacor, Mallorca
Manacor has a long tradition of furniture-making dating back to the 17th century, when it became a centre for wood craftsmen. Its main claim to fame, however, lies in the production of pearls, an important industry in Mallorca and internationally known. You can visit the factory and see how the pearls are produced in a simulated process that resembles the natural one.

A Roman theatre (about 1.5km (1 mile) south is situated in some fields. The theatre was carved from rock, and items uncovered here are to be seen in the museum in the Castell de Bellver, Palma.

▷ *Take the C712 southeast to Artà. Continue southeast on a minor road to the Coves d'Artà (Caves of Artà), 45km (28 miles).*

8 Coves d'Artà, Mallorca
On the beach of Canyamel are the caves of Artà. The largest known caves on the island, they are said to have provided the inspiration for Jules Verne's famous story *Journey to the Centre of the Earth.* They are reached by a huge opening in the cliff,

Recent development at Porto Cristo has changed the little port but not spoilt its character

---

BACK TO NATURE

Birdwatchers should stop at L'Albufera, a partly dried-up lagoon in swamp lands southwest of Alcúdia, where you can see many species of birds. Look for black-winged stilts, stone curlews and little egrets. In the south of the island Sa Marina de Llucmayor is an area of strange rock formations that are of geological interest, with extensive views from the top. The rocks and lagoons are also a natural habitat for sea birds and marine plants.

FOR HISTORY BUFFS

Petra (northwest of Manacor) is the birthplace of the Franciscan, Fray Junípero de la Sierra (1713–84), famous for his mission work in California and Mexico. San Francisco, San Diego and Santa Barbara are three of his former missions that grew into large towns. Junípero's home is now the museum of the Casa Museu Fray Junípero de la Serra, and a his statue stands in the town.

Other places of interest include the Gothic Iglesia de San Vicente, the Museo Arqueológico and the remains of the old tower, which was once the summer residence of Jaime II, the conqueror of Mallorca.

▷ *Take the road southeast to Porto Cristo*

⑩ Porto Cristo,
Mallorca
The attractive little port of Porto Cristo is one of the oldest anchorages on the island, confirmed by the discovery of a sunken Roman ship in the area. In the Middle Ages the port flourished for it was the main entry point for the island's imports. As with so many other seaside villages and towns in mainland Spain and in the Balearics, it has developed over recent years into a popular holiday destination, which has inevitably changed its old character. Nevertheless it still remains a picturesque little resort with considerable charm.

▶ *Near by are the Coves del Drac.*

Giant saguaro cacti flourish in Mallorca's warm climate

Post boxes in Mallorca are easy to spot – their bright yellow paint enlivens the street scene

⑪ Coves del Drac, Mallorca
The caves of Drach are the best known in Mallorca, and no tourist trip is complete without a visit here. They stretch for some 2km (1½ miles) and visitors travel through a wonderland, over bridges and past a series of underground pools. Lago Martel (Lake Martell) is the largest underground lake in Europe and its transparent waters reflect the weird and wonderful shapes of the rock formations. In summer, concerts are held aboard a small vessel which floats on the lake. If you want to see more caves, the Coves dels Hams (Caves of Hams) near by are also magnificent, noted for the pure white of the stalactites, and lovely underground lakes.

▶ *Return to Manacor and take the C/14 south to Felanitx.*

⑫ Felanitx, Mallorca
The old town of Felanitx dates back to the 13th century. Visit the Convent de Sant Augustín and the parish church, which has a fine Gothic façade. Felanitx is the birthplace of the

---

BACK TO NATURE

Located within the municipality of Santanyi is the Mondragó Natural Park, with many species of birds, mammals and reptiles, aquariums and several beaches.

---

artist Miguel Barceló who still keeps a studio here.

South of Felanitx is the old convent of Castillo de Santueri, perched on a huge rock mass.

▶ *Continue for 16km (10 miles) on the C714 south to Santanyi (Santani).*

⑬ Santanyi, Mallorca
A massive gateway, known as Porta Murada, still remains from the town fortifications. These were built as a defence against piracy, which was once a recurrent problem in this part of the island. The parish church has an excellent rococo organ, and there is a fine Romanesque–Gothic oratory in the Roser's chapel. Near by are the remains of some prehistoric sites and fortifications.

▶ *Take the C717 for 51km (32 miles) back to Palma.*

SPECIAL TO...

Among the many festivals that take place in Mallorca, two are outstanding. In January the fiesta of Sant Antoni Abat, patron saint of domestic animals, is celebrated all over the island. The main day is 17 January and celebrations are especially colourful in Pollença. The Feites de Sant Pere (St Peter), patron saint of fishermen, is held on 29 June. Celebrations in his honour are a particular attraction in Port d'Alcúdia, where his statue is carried along the seafront by barefoot fishermen, followed by a procession of local people.

FOR CHILDREN

In Porto Cristo, near the Coves del Drac, is a water amusement park called Aquarius; and on the Porto Cristo/San Severa road is the AutoSafari Park where the animals can be seen from the car.

ANDALUCIA

To many people the image of Spain is the reality of Andalucia: dazzling white villages perched on mountain tops silhouetted against brilliant blue skies, sun-soaked beaches and high-rise blocks Its past has included some 600 years of Roman domination and almost 800 years of Moorish occupation. This brought the region rich cultures and some unique monuments, of which the Alhambra in Granada, the Mosque of Córdoba and the Alcázar in Sevilla are the finest examples. The Moorish past is more evident in Andalucia than in any other part of Spain.

The region is renowned for its song and dance, from the gypsy lament of the flamenco to the twirling rhythms of the Andalucian dances known as sevillanas. It is also famed for its festivals. Sevilla's Holy Week Processions and Spring Fair are outstanding.

Andalucia is a vast region made up of the provinces of Huelva, Cádiz, Sevilla, Córdoba, Jaén, Almería, Granada and Málaga, with Sevilla as its capital. To the west is Portugal and south is a long coastline, washed by both the Atlantic and the Mediterranean. Named the Costa de la Luz (Coast of Light), from Portugal to the Straits of Gibraltar, then the Costa del Sol (Sunshine Coast), which stretches eastward and leads in turn to the Costa de Almería.

In the north is the Sierra Morena, while the land further south is dominated by the Andalucian Mountains, incorporating the beautiful snowcapped peaks of the Sierra Nevada including Spain's highest peak, the Mulhacén, 3482m (11,424 feet).

Around the basin of the River Guadalquivir olive groves and cereals create patterns of green and gold, and forests of cork-oaks flourish. Further south are sugar-cane and banana plantations and cotton fields while important wine-growing regions lie around Jerez de la Frontera, Málaga and south of Córdoba. In the southwest is a great expanse of salt marshes and fenland, called the 'Marismas', which contains one of Spain's most important nature parks.

Take some carriage exercise from the Plaza de Espana, Sevilla; a pleasant way to sightsee

Tour 7

This tour of eastern Andalucia takes you off the beaten track through a sparsely populated area of rugged mountains, deep valleys and vast plains, suggesting a journey into the unknown. Further north is one of Spain's best-known nature parks in a magnificent setting of high mountain peaks, fresh green forests and rivers. Dotted about the landscape are interesting little towns with their roots deep in the past. Old cave dwellings also add interest to the journey through this unusual part of Spain.

Tour 8

On this tour you travel through some of the most impressive scenery to be found in southern Andalucia, combining beautiful mountain roads, woods and valleys, with a drive along one of the most attractive parts of the coast. The highlight of the trip is a visit to one of Spain's most important Moorish legacies. Added to this is the splendid setting with the snowcapped mountains of the Sierra Nevada in the background.

Tour 9

The sun-soaked coastline of Spain's southern coast with its familiar skyline of modern high-rise blocks contrasts sharply with the magnificent mountain landscapes and charming Andalucian villages of the hinterland. Two special features on this tour are the view of the coast's famous landmark, the rock of Gibraltar, and one of Spain's best bridges.

Tour 10

This drive through the basin of the River Guadalquivir goes through cornfields and groves of old twisted olive trees , and past small farmhouses. There are wine-growing areas among the gentle hills, and views of distant mountains. The villages are Moorish in appearance – square white houses, red-tiled roofs and little old streets. The highpoint s Spain's Moorish Mosque, magnificent in its entirety.

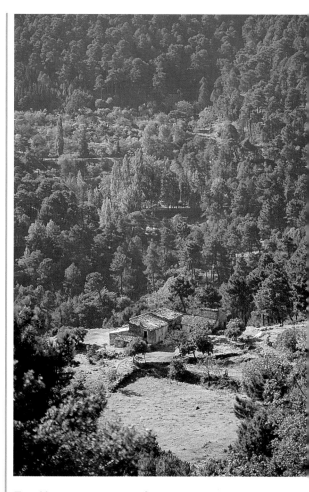

A 'cortijo' or farm deep in the countryside near Cazorla

Tour 11

The first part of the tour passes through the forested mountains of the Sierra Morena, and then down, passing through olive groves and fig plantations. These, in turn, lead to the shores of the Atlantic. In the southwest corner, close to the Portuguese border, is the area referred to as the 'cradle of new civilisations'. It was from here that many expeditions by Spanish explorers set sail across the Atlantic in the 15th and 16th centuries to the lands of golden promise.

Tour 12

Andalucia's 'white towns' are famous and some of the most beautiful are included on this route. You will find that the names of many of these towns are followed by 'de la Frontera', an appellation dating from the 200 years of fighting between the Moors and Christians, when these towns determined changing frontiers, until Granada, last stronghold of the Moors, fell to the Christians. The tour also explores the coastline of sandy beaches and pine-woods, and several of Andalucia's ports and holiday resorts. A trip into Andalucia's foremost wine-growing region culminates in a visit to its renowned sherry-producing area.

Lunar Landscapes of the South

Almería was a flourishing Roman port; to the Moors it was Al-Mariyya – 'mirror of the sea'. The Alcazába (fortress) overlooks the city, and the cathedral, rebuilt in the 16th century on the site of a former mosque, also resembles a fortress, to counter raids by Barbary pirates.

2/3 DAYS • 645KM • 402 MILES

ITINERARY

ALMERÍA	► Tabernas (30km-19m)
TABERNAS	► Sorbas (27km-17m)
SORBAS	► Mojäacar (34km-21m)
MOJÁCAR	► Huércal-Overa
	(48km-30m)
HUÉRCAL-OVERA	► Vélez Rubio (43km-27m)
VÉLEZ RUBIO	► Vélez Blanco (6km-4m)
VÉLEZ BLANCO	► Baza (73km-45m)
BAZA	► Cazorla (102km-63m)
CAZORLA	► Úbeda (48km-30m)
ÚBEDA	► Guadix (114km-71m)
GUADIX	► Almería (120km-75m)

i *Parque San Nicolás Salmerón*

▶ *Take the N340 for 30km (19 miles) to Tabernas.*

SCENIC ROUTES

Areas of outstanding scenery include the stretch north of Almería through the 'Wild West' mountains around Tabernas to Sorbas (A370/N340); the area around Mojácar; Mojácar north up to Vélez Rubio (N340, C321 and A327); the approach to the Sierra de Cazorla; from Jódar (south of Ubeda) down to Moreda and beyond (C325 and N401/N324); and Guadix southeast on the A921/N324 nearly all the way to Almería.

❶ Tabernas, Almería

The little town of Tabernas has a definite Moorish look about it, but has Roman origins. Tucked away at the foot of a hill, it lies on a vast plain between the Sierra de los Filabres and the Sierra de Alhamilla. There are remains of an old Moorish castle, and the church has a fine Mudejar coffered ceiling. The wild, desert-like landscapes in this area provided the setting for many 'spaghetti Westerns' during the 1960s and 1970s, and some of the scenes for *Lawrence of Arabia* were shot around an area to the northeast, which provided an excellent location.

▶ *Continue northeast on the A370/N340 for 27km (17 miles) to Sorbas.*

❷ Sorbas, Almería

Sorbas rates as one of the most picturesque towns in the region. A cluster of white houses is perched on top of a high cliff that descends sharply down to the River Aguas and other small streams. The remains of an old Moorish castle form part of the skyline. Sorbas is noted for pottery and some of its workshops can be visited. There are also cave dwellings in the area.

▶ *Continue north on the A370/N340. Branch off right to Mojácar.*

Fortifications of the 16th-century Moorish Alcazába which still dominates Almería

❸ Mojácar, Almería

A few kilometres from the sea is the stunning little Moorish town of Mojácar. Its flat white buildings sprawl up a steep hill, and it holds a commanding position over the coast and surrounding plains. Its former name of Meschech-Masstia is

BACK TO NATURE

A road southeast of Sorbas leads to the Cortijada de los Molinos del Río Aguas, a good point from which to explore the River Aguas, where you may find tortoises and a wonderful range of colourful flowers typical of this area. Near by are some caves in crystallised gypsum with an inner lagoon. Further along is the Parque Natural de Cabo de Gata-Nijar, situated in the volcanic mountain range of the Sierra del Cabo de Gata.

one of the oldest known names in Spain. Of Carthaginian origin, the town was of some importance during Roman times, and strong influences remain from the Moorish occupation. Steep, winding streets lead to the top of the village, with fine views of the sea and countryside.

[i] *Plaza Nueva*

▷ *Return to the N340 and continue north to Huercal-Overa, making a short detour to see the Cuevas de Almanzora cave dwellings just north of Vera.*

4 Huercal-Overa, Almería
Huercal-Overa is an important agricultural centre. Formerly inhabited by the Moors, the town became deserted when they were driven out of Spain. It was gradually repopulated during the 16th century. The most notable buildings in the town are the Iglesia de Nuestra Señora de la Asunción (Church of Our Lady of the Assumption), with a fine altar; the Ayuntamiento and the Plaza de Toros (bullring), which dates back to the beginning of this century. Embroidery features among the traditional crafts practised here.

▷ *Take the A327/C321 north and join the N342 west to Vélez Rubio.*

5 Vélez Rubio, Almería
Right in the middle of a wild, barren landscape lies Vélez Rubio, capital of the area since the beginning of the 18th century. The Convento de San Francisco, the parish church and the Iglesia de Nuestra Señora del Carmen (Church of Our Lady of Carmen) are all fine examples of baroque architecture. The old hospital and the Ayuntamiento are also notable buildings, and there are many

The flat-topped, white houses of the Moorish village of Mojácar can be seen for many miles

elegant private mansions from earlier centuries.

▷ *Take the A327/C321 north for 6km (4 miles) to Vélez Blanco.*

6 Vélez Blanco, Almería
Built on the slopes of a mountain, Vélez Blanco has a rich heritage, with Roman origins. Buildings of special interest include the Iglesia de Santiago (Church of St James), with a fine Mudejar ceiling, and the Convento de San Luís, both showing Mudejar and Renaissance styles. Its chief splendour, however, is the magnificent Renaissance castle on top of the hill overlooking the town and offering panoramic views of the surrounding landscape. The flamboyantly decorated 16th-century courtyard, however, is now in the Metropolitan Museum in New York.

On the outskirts of town are the Cuevas de los Letreros, with Neolithic cave paintings.

(
▷ *Rejoin the N342 and continue on this road west to Baza.*

7 Baza, Almería
The old Iberian settlement of Baza lies in the valley of Baza, in the heart of a fertile plain surrounded by rather barren mountains. The discovery of an Iberian stone figure, the Dama de Baza (Lady of Baza), exca-

---

SPECIAL TO...

An unusual celebration takes place between Guadix and Baza on 6 September in honour of Nuestra Señora de la Piedad, Patron Saint of Baza. A character from Guadix (known as 'El Cascamorras') has to travel to Baza to take possession of the statue of the Virgin, enduring insults and all sorts of abuses from the people of Baza during the course of the journey.

---

vated here in 1971, was a find of some importance. Buildings of note include the 16th-century Iglesia Colegiata, built in the Renaissance style; the Iglesia de Santiago, also from the 16th century, with elegant Mudejar coffered ceilings; and the Iglesia de San Juan y Los Dolores (Church of St John and the Sorrows). The Iglesia de Santo Domingo has fine cloisters. In the Iglesia de la Merced is the

The Santa María fountain in Baeza, close to Ubeda

image of Nuestra Señora de la Piedad, the town's patron saint. The Moorish Baths in the town centre have been preserved as a National Monument,

▷ *Continue on the N342 for a short distance before turning right on to the C323 north. At Peal de Becerro take the regional road east to Cazorla.*

8 Cazorla, Jaén
Capital of the area, Cazorla is dominated by the mighty mountain ranges of the Sierra de Cazorla and Sierra de Segura. Its two attractive main squares are surrounded by fine mansions. The ruins of the Iglesia de Santa María show the Plateresque style, and the two castles, Castillo de las Cinco Esquinas (Five Corners) and La

RECOMMENDED WALKS

The Sierra de Cazorla is a superb area for walking in magnificent surroundings offering a wide variety of landscapes. Its rugged peaks will doubtless lure the serious hiker, while its green pine forests, lakes and river offer some gentler strolls. The park also has facilities for canoeing and horse-riding.

designated a nature park and provides excellent walks for serious hikers and a wonderful area for nature-lovers. There are good views of the area from here over the Valley of the Guadalquivir.

i Juan Domingo 2

▶ *Return to Peal de Becerro and take the C328 westwards. Where it joins the C325 turn right on that road to Ubeda, 48km (30 miles).*

BACK TO NATURE

The Parque Natural de Cazorla is an area of great natural beauty and of considerable ecological importance. Among its wild rugged mountains, dense forests and rivers there is a wealth of wildlife. The Visitors' Centre at Torredelvinagre has a small museum and presents slide shows about the flora and fauna.

Yedra, are both medieval. The town is lovely in spring, when the purple blossoms of the many Judas trees are out.

Just north of Cazorla is the tiny village of La Iruela, perched on a high cliff, with a castle at the top. Just beyond this is the gateway to the Sierra de Cazorla and the Sierra de Segura. The area has been

8 Ubeda, Jaén
Ubeda has some great palatial buildings and many fine churches. The Sacra Capilla del Salvador (Sacred Chapel of St Salvador) was built in an elaborate Renaissance style in the 16th century, and has a superb sculpture of the *Transfiguration* by Alonso Berruguete. The Iglesia de Santa María was

begun in the 13th century and not completed until several centuries later. Of note inside are its lovely cloister and splendid grilles. The 13th-century Iglesia de San Pablo (Church of St Paul) boasts a fine portal.

From Ubeda the view is stunning, out over the ranks of olive groves to the distant hills

The heart of the old town is the Plaza Vázquez de Molina, an attractive square surrounded by elegant buildings. The Ayuntamiento is in the Palacio de las Cadenas (House of Chains), named after the iron

A few of the cave dwellings carved out of the soft tufa rock near Guadix are still inhabited

chains that were once placed around the courtyard. It is a graceful building, flanked by arcades and with an unusual 16th-century fountain built into the wall.

Other buildings worth a mention are the Montiel Palace, Bishop Canastero's Mansion (note the coat-of-arms on the outside) and the Palacio de los Marqueses de Mancera, formerly the property of the Viceroy of Peru. In the centre of the old Plaza del Mercado is a monument to San Juan de la Cruz (St John of the Cross), famous poet and mystic. He died here in the Oratory, near the Plaza, in 1591.

FOR HISTORY BUFFS

Literary enthusiasts may wish to make the short trip from Úbeda to Baeza (9km, 6 miles west), where the great Spanish poet Antonio Machado (1875–1939) lived from 1913 to 1919. He was known for his philosophical writing, and produced much work during his time here, as well as giving French classes. A monument in his memory stands in the large courtyard of the University.

▶ Take the C325 south, join the N324 south and continue on this road east to Guadix, 114km (71 miles).

🔟 Guadix, Jaén

The Renaissance cathedral is the most prominent building of the town, and features a massive tower and a baroque portal. The churches of Santiago (St James) and Santa Ana (St Anne) have fine Mudejar coffered ceilings. In the upper part of the town is the Alcazába (Moorish palace). Other buildings of note are the Palacio Episcopal and the Palacio Peñaflor. The main square, Plaza Mayor, is a fine example of Renaissance architecture and offers an attractive view of the rooftops and the cathedral tower.

Cave dwellings, hollowed out of the soft tufa rock, are to be found in the Barrio Santiago behind the town and are one of Guadix's most visited features. Some open up into further caves within, and a few have two storeys. Conical chimneys protrude from the pathways above, creating an odd spectacle. Nowadays only a few of the caves are inhabited by gypsies.

[i] *Carretera de Granada*

▶ Return to Almería on the A92/N324, 120km (75 miles).

Spain's
Moorish Legacy

Málaga is the 'capital' of the Costa del Sol, the main gateway to its famous resorts. Founded by the Phoenicians, it was held by the Moors from 711 until 1487, and the Alcazába (Moorish palace), set in attractive gardens, is now a museum. Pablo Picasso was born in Malaga, and some of his early works are in the Museo de Belles Artes.

2/3 DAYS • 347KM • 217 MILES

ITINERARY		
MÁLAGA	▶	**Vélez-Málaga (37km-23m)**
VÉLEZ-MÁLAGA	▶	**Nerja (25km-16m)**
NERJA	▶	**Almuñécar (22km-14m)**
ALMUÑÉCAR	▶	**Motril (21km-13m)**
MOTRIL	▶	**Vélez de Benaudalla (14km-9m)**
VÉLEZ DE BENAUDALLA	▶	**Granada (54km-34m)**
GRANADA	▶	**Loja (52km-32m)**
LOJA	▶	**Antequera (43km-27m)**
ANTEQUERA	▶	**Álora (39km-24m)**
ÁLORA	▶	**Málaga (40km-25m)**

Above: the Balcon de Europa at Nerja. *Left:* looking down from the Balcon, over the beach and the town to the mountains beyond

lookout point over the Mediterranean, so named by King Alfonso XII when he passed in 1885.

About 2km (1½ miles) away, near the village of Maro, are the impressive Cuevas de Nerja. They were discovered in 1959 and contain paintings from palaeolithic times.

ℹ *Puerta del Mar 2*

➤ *Continue on the N340 for 22km (14 miles) to Almuñécar.*

3 **Almuñécar,** Granada

This enchanting little town is a cluster of whitewashed houses sprawling up a steep hill, crowned by the remains of an old Moorish castle. The ancient aqueduct and the Torre del Monje (Tower of the Monk) are Roman. Also of interest is the Cueva de los Siete Palacios (Cave of Seven Palaces, or

ℹ *Pasaje de Chinitas 4*

➤ *From Málaga take the N340 east. At Torre del Mar turn north on to the C335 to Vélez-Málaga.*

1 **Vélez-Málaga,** Málaga

Lying towards the end of a valley among subtropical vegetation is the little white town of Vélez-Málaga. On top of the hill stands the old Moorish Alcázar, or castle. Take a look at the Iglesia de Santa María la Mayor (St Mary Major), the Iglesia de San Juan (St John) and the Ayuntamiento. Thursday is market day, always a colourful event.

➤ *Return south and continue on the N340 to Nerja.*

FOR CHILDREN

Located in the residential area of El Tomillar, between Torre del Mar and Vélez-Málaga, is Aquavelis, a splendid aquapark for children, which offers 11 sorts of aquatic delights, including a large swimming-pool, waterchutes and fast kamikaze slides. There are also American slopes, a spiral slide and a children's playground.

---

2 **Nerja,** Málaga

Its clifftop setting is one of Nerja's main attractions, with lovely views of the rocky coves below. Near the main square is a terrace with the famous Balcón de Europa (Balcony of Europe)

Vaults). The beaches of La
Herradura and Punta del Mar
have contributed to the growth
in tourism. The near by Punta
de la Mona is a wonderful lookout point for views over the
Mediterranean.

ⓘ *Avenida Europa Palacete la
Najarra*

▶ *Continue east to Motril.*

4 Motril, Granada
Make a brief stop here before
continuing on the next lap of
your journey. Among the town's
most important buildings are
the Iglesia Colegiata de la

Encarnación (Collegiate Church
of the Incarnation) and the
Santuario de Nuestra Señora de
la Cabeza, said to have been the
home of the mother of Boabdil,
the last of the Moorish kings of
Granada.

▶ *Take the regional road north
to Vélez de Benaudalla.*

5 Vélez de Benaudalla,
Granada
Vélez de Benaudalla is a typica
Andalucian village of white
houses and red-tiled roofs clus-
tering below a large hexagonal
tower and with beautiful moun
tains around it. A good place fo
a break before you continue th
next stage which is quite a driv

Granada, the Alhambra. *Left:* intricate decoration in the Mexuar Court. *Inset: an overall view*

RECOMMENDED WALKS

A road branching off northeast from Vélez de Benaudalla leads to the region of Las Alpujarras (which stems from the Moorish 'Al-Busherat' meaning the grassland) and this offers some excellent walking in surroundings that are very agreeable without making too many demands on your stamina.

▶ *Continue north on the regional road for a short distance, then turn right on to the N323 north for 54km (34 miles) to Granada.*

❻ Granada, Granada
The city of Granada is built on three hills: the Alhambra, the Albaicín and the Sacromonte, dominated by the beautiful snowcapped mountains of the Sierra Nevada. It is thought to have been founded by the Iberians. The Romans and the Visigoths were here later, and in 711 it was conquered by the Moors. The town was called Gharnatha and a fortress was erected on the Alhambra Hill. During the Reconquest it became the last stronghold of

SCENIC ROUTES

Solynieve is a winter resort in the Sierra Nevada that offers excellent facilities for winter sports, normally under a brilliant blue sky. The area is reached by a very winding mountainous road southeast of Granada in beautiful scenery. A further drive takes you along one of the highest roads in Europe to the Pico de Veleta, second-highest peak in the Sierra Nevada. In spring the whole area is a fairyland of pink blossoms.

the Moors until 2 January 1492, when the Moorish Caliph, Emir Abdallah Mohammad XI, known to the Spaniards as Boabdil, the Boy King, was deposed and Moorish domination of Spain came to an end.

You can either walk up the hill to the Alhambra or take the longer route by car. The entrance is through the Puerta de las Granadas (Gateway of the Pomegranates), built by the Habsburg Emperor Charles V. A short walk up a pathway lined by elm trees (planted by the Duke of Wellington) leads to the Puerta de la Justicia (Gate of Justice). On the west side of the square stands the oldest

structure of all, the Alcazába. Dating back to the 9th century, only its outer walls remain.

To the east is the Palacio de Carlos V (Palace of Emperor Charles V). Begun in 1526 and never completed, it was built in classical Renaissance style, in sharp contrast to the style of architecture which characterises the Alhambra. Many beautiful treasures can be seen in the two museums here, the Museo Provincial de Bellas Artes (Museum of Fine Arts) and the Museo de la Alhambra (Museum of the Alhambra), noted for its priceless Alhambra Vase, which dates back to 1320.

To the north is the masterpiece itself, the Alcázar, or Casa Real (Royal Palace). Started in 1334 and completed in 1391, it is a remarkable architectural achievement, characterised by rich and elaborate decorations. Entrance is through the Patio del Mexuar (Mexuar Court), formerly the council chamber and later used as a chapel, which leads to the lovely Patio de los Arrayanes (Court of the Myrtle Trees). Adjoining this is the Sala de los Embajadores (Hall of the Ambassadors). Originally used as a throne room for the Moorish kings, it is noted for its rich decorations and magnificent domed ceiling.

The Italian-style gardens, refreshed with fountains, at the Generalife Palace, once the summer residence of the Moorish kings.

The Mozárabes Gallery leads to the splendid Patio de los Leones (Court of Lions), a main feature of the palace and the old heart of the harem. Chambers leading from here include the Sala de los Abencerrajes (Abencerrajes Gallery) to the south, with an impressive stalactite ceiling and a marble fountain; and the Sala de los Reyes (King's Chamber) to the east, noted for its alcove paintings of historical scenes. The Sala de

The white houses of Andalucía set off the flowers the Spanish love to tend; here, in Antequera

las dos Hermanas (Hall of the Two Sisters), on the north side, features an intricately decorated honeycomb dome. This leads, in turn, to the Sala de los Ajimeces (Ajimeces Gallery) and on to the Mirador de Daraxa, a charming little look-out balcony. The Patio de Daraxa (Daraxa Courtyard) is a lovely inner courtyard with cypresses and orange trees.

More galleries and patios may be visited before you make your way to the Generalife, on the Cerro del Sol (Hill of the Sun). The Palacio del Generalife was completed in 1319 and served as the summer residence of the Moorish kings. The Patio de la Acequia (Canal Court) is planted with roses, laurels and orange trees and the surrounding gardens are laid out in Italian style.

Allow time to explore the town itself. The heart of the city is a large square called Plaza de Isabel la Católica. Here stands a monument to commemorate the Santa Fé Agreement of 1492 made between Isabel la Católica and Columbus. The 19th-century Ayuntamiento stands in the smaller Plaza del Carmen. Near by is the 18th-century Palacio Arzobispal (Archbishop's Palace). A little further on is the Catedral de Santa María de la Encarnación (St Mary of the Incarnation). Begun in 1523 and consecrated in 1561, it stands as a memorial to the victory of Christianity in Spain. It has a richly decorated interior and a fine Capilla Mayor (Main Chapel), which is noted for its high dome and beautiful stained-glass window. Other buildings of interest include the Carthusian Monastery, the Audiencia (Law Court), the 16th-century Iglesia de Santa Ana and the Casa de Castríl, which houses the Museo Arqueológico (Archaeological Museum). On the right bank of

the Darro ravine is the Albaicín, the old Moorish quarter, where a wander around its narrow, cobblestoned streets and hidden corners recaptures the past. Behind the Albaicín is the Sacromonte Hill, where the gypsies live in caves and put on flamenco shows.

Beware when the bullfight is on. All streets become one-way, leading right to the bull-ring, where you might find yourself inadvertently spending the rest of the day!

[i] *Plaza de Mariana Pineda 10*

▶ *Take the A92/N342 west to Loja.*

7 Loja, Granada
Located in the west of the province of Granada, Loja is dominated by the ruins of an old Moorish castle. Buildings of interest in the town include the 15th-century Iglesia de la Encarnación, the 16th-century Iglesia de San Gabriel and the Convento de Santa Clara

(Convent and Church of Santa Clara), which has a fine Mudejar ceiling. Take a look also at the Ayuntamiento, the Granary, the Hospital de la Misericordia and the old Alcazába (fortress) that over-looks the town.

In the vicinity are two lovely waterfalls, the Colas de Caballo (Horsetail Falls), and Los Infiernos (Hell), which cascade into the River Genil.

SPECIAL TO...

The Renaissance Palacio de Carlos V (Palace of Emperor Charles V) provides a beautiful setting for the Festival of Music and Dance, which is held here annually at the end of June/ beginning of July and is recog-nised as an important inter-national event. The programme includes concerts, ballet, guitar recitals and other events, with performances by famous artists and orchestras.

▶ *Continue on the N342 west, turning off left on A345/ C337 to Antequera shortly after passing Archidona.*

❽ Antequera, Málaga

The presence of prehistoric dolmen caves in the area indicates this market town's ancient origins. The old castle on top of the hill was the first fortress to be taken by the Christians (in 1410) during the reconquest of the Province of Granada, although it was later recaptured by the Moors. There is a fine view across the plains from its well-preserved ramparts. Close to the castle is the 16th-century Colegiata de Santa María la Mayor, noted for its Mudejar ceiling. The churches of San Sebastián and St Augustín feature Mudejar belfries and the churches of El Carmen and los Remedios have fine baroque interiors. If you visit the Museo Municipal, look for the bronze statue of a Roman boy called Efebo.

The dolmen caves are to the left of the Granada road. These prehistoric caves served as burial places in neolithic times and have great historical significance.

ℹ *Infante Don Fernando – Ed San Luis*

▶ *Take the C337 south-west for 39km (24 miles) to Álora, which lies slightly off the road.*

❾ Álora, Málaga

Álora stands high above the River Guadalhorce in an area of olive and citrus groves. This charming town has a ruined castle, a 17th-century church with an unusual wooden roof and a few fine buildings.

▶ *Go back to the C337, turn right and return to Málaga.*

The large and dramatic tower of the cathedral at Málaga

BACK TO NATURE

Some 15km (9 miles) south of Antequera is El Torcal de Antequera, an area of deep ravines, where great limestone boulders have formed bizarre shapes, suggesting a petrified forest. It is rich in plant life, including the Spanish bluebell, rare species of iris and a number of different types of orchid. Twenty-four kilometres (15 miles) northwest of Antequera, off the N334, is the Laguna de la Fuente de Piedra, Andalucia's largest lake and an important breeding ground for flamingos. Other species of birds seen here include black-headed gulls, mallards, red-crested pochards and even the occasional white stork.

FOR HISTORY BUFFS

Santa Fé, west of Granada, was the scene of two great historical events; the signing of the surrender of Granada in November 1491, and the signing, on 17 April 1492, of the agreements with Christopher Columbus that paved the way for his first voyage of discovery across the ocean.
A few kilometres away is the village of Fuentevaqueros, where the famous Spanish poet Federico García Lorca was born in 1899; his former home is now a museum. La Huerta de San Vicente (San Vicente Orchard), where he spent many summers writing, has also been converted into a museum and is a centre for studies on the poet. The Federico García Lorca Memorial Park, between Viznar and Alfacar (northeast of Granada), marks the place where he is said to have been shot in 1936.

The Sun Coast
& Medieval Villages

Pleasant features of Málaga are its lively harbour and the seafront promenade, or Paseo Marítimo. The nearby Mercado (Market Hall), is a busy, bustling place when the fresh catch of the day comes in. The old quarter has narrow, twisting streets and plenty of old *bodegas* (wine vaults); Málaga is known for its production of sweetish wines from the muscatel grape.

3 DAYS • 403KM • 250 MILES

ITINERARY

MÁLAGA	▶ Torremolinos (15km-9m)
TORREMOLINOS	▶ **Benalmádena-Pueblo** (9km-6m)
BENALMÁDENA-PUEBLO	▶ Mijas (8km-5m)
MIJAS	▶ Fuengirola (7km-4m)
FUENGIROLA	▶ Marbella (27km-17m)
MARBELLA	▶ Puerto Banus (7km-4m)
PUERTO BANUS	▶ Casares (49km-30m)
CASARES	▶ San Roque (44km-27m)
SAN ROQUE	▶ La Línea (7km-4m)
LA LÍNEA	▶ **Castellar de la Frontera** (27km-17m)
CASTELLAR DE LA FRONTERA	▶ Jimena de la Frontera (29km-18m)
JIMENA DE LA FRONTERA	▶ Ronda (62km-39m)
RONDA	▶ Coin (75km-47m)
COIN	▶ Málaga (37km-23m)

i *Pasaje de Chinitas 4*

▷ *Take the N340 to Torremolinos, turning left into the town.*

❶ Torremolinos, Málaga
A tiny fishing village in the 19th century, with towers (*torres*) and windmills (*molinos*) in the vicinity, Torremolinos was one of the first places to cater for mass tourism, and appeals particularly to families. Its beaches are of fine grit and have facilities for watersports. One of its more agreeable areas is the Carihuela district, which has a pedestrian esplanade with bars, cafés and good fish restaurants.

i *Plaza Blas Infante 1*

▷ *Continue along the coast road to Benalmádena Costa. Turn right for 4km (2½ miles) to Benalmádena-Pueblo.*

❷ Benalmádena-Pueblo,
Málaga
Benalmádena Costa is a popular resort, with beaches, an impressive yacht harbour, casino and golf club. A short drive inland leads to Benalmádena-Pueblo, a delightful Andalucian village dating back to the Phoenicians, Romans and Moors. At Arroyo de la Miel, near by, you can see the ruins of a Roman arch, once the entrance to a building known as El Tribunal (Tribune). A museum displays archaeological finds from the area.

i *Avenida Antonio Machado 12*

▷ *Continue on the regional road west for 8km (5 miles) to Mijas.*

❸ Mijas, Málaga
The little town of Mijas is so picturesque that it was quickly 'discovered' by tourists, with all the inevitable changes that result. The village is still appealing, however, with pretty whitewashed houses, tiny winding streets and flowers every-

The view from Mijas

where. There are wonderful views down to the coast. Renowned as a crafts centre, it specialises in ceramics and basket weaving.

▷ *Take the regional road south for 7km (4 miles) to Fuengirola.*

SCENIC ROUTES

Although parts of the coast road are dominated by high-rise blocks, the sea views and dramatic silhouette of the mountains in the hinterland make up for it. The drive to Mijas and back through the pine-clad mountains offers lovely views of the coast. The mountain road up to Casares is also very attractive. From San Roque the road winds up to Jimena de la Frontera (on the C3331), then goes through the dramatic landscapes of the Serranía de Ronda, with its wild, eroded rock formations.

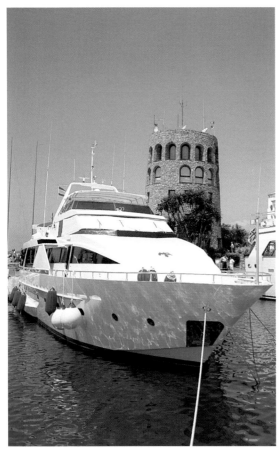

Boats of many nationalities crowd the marina at Puerto José Banús

decked balconies. These open out on to the Plaza de los Naranjos (Square of Oranges), an enchanting square edged with orange trees and surrounded by restaurants and boutiques. A walk along the old fortifications overlooks the area, with the old Moorish castle way above.

The town of Ojén, 8km (5 miles) inland, is reached by a winding road. It has a pleasant 16th- to 18th-century church, a beautifully laid-out Andalucian cemetery, and is well known for its pottery.

[i] *Gloriete de la Fontanilla s/n*

▶ *Continue for a short distance along the coast road. Branch off to Puerto José Banús, 7km (4 miles).*

6 Puerto José Banús, Málaga

This short stretch between Marbella and Banús, known as the Golden Mile, is one of the most attractive parts of the Costa del Sol, with luxurious properties set in lovely gardens. The area is lush and green, with tropical flowers and vegetation, framed by the dramatic silhouette of the mountains in the background. Puerto José Banús was created as a marina for Marbella, and is an Andalucian type village of white houses lining a yacht harbour. Bars, restaurants and boutiques sprang up and it became a very fashionable resort.

▶ *Continue along the N340 coast road. Just past Estepona take a right turn to Casares, 20km (12 miles).*

4 Fuengirola, Málaga

Fuengirola has also changed beyond recognition, from a sleepy fishing port to a resort of high-rise blocks. It has extensive beaches, bars, restaurants, lively evening entertainment, and attracts the crowds in the summer. It has also become a favoured winter retreat for retired people. Culture is minimal here, though there are the ruins of a 10th-century castle.

[i] *Avenida Jesús Santos Rein*

▶ *Continue on the N340 for 27km (17 miles) to Marbella.*

5 Marbella, Málaga

Marbella is the centre of the Costa del Sol. The description 'playground of the rich' refers to the jetsetters and pop stars who stay in luxurious surroundings and frequent the smart restaurants and nightspots to be found along this part of the coast. The appearance of tall, modern blocks over the years has inevitably changed Marbella's skyline and character. However, it has some attractive areas, including its busy harbour and a seafront promenade with bars and restaurants.

On a clear day Africa is faintly visible, while at the western end of the scene is the unmistakable outline of the Rock of Gibraltar. Its real delight, however, is the old town behind the main street, with its narrow streets, white-washed houses and flower-

7 Casares, Málaga

This part of the tour takes you inland to the Sierra Bermeja and, although it means returning to the coast by the same road, you will not regret it when you catch your first glimpse of Casares on the hill high above

The medieval village of Casares overlooked by a Moorish castle

This medieval village is one of the most attractive in the area. A gentle stroll up the steep, winding streets leads to the ruins of its Moorish castle. There are two churches, the parish church and the Iglesia de San Sebastián, both 18th-century, and a beautifully laid out cemetery adorned with flowers.

▶ *Return to the N340 and continue to San Roque.*

8 San Roque, Cádiz
San Roque was founded in the 18th century by the Spanish inhabitants of Gibraltar, who left after it was taken by the British in 1704. The town is situated on a low hill, with pleasant views. Places of interest include the Iglesia de Santa María and the Palacio de los Gobernadores.

▶ *Take the N351 for 7km (4 miles) to La Línea de la Concepción.*

9 La Línea, Cádiz
La Línea de la Concepción stands at the foot of the Rock of Gibraltar and is the border town between Spain and the British colony of Gibraltar. Closed for many years, the frontier is now open for travel between the two countries. Whether or not you decide to visit, it is worth making the drive to get a close look at this gigantic piece of rock silhouetted against the sky,
an impressive sight and the landmark of the whole coast.

▶ *Return to San Roque and take N340 west for 3km (2 miles); turn right on C3331 to Castellar de la Frontera, 7km (4 miles) off this road on an unclassified road.*

FOR HISTORY BUFFS

The Cueva de la Pileta, some 27km (17 miles) south-west of Ronda, shelter paintings of animals in shades of red and black and drawings of huge fish, believed to date back some 25,000 years. The paintings resemble those in the Altamira Caves in northern Spain.

Bridge over the gorge of the River Guadalevín which divides Ronda

🔟 Castellar de la Frontera, Cádiz

Your route now takes you into the hinterland of southern Spain, where you can enjoy superb mountain scenery and visits to some of Andalucia's famous white towns.

Castellar de Frontera is one of these lovely old walled cities, crowned by a large Moorish castle. Its white houses, red-tiled roofs and surrounding forests all add to its attractions. Ancient walls dating back to the 13th century enclose the old part of town, which has tiny streets and pretty squares.

▶ *Return to and continue north on the C3331 for 29km (18 miles) to Jimena de la Frontera.*

🔟 Jimena de la Frontera, Cádiz

The little town of Jimena de la Frontera is also an attractive cluster of whitewashed houses built up a hillside. It was under Moorish occupation for a considerable time and has a well-preserved castle from that period, reached through a triple-arched gateway.

▶ *Take the C341 northeast for 62km (39 miles) to Ronda.*

RECOMMENDED WALKS

The Parque Natural de Grazalema offers good walking. Specific routes are laid out for serious hikers (information from the park wardens). If you want the best shots of the famous Puente Nuevo bridge over the gorge, take your camera and steel yourself for a scramble down the hillside, where you will be rewarded by the famous view that is associated with Ronda. Take care how you go, however, as it is a steepish climb.

SPECIAL TO...

The bullring in Ronda was built in 1785 and is one of the oldest and most famous in Spain. The museum beneath the ring has posters of the earliest fights that took place, as well as other memorabilia. Bullfights are normally held in Ronda only during its major festivals in May and September.

🔟 Ronda, Málaga

Ronda is well known for its spectacular setting, in particular the dramatic view of the bridge over the gorge of the River Guadalevín, which splits the town in two. It lies on the edge of the Serranía de Ronda, against a backdrop of sheer rock. Its unique situation, together with its attractive old quarter and historic interest, makes it a fascinating place to visit. It is one of the oldest towns in Spain and was for a long time capital of an independent Moorish kingdom, conquered by the Catholics in 1485. In the new part of town is one of the oldest bullrings in Spain.

There are magnificent views from here of the deep river valley and rugged splendours of the Serranía de Ronda. Across the famous Puente Nuevo bridge is La Ciudad, the old part. The bridge was built between 1775 and 1793 and is an outstanding architectural achievement. The old town is a maze of narrow, twisting streets and houses. The Colegiata de Santa María la Mayor was originally a Moorish mosque, and is now the cathedral of Ronda. The Puerta de Almocobar (Moorish gates) were entered by the victorious Ferdinand with his troops in 1485. The Casa del Rey Moro (House of the Moorish King) is a beautiful old mansion with lovely terraced gardens. A long flight of steps from here runs down the rocks to the river far below.

▶ *Take the C344 to Coín.*

A typical Ronda house with doorway carvings and balcony

🔟 Coín, Málaga

Coín is a good place for a break on the last part of the return journey to Málaga. Set in the Valley of Orange Blossoms, this is a typical Andalucian market town of whitewashed houses and pretty squares, known for its colourful Saturday market.

▶ *Take the C344 and almost at once branch off left on a minor road northeast towards Cártama. Cross the Río Guadalhorce and turn right for Málaga, 37km (23 miles).*

BACK TO NATURE

A few kilometres west of Ronda is the Parque Natural de Grazalema, a vast wilderness reputed to be one of the wettest spots in Spain, known for its forest of a rare species of fir (pinsapos). The charming village of Grazalema is a good base from which to make excursions. Birdwatchers may spot owls, eagles, blue rock thrushes and chaffinches among many species to be seen here. Botanists can look out for rare species of plants, such as the yellow-flowered knapwood and for the 'maquis', growing among the forest.

The Great
Mosque &
Moorish Towns

The capital of Andalucia, Sevilla stands on the River Guadalquivir, with the 13th century Torre del Oro, built to guard the river, as a landmark. The town was ruled by the Moors from 712 to 1248 and the Giralda, minaret of the Great Mosque, is Sevilla's most prominent feature. The Palace of the Alcázar was built by Pedro the Cruel (1350–69) on a 12th-century Moorish fortress.

ITINERARY		
SEVILLA	▶	**Carmona** (32km-20m)
CARMONA	▶	**Ecija** (55km-34m)
ECIJA	▶	**Córdoba** (54km-34m)
CÓRDOBA	▶	**Baena** (61km-38m)
BAENA	▶	**Priego de Córdoba**
		(29km-18m)
PRIEGO DE CÓRDOBA	▶	**Cabra** (27km-17m)
CABRA	▶	**Lucena** (11km-7m)
LUCENA	▶	**Estepa** (45km-28)
ESTEPA	▶	**Osuna** (24km-15m)
OSUNA	▶	**Sevilla** (90km-56m)

2/3 DAYS • 428KM • 267 MILES

ℹ Avenida de la Constitución 21B, Sevilla

▶ *From Sevilla take the NIV east for 32km (20 miles) to Carmona.*

❶ Carmona, Sevilla

The town of Carmona stands on the highest point of a flat plain. It has a Moorish fortress, which holds a commanding position and offers good views of the countryside. This delightful little town has two old entrance gates, known as the Córdoba Gate and Sevilla Gate.

SCENIC ROUTES

The first part of the journey takes you through the fertile plains of the Guadalquivir valley, with patches of yellow and green fields relieved by olive groves and gently rolling hills, offering pleasant rather than remarkable scenery. There is a very scenic stretch between Priego de Córdoba and Cabra on the C336, and some attractive scenery round Lucena.

The Iglesia de Santa María de la Asunción is 15th-century late Gothic, and you can see the patio of the Great Mosque on whose foundations the church was erected. The Santuario (1525–51) has a notable retable while Roman mosaics decorate the Ayuntamiento.

West of the town is a Roman necropolis. This network of underground tombs was arranged in groups, with a crematorium at the front. Look out for the tomb known as El Elefante for its unusual carving of a young elephant.

▶ *Continue northeast on the NIV for 55km (35 miles) to Ecija.*

❷ Ecija, Sevilla

The ancient town of Ecija lies beside a small basin on the River Genil. Thought to date back to Greek times, it was known to the Romans as Astigi and pottery, mosaics and other items found during excavations have given some insight into its early history. Its baroque belfries, decorated with colourful tiles, are an attractive feature

Delicate stonework ornaments the Renaissance façade of Sevilla's splendid Ayuntamiento

of the town. The Iglesia de Santiago, entered through an 18th-century patio, has Mudejar windows from a previous building, and an elaborate Gothic retable. There are several handsome 18th-century palaces in the town including the Palacio Benamej, the Palacio Peñaflor, decorated with paintings on the outside, and the Palacio Valdehermoso, which has a fine Renaissance exterior.

▶ *Continue on the NIV northeast for 54km (34 miles) to Córdoba.*

RECOMMENDED WALKS

A detour north of Ecija takes you to the village of Hornachuelos, which is on the edge of a large game-hunting area. This stretches away to the north of the region and offers some excellent walking.

3 **Córdoba,** Córdoba

Córdoba, a town of narrow streets and alleyways, is situated on a plain between the Sierra de Córdoba and the River Guadalquivir. Córdoba suffers from extremes of climate, with very hot summers and cold weather during the winter.

Already quite prominent when the Romans arrived, the town continued to flourish and

The red-and-white striped arches in the the mosque at Córdoba

in 152BC became the capital of Hispana Ulterior.

It developed into a prosperous city under the Moors and was an important cultural and artistic centre. The town was conquered by the Catholic King Ferdinand in 1436, having long been used by Christian leaders as a centre for plotting the retaking of Granada from the Moors. It was in Córdoba that Christopher Columbus was granted the commission by Queen Isabella for his first exploratory expedition to the New World.

The great Mezquita (mosque) was constructed by the Moors between the 8th and 10th centuries. It is one of the largest mosques in the world and is a remarkable achievement of Moorish architecture. Its beauty lies in its interior. As you enter you are confronted by hundreds of columns made of onyx, marble and other materi-

als, designed to catch the light, forming a myriad of colours. The columns are topped by capitals and crowned with striking red-and-white-striped arches, typical of Moorish art. An important feature of a mosque is the Mihrab, a sacred niche hollowed out from the wall. They are always built to face Mecca in the east, although this one points more south than

east, owing to a miscalculation. From 1436, when Córdoba was taken by the Christians, the mosque became the cathedral. The Patio de los Naranjos (Court of Orange Trees) is

particularly attractive in spring when it is filled with the scent of orange blossom. Through the Puerta del Perdón (Gate of Forgiveness) a flight of steps leads up to the baroque Campanario (bell tower). It provides a superb view of the rooftops of Córdoba and the sweep of the River Guadalquivir.

The Museo Arqueológico and the Museo de Bellas Artes have interesting exhibits of sculptures and Roman antiquities in the first case, and a fine collection of paintings in the latter. Those with an interest in bullfighting should visit the Museo Taurino (Museum of Bullfighting). A statue of the famous Spanish bullfighter, Manolete, stands in the Plaza San Marina de las Aguas.

The Zoco (from the old Arab souk) has displays of handicrafts and occasional flamenco performances.

[i] *Torrijos 10 (Palacio de Congresos)*

FOR HISTORY BUFFS

On the N432 between Córdoba and Baena is the small town of Castro del Río, where Spain's famous author, Miguel Cervantes, was imprisoned for a time in 1592. You can take a look at his old prison, which is housed in the Ayuntamiento. The town also features the ruins of an ancient castle and a Roman bridge.

▶ Take the N432 southeast for 61km (38 miles) to Baena.

4 **Baena,** Córdoba

The route continues through some of Andalucía's delightful pueblos blancos, or white towns. While sharing many common characteristics, each has its own style. Baena is an oil-producing town and is typically Andalucian. A cluster of whitewashed houses climbs up a slope, dominated by the remains of old Moorish battle-

FOR CHILDREN

Córdoba's zoo, located on Avenida Linneo (in front of the Jardín Botánico), has a wide variety of animals, with an unusual black lion. Another treat for children could be a tour around town in an elegant horse-drawn carriage. Aquatic parks near Córdoba include the Guadalpark, located at Polígono Aeropuerto-Sevilla-Este (open May to September) and Aquasierra in Villafranca de Córdoba.

ments. The Iglesia de Santa María la Mayor dates back to the 16th century. The Convento de la Madre de Dios was built in the Mudejar style and has an interesting carved retable.

▶ *Continue southeast on the N432. Close to the River Guadajoz turn south on the N321 to Priego de Córdoba.*

5 **Priego de Córdoba,** Córdoba

Priego de Córdoba is one of the region's little gems. Its dazzling white houses, flower-decked windows and tiny, winding streets give it a very Moorish look. Elegant 17th- and 18th-century mansions reflect prosperous times when Priego was the centre of the silk and textile industries. Several churches including La Asunción and La Aurora are masterpieces of fine baroque architecture. An abundance of springs here feed the splendid Fuente del Rey.

Alcalá Zamora, first president of the Second Republic of Spain (1931–6), was born here in 1877. His former home is now a museum (Museo de Niceto Alcalá Zamora). A viewpoint from El Adrave, high on the hill, shows the fertile lands around and distant mountains.

▶ *Take the C336 west, turning right on to the C327 for 2km (1 mile) to reach the town.*

6 **Cabra,** Córdoba

A pleasant park, the Parque del Fuente del Río (Park of the Source of the River) welcomes you to Cabra. The town is another Andalucian delight, with white houses, red-tiled roofs and old narrow streets. The Iglesia de San Juan Bautista, dates back to the time of the Visigoths.

▶ *Take C327 southwest for 11km (7 miles) to Lucena, just off the road.*

7 **Lucena,** Córdoba

At the foot of the Sierra de Arcos is the attractive little town of Lucena renowned for its bronze, furniture-making and copperware. Fine churches are the 15th-century Renaissance Iglesia de San Matéo, the Iglesia de Santiago and the Convento de San Francisco. Lucena was the scene of the capture of the boy-king Boabdil, the last Moorish ruler, by the Count of Cabra in 1483, during an unsuccessful revolt against the Christians.

▶ *About 2km (1 mile) west of town take C338 to Estepa.*

The main square at Lucena and the Iglesia de San Mateo. *Inset:* detail of the doorway of Iglesia de Santiago

Carriage rides are a restful way of sightseeing in Sevilla, especially through the Parque de Maria Luisa

8 Estepa, Córdoba

Estepa, lying among farmlands, is known throughout Spain for its confectionery, especially its Christmas cakes known as *mantecados* and *polvorones*. As well as the churches of Santa María la Mayor, La Asunción and Los Remedios, the 18th-century Palacio de los Marqueses de Cervales is

worth a look, along with the Gothic interior of the old castle keep and the splendid Torre de la Victoria (Tower of Victory), all that remains of a former convent. There are good views from a nearby lookout-point called El Balcón de Andalucía.

▶ *Take N334 west to Osuna.*

9 Osuna, Córdoba

The history of Osuna dates back to the time of the Iberians. Like so many towns in southern Spain, it was taken by the Romans and then ruled by the Moors until 1239, when the town was captured by Ferdinand III. Of the many fine monuments note the Colegiata, a Renaissance church that houses valuable works of art. La Universidad (University) is another important building, with its two towers built like minarets. The Casa de los Cepeda, Palacio del Cabildo Colegial and Palacio de la Antigua Audiencia have elegant façades. The Museo Arqueológico is in the old Torre de Agua (Water Tower).

▶ *Return to Sevilla on the N334.*

BACK TO NATURE

The Lagunas de Córdoba, a series of salt-water lakes around Aguilar de la Frontera northwest of Cabra, are inhabited by many different species of waterfowl in the winter. An attractive and rare visitor is the white-headed duck, with its lovely blue bill. Some of the lakes shrink or dry up during summer, but fill again after the rains. Flamingos and shelduck inhabit the Laguna del Salobral, the largest of the lakes.

SPECIAL TO...

A turn to the right just before Cabra leads to El Picacho and the Ermita Virgen de la Sierra (Shrine of the Virgin of the Mountains), which contains the much-venerated image of the patron saint of Cabra.
The province of Córdoba has quite a reputation for wines and enthusiasts can follow the Ruta del Vino (Wine Route) which leaves Córdoba on the NIV and goes southwest to Montemayor and Montilla. You can visit many of the wine cellars, which offer a number of different sherry-type wines.

Exquisitely carved detail defines the little balcony of the church of La Merced at Osuna

Trail of the
New World
Explorers

3 DAYS • 353KM • 218 MILES

ITINERARY	
SEVILLA	▶ **Santiponce** (11km-7m)
SANTIPONCE	▶ **Itálica** (1km-1m)
ITÁLICA	▶ **Aracena** (81km-50m)
ARACENA	▶ **Cortegana** (26km-16m)
CORTEGANA	▶ **Zalamea la Real**
	(49km-30m)
ZALAMEA LA REAL	▶ **Valverde del Camino**
	(20km-12m)
VALVERDE DEL CAMINO	▶ **Gibraléon** (39km-24m)
GIBRALÉON	▶ **Huelva** (18km-11m)
HUELVA	▶ **Monasterio de la Rábida**
	(9km-6m)
MONASTERIO DE LA RÁBIDA	▶ **Moguer** (10km-6m)
MOGUER	▶ **Niebla** (24km-15m)
NIEBLA	▶ **La Palma del Condado**
	(12km-7m)
LA PALMA DEL CONDADO	▶ **Sevilla** (53km-33m)

Sevilla has three major museums: the Museo del Bellas Artes in the old Merced Monastery, with superb Spanish works, the Museo de Arte Contemporáneo, in the old chapel of the Cathedral Chapter, and the Museo Arqueológico in the Palacio del Renacimiento. Among Sevilla's parks and gardens, those of the Alcázar are outstanding, with Moorish to Renaissance sections.

ⅰ *Avenida de la Constitución 21B*

▷ *From Sevilla take the motorway west over the river. Turn right on to the N630 to Santiponce.*

❶ Santiponce, Sevilla

The chief monument in Santiponce is the former Monasterio de San Isidro del Campo, which was founded in 1298 by Alfonso Guzmán as a Cistercian house. Guzmán, known as 'El Bueno' ('The Good One') was renowned for the heroic role he played in defending Tarifa castle against the Moors. The church contains a remarkable 17th-century retable by the artist Martínez Montañés, noted for the figure of St Jerome. Montañés also carved the effigies on the tombs of Guzmán and his wife. A second church marks the first resting place of the body of Cortés, conqueror of Mexico, before it was taken to Mexico.

▷ *Take an unclassified road northwest to Itálica, on left.*

❷ Itálica, Sevilla

The Roman ruins of Itálica are considered of major significance. Originally founded in 206BC by Scipio Africanus as a place of retirement for his veteran soldiers, the city flourished and by the 2nd century AD had become one of the most important Roman cities in Spain. Two great Roman emperors – Trajan (AD 52–117) and Hadrian (AD 76–138) – were born here. The most important building is the Amphitheatre, which was one of the largest in the Roman Empire, with a capacity of up to 40,000 spectators. Faintly visible traces can still be seen of a forum, city streets, the foundations of villas, mosaic floors: evidence of the old city. The treasures found here are on display in Sevilla's Museum of Archaeology.

▷ *Keep on this unclassified road to rejoin the N630. Turn left to go north on the N630, then after 25km (15 miles) turn left on to the N433 northwest to Aracena.*

Imagine a spectacle in this Roman amphitheatre at Italica with 40,000 spectators cramming the terraces

❸ Aracena, Huelva

The Convento de Santa Catalina (Convent of St Catalina) has a notable doorway. On top of the Cerro del Castillo (Castle Hill) are the remains of a castle, which was built in the 13th century by the Knights Templar. Of mixed Gothic and Mudejar styles, it features an old tower, originally a minaret

---

SCENIC ROUTES

This route becomes very scenic after you have joined the N435 from Cortegana through to Zalamea la Real and on to Valverde del Camino There is also some appealing scenery around Moguer. The route from Huelva to Matalascañas, should you decide to visit Coto Doñana, offers a beautiful drive along miles of deserted beaches.

---

nd decorated in similar style to he Giralda of Sevilla.

Near Aracena are the Grutas e las Maravillas (Grottos of arvels). Over 1,000m (1,094 ards) in length, they are noted or the variety of shapes and olours in the stalactites and talagmites which are reflected n underground pools and rivers.

▶ Take N433 west to Cortegana, just south of this road.

RECOMMENDED WALKS

Aracena is a good base for walks in the Sierra de Aracena, where you will find orange and lemon groves, great oak forests and tiny isolated villages. There is a superb view of the area from the top of La Peña Arias Montano.

4 Cortegana, Huelva
The small town of Cortegana was originally a Roman settlement known as Corticata. Its main assets are its beautiful setting, an interesting little parish church and an old castle.

▶ Take the regional road southeast. Turn right on N435 to Zalamea la Real.

5 Zalamea la Real, Huelva
The town's most notable building is the Iglesia de la Asunción (Assumption), an elegant neoclassical monument from the 17th century. There are several interesting old hermitages.

The impressive Minas de Ríotinto (Rio Tinto Copper Mines) are about 6km (4½ miles) east of town. Already in use during Iberian and Roman times, the mines were abandoned when the Visigoths came, and only regenerated in the last century. For a long time they were a British concern, reverting to Spanish ownership in 1954. There are still English-style houses, and a small museum in an old engine shed.

Kite-flying by Aracena's castle ruins
Left: the 13th-century church

➤ Continue on the same road south towards Valverde del Camino. Turn left where signposted into the town.

6 Valverde del Camino, Huelva

The town of Valverde del Camino is noted for its production of wood, metal and leather goods, including leather wine bottles. Buildings of note include the attractive Ermita de la Trinidad and the Iglesia de Nuestra Señora del Reposo (Church of Our Lady of Rest).

➤ Rejoin and take the N435 south. At Trigueros turn right on an unclassified road to Gibraleón.

7 Gibraleón, Huelva

Gibraleón is a town with ancient roots. Some of the people may be descendants of the slaves brought here by the Spaniards in the 15th century. Among the most interesting buildings in the town are the Iglesia de Santiago, the Iglesia de San Juan and the Chapel of El Carmen. The 16th-century Convento del Vado still preserves the remnants of its old walls.

➤ Take the N431 south. Continue straight on to Huelva when the N431 branches off east.

8 Huelva, Huelva

The region played an important role in the events leading to the Voyages of Discovery across the ocean. Christopher Columbus came to Huelva with his son in 1485 and stayed in the nearby Monasterio de la Rábida. The first expedition set sail from the area in 1492, to reach land two months later. At the end of the Paseo del Conquero is the modest white shrine of Nuestra Señora de la Cinta, with a Mudejar roof and a wall painting of the Virgin, patron saint of the city. A tile painting by the artist Zuloaga commemorates a visit made here by Columbus on his return from one of his voyages.

Huelva was severely damaged by an earthquake in 1755 and only a handful of buildings remain from the past. The 17th-century Iglesia de la Merced (now the cathedral) has an elegant doorway of mixed styles and houses an image of the Virgen de la Cinta. The 16th-century Iglesia de San

Pastel-washed houses with graceful balconies beside the Church of Our Lady of Rest at Valverde

Pedro features a tower with attractive tile decorations. The Iglesia de la Concepción, also dating from the 16th century, is noted for its paintings by the Spanish artist Zurbarán.

BACK TO NATURE

The Coto Doñana is one of Spain's largest and most important nature parks. This vast expanse of flat salt marshes (*marismas*), dunes and pine forests lies in the delta of the River Guadalquivir, covering an area of some 50,625 hectares (125,000 acres). Thousands of migratory birds come here, and large colonies of birds nest in the cork-oak trees. It is also the home of a variety of other animals, and has many rare species of flower and plant life. Matalascañas, located down the coast southeast of Huelva, is the usual starting point for visiting the reserve. It can only be visited as part of a guided tour or with special permission.

The Museo Provincial Arqueológico has a collection of antiquities from the region, including some beautiful Roman amphorae (vessels). Its fine arts section features works from the Flemish school of painting as well as paintings by local artists.

ⓘ *Avenida de Alemania 12*

▶ *Take the N442 and cross over the Río Tinto. Shortly after, take a left turn to the Monasterio de la Rábida.*

9 Monasterio de la Rábida, Huelva

This old Franciscan monastery lies in beautiful surroundings at the mouth of the Río Tinto. It is the place where Columbus received the necessary stimulus to persevere with his plans to sail across the ocean in search of the Indies. Columbus came to the monastery in 1485 with his son. He was well received by the monks, and Father Antonio Marchena, in particular, was instrumental in bringing influence to bear with Queen

---

FOR CHILDREN

One attraction for children on this tour is the Zoo, in the Jardines del Muelle. Otherwise there are splendid beaches in Huelva province. Just south of Huelva is Punta Umbria, the main resort on this coast, with the nearby beach of La Bota and the lagoon of El Portil, which provides a delightful place to stop for a swim.

Isabella. After lengthy negotiations, the agreement was finally signed and Columbus was able to fulfil his dreams. The Lecture Cell is where Columbus held many meetings with the monks; the Chapter House displays relics of the explorer, and the Gallery has models of the three caravels that undertook the first voyage. The church and courtyard date

back to the early 15th century and are very attractive. Note the 14th-century statue of the Virgen de los Milagros, to whom Columbus offered his prayers before setting sail. In the beautifully laid out garden is the Latin-American University, a centre for American studies, and a monument to the Discoverers of America.

▶ *Continue on the same road northeast to Moguer.*

10 Moguer, Huelva

Moguer is renowned as the birthplace and home of the great Spanish poet, Juan Ramón Jiménez (1881–1958), Nobel prize-winner for literature in 1956 and author of the delightful Spanish classic *Platero y Yo*, about a boy and his donkey. His former home is now a museum with relics from the poet. The 14th-century Gothic-Mudejar Convento de Santa Clara contains the tombs of the convent's founders and has been declared a National Monument. The parish church is noted for its tall, impressive tower.

▶ *Continue on the regional road east, along the south bank of the Río Tinto, bearing north at Bonares. Join the N431. Turn left to Niebla, 24km (15 miles).*

FOR HISTORY BUFFS

Palos de la Frontera, 13km (8 miles) southeast of Huelva, is the place from which Christopher Columbus set sail on 3 August 1492 in the *Santa Maria* on his first voyage of discovery. Columbus sighted land on 12 October and set foot on Cuba and Haiti, where he left some of his men to establish a colony before returning to Palos on 15 March 1493. In May 1528, Hernán Cortés landed in the port after he had overthrown the mighty Aztec Empire and conquered Mexico.

The Monasterio de la Rábida, where Columbus prepared for his voyage west, now has a centre for American studies in the garden

11 Niebla, Huelva

The ancient town of Niebla (its name means mist) lies on the bank of the Río Tinto. It was the last town in the Guadalquivir valley to fall to the

---

SPECIAL TO...

South of Almonte in the village church of El Rocío is the Shrine of El Rocío, scene of Spain's most famous *romeria* (pilgrimage to a church or shrine). This takes place at Whitsun. People from all over the region process to El Rocío on foot, horseback or in gaily decorated horse-drawn wagons, dressed in traditional costumes. Upon arrival in the village they celebrate with music, dancing and drinking until the climax of the festival, when the statue of the Virgin is brought from the church at dawn and paraded among the crowds by members of the Brotherhoods. Bells peal, fireworks explode and there is much celebration.

Christians during the Reconquest of Spain, and is noted as being the first place in Spain where gunpowder was used in battle. Its main historical monuments are the Roman bridge over the river and four splendid Moorish entrance gates, known as the Puertas de Sevilla, Socorro, del Buey and del Agua. Of particular charm is the little chuch of Nuestra Señora de Granada (Our Lady

of Granada). The Iglesia de San Martín and the 12th-century Castillo de Los Guzmanes also warrant a visit.

▶ Continue on the N431 to La Palma del Condado.

🄬 La Palma del Condado, Huelva

La Palma del Condado has long been the centre of a wine-producing area and is known for its pleasant white table wine. One of its main attractions is the 16th-century Iglesia de San Juan Bautista, a beautiful white monument with an attractively decorated steeple. The Ermita del Valle (Hermitage of the Valley), which was built in the 15th century, is a fine example of the Mudejar style.

▶ Return to Sevilla east on the N431, 53km (33 miles).

71

ITINERARY

SEVILLA	▶ Utrera (38km-24m)
UTRERA	▶ Arcos de la Frontera (62km-39m)
ARCOS DE LA FRONTERA ▶	Medina Sidonia (39km-24m)
MEDINA SIDONIA	▶ Vejer de la Frontera (29km-18m)
VEJER DE LA FRONTERA	▶ Chiclana de la Frontera (29km-18m)
CHICLANA DE LA FRONTERA	▶ Cádiz (23km-14m)
CÁDIZ	▶ El Puerto de Santa María (13km-8m)
EL PUERTO DE SANTA MARÍA	▶ Rota (27km-17m)
ROTA	▶ Chipiona (16km-10m)
CHIPIONA	▶ Sanlúcar de Barrameda (9km-6m)
SANLÚCAR DE BARRAMEDA	▶ Jerez de la Frontera (24km-15m)
JEREZ DE LA FRONTERA	▶ Sevilla (90km-56m)

The White Towns
of Andalucia

3 DAYS • 399 KM • 249 MILES   Sevilla's festivals are world-famous. During Holy Week there are processions every day and one at dawn on Good Friday. *Pasos* (platforms), carried by Penitents, show scenes of the Passion of Christ. The Feria de Sevilla takes place on six days in April, with horseback parades.

i *Avenida de la Constitución 21B*

▶ *From Sevilla take NIV south. Turn left to Dos Hermanas. After a few kilometres towards Alcalá de Guadaira, turn right on C432 and go south to Utrera, 38km (24 miles).*

❶ Utrera, Sevilla

The old town of Utrera features an impressive Alcázar with a square tower, some fine Gothic churches and an attractive little main square. The Convento de Nuestra Señora de la Consolación on the edge of the town has a much venerated image of the Virgin, which is believed to work miracles. An annual pilgrimage takes place in September.

▶ *Take N333/A443 south to NIV then C343 to Arcos de la Frontera, 62km (39 miles).*

❷ Arcos de la Frontera, Cádiz

The first stop in the province of Cádiz is Arcos de la Frontera, one of the most attractive towns in the region. It is perched on top of a high rock, surrounded by steep ravines that descend to the River Guadalete.

The mass of white and stone-coloured houses is dominated by a castle and two churches. Tiny narrow streets and alleys wind their way up the steep slopes, offering splendid views. The Hospital de San Juan de Dios has a white baroque façade and a 16th-century crucifix in the temple. Other outstanding churches are those of Santa María, with a Plateresque west façade, and San Pedro, a massive Gothic structure which has a baroque bell tower, a landmark for miles around.

Arcos de la Frontera, high on a rock above the River Guadalete. *Left:* church clocks were timepieces for everyone in the town

▶ *Continue south on the C343 to Medina Sidonia.*

❸ Medina Sidonia, Cádiz

This is an historic little town whose origins can be traced back over 1,000 years. It was once the seat of the dukes of Medina Sidonia –the seventh duke was the Commander-in-Chief of the Armada. The

---

SCENIC ROUTES

Some of the most attractive scenery along this route is to be found around Arcos de la Frontera, which lies amid rugged mountains and green woods. The drive from Vejer de la Frontera through to Cádiz and on to El Puerto de Santa María is also very pleasant, with long stretches of white sandy beaches and pinewoods, indented at times by tall cliffs.

Iglesia de Santa María Coronada was built in the Gothic style at the time of Granada's recapture by the Christians. Some important religious paintings may be seen in the church. The Arch of 'La Pastora' (the Shepherdess) is set in the old Moorish walls in a horseshoe shape. Built in the 18th-century, the Ayuntamiento features an elegant, tiled staircase and the churches of San Agustín and Santiago are also worth a visit.

Some 7km (4½ miles) away are caves known as the Tajo de las Figuras.

▶ Continue south on the C343 to Vejer de la Frontera.

❹ Vejer de la Frontera, Cádiz

The medieval town of Vejer de la Frontera is situated on the banks of the River Barbate high above Cabo de Trafalgar (Cape Trafalgar). The place is Moorish

The Moorish look of the White Town of Vejer de la Frontera

in appearance – in the dazzling white houses and tiny twisting streets, and also in its women-folk, some of whom dress in black from head to toe, Arab-style, and are known as *Las Cobijadas* (the covered ones). The town features little hidden squares and flower-filled patios with streets so precipitous that handrails have been added for safety. Its most important building is the Iglesia de El Divino Salvador. Built in the 13th century, soon after the town was taken from the Moors, it shows a combination of Romanesque, Gothic and Mudejar styles and contains some fine 17th-century paintings.

From here, make a detour to Tarifa southeast on the N340. When you stand on the Punta Marroquí, also called Punta de

FOR HISTORY BUFFS

Fourteen kilometres (9 miles) southwest of Vejer de la Frontera is Cabo de Trafalgar (Cape Trafalgar). It was off this Cape that the famous battle of Trafalgar took place in 1805, resulting in victory for the British over the French and Spanish fleets and confirmation of British domination of the seas. The battle also resulted in the death of Lord Nelson.

Tarifa, you are on the southernmost tip of Europe, with the African continent only 14km (8 miles) away. This is where the Mediterranean and the Atlantic meet. Tarifa has a Moorish look and some Roman remains.

▷ *Take the N340 northwest to Chiclana de la Frontera.*

❺ Chiclana de la Frontera, Cádiz

Chiclana has neat white houses rising up the hillside and a Mosque-like parish church. A few kilometres away to the west is the splendid sandy beach of La Barrosa, a popular summer resort bordered by pinewoods.

▷ *Continue on N340 northwest, then join the NIV for 23km (14 miles) to Cádiz.*

❻ Cádiz, Cádiz

The old port of Cádiz is noted for its lovely setting. It is built on a rock platform jutting out into the Atlantic Ocean and is

RECOMMENDED WALKS

Cádiz has several promenades along the seafront with views of the sea and harbour. A walk along the promenade to the Castle of San Sebastián is especially recommended in the evening, when you can see some stunning sunsets.

connected to the mainland by a bridge. The town's massive ramparts serve protect it against the force of the waves. It has tall white houses, many of which have *miradors* (lookout towers) and *azoteas* (roof terraces).

Cádiz is thought to be one of the oldest towns on the Iberian peninsula. It was founded by the Phoenicians in 1100BC under the name of Gadir and was a trading port. It

Cadiz jutts out into the Atlantic and men still fish from the sea front

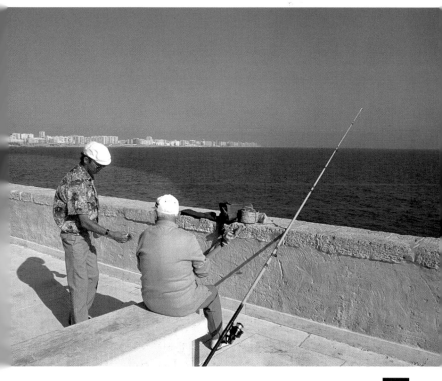

BACK TO NATURE

On this tour, look out for bee-eaters perched on wires beside the road – they are arguably Spain's most colourful birds. Bee-eaters are summer visitors and excavate nest burrows in soft, sandy banks.

La Algaida, northeast of Sanlúcar de Barrameda, is a continuation of the Coto Doñana on the eastern side of the River Guadalquivir. This area of dunes is used by migratory birds in the winter and is also home to the chameleon.

was later under the control of the Carthaginians, then the Romans.

Cádiz was used as a base for Spanish treasure fleets. In 1587 Sir Francis Drake burned ships of the Spanish Armada gathered in Cadiz harbour before setting out against England. In 1805 the French fleet left from Cádiz before the Battle of Trafalgar. And, here, in 1812, the Spanish Parliament met to establish the first liberal constitution.

One of the town's most pleasing aspects is its lovely parks, among which those of Genovés, Alameda Marqués de Comillas and Alameda de Apodaca are the most attractive. The cathedral features a golden dome and a baroque façade. It was built in the 18th and 19th centuries and hoards of gold and silver treasures and gems may be seen in the museum. Its most precious piece is a processional cross by Enrique de Arfe, which is brought out for the Corpus Christi processions. In the crypt is the tomb of the Spanish composer, Manuel de Falla (1876–1946), who was born in Cádiz and drew inspiration from Andalusian folklore.

The Museo de Bellas Artes features some great canvases by Zurbarán and works by Murillo. An interesting item in the Museo Historico Municipal is a 19th-century mural of the drawing up of the 1812 constitution.

Its masterpiece, however, is an intricate model of the town as it was in the 18th century, beautifully worked in ivory and mahogany and showing all the streets and houses in minute detail. Spain's first constitution was declared in 1812 in the Oratorio de San Felipe de Neri. Over the altar hangs a painting of the Immaculate Conception by the great Sevillian artist, Murillo.

The old town is a labyrinth of narrow streets opening out on to pleasant squares. Its central point is the attractive Plaza de Miña, shaded by palms and lined by elegant buildings.

[i] *Calderón de la Barca 1*

▶ *Leave by the toll bridge and join the NIV north to El Puerto de Santa María, 13km (8 miles).*

7 **El Puerto de Santa María,** Cádiz

The small fishing port of El Puerto de Santa María is noted for its sherry and brandy *bodegas* (cellars) and a tour of one is recommended. The town lies at the mouth of the Guadalete River and features a busy port, lively streets and miles of sandy beaches. The Moorish Castillo de San Marcos (St Mark's Castle) is a watchtower over the river, where you can enjoy a lovely view of the coast.

[i] *Guadalete 1*

▶ *Take the regional road for 27km (17 miles) northwest to Rota.*

8 **Rota,** Cádiz

The Spanish-American naval base is the major feature of Rota and has brought a cosmopolitan atmosphere to the town, with lively bars, shops and evening entertainment. The town has several pleasant beaches, some old walls and the Luna Castle by the fishermen's quarters. Rota is also an agricultural centre, noted for its tomatoes and watermelons.

▶ *Continue north on minor roads to Chipiona for 16km (10 miles).*

9 **Chipiona,** Cádiz

The lighthouse of Chipiona, visible from a great distance, is a famous landmark for navigators. This is a popular holiday resort with beaches of fine white sand and good fishing in some areas. The little town has whitewashed houses, quaint streets and a profusion of flowers. The Iglesia de Santa María de la Regla contains a shrine to the Virgin, venerated by seamen.

▶ *Take the C441 east for 9km (6 miles) to Sanlúcar de Barrameda.*

10 **Sanlúcar de Barrameda,** Cádiz

Lying at the mouth of the River Guadalquivir, the little port of Sanlúcar de Barrameda was the dpearture point for Columbus's third voyage to the New World in 1498, and the Portuguese Magellan also sailed from here in 1519 on his first voyage around the world.

There is a lively fish auction in the afternoons and this is the home of Manzanilla wine, a fine accompaniment to seafood.

Take the C440 southeast to Jerez de la Frontera.

SPECIAL TO...

Jerez de la Frontera is famous the world over for its fortified wine, known to the English as sherry. Every visitor to Jerez will undoubtedly want to do the rounds of the bodegas. Visits to the large ones can be made by prior arrangement or on an organised tour. These usually take place in the mornings with a guide and a tasting at the end. September is the month for the Vintage Festival. A ceremony for the blessing of the grapes is held on the cathedral steps with music, flamenco and much festivity.

A palm tree avenue leads up to the cathedral in Jerez de la Frontera

FOR CHILDREN

Horse-mad children will love a visit to the Royal Andalucian School of Equestrian Art. It was founded in 1973 and is situated some 4.5km (2 1/2 miles) southeast of Jerez de la Frontera. Shows of horsemanship are put on weekly.

⓫ Jerez de la Frontera,
Cádiz

Set among vineyards, the town of Jerez is the home of sherry, to which it has given its name. The bodegas, some of which are very grand, are the great attraction and tours can be made.

The town has a somewhat aristocratic air, with broad avenues and large squares. The Colegiata, built in the 17th and 18th centuries in Gothic style, contains paintings by Zurbarán. The Alcázar is an impressive 11th-century building with a Gothic church and Arab baths.

ℹ️ *Doña Blanca s/n*

▶ *Return to Sevilla on the A4.*

ARAGON, NAVARRA & LA RIOJA

Aragon, Navarra and La Rioja lie to the north and south of the basin of the River Ebro, which runs from the Cantabrian Mountains in the northwest through the Catalonian Mountains and down to the Mediterranean. Along the banks of the Ebro are the green irrigated lands known in Spain as *huertas*. The capital of Aragon, Zaragoza (Saragossa), lies in the Ebro depression on the right bank of the river and is a major agricultural centre. Southern Aragon is an area of arid plains and the bleak windswept plateaux that form part of the Montes Universales mountain range. Temperatures here are extreme.

To the northwest is the small province of La Rioja, one of Spain's most important wine-growing regions, known particularly for its red wines, which have an unmistakable flavour. The Upper Rioja is mountainous and humid, while the Lower Rioja consists of irrigated flatlands and enjoys a mild climate.

Upper Aragon and the northern part of Navarra lie within the great Pyrenees chain. Mountain peaks, lush green valleys and waterfalls, and rough stone houses with steep slate roofs are typical. To the west, the countryside changes and is divided into small fields.

Navarra has links with the Basque country and was once the home of the 'Vascons', the Basque ancestors. Late in the 8th century Charlemagne wrested it from the Moors. During the 11th century Navarra was annexed for some time by the kingdom of Aragon. It was ruled by the kings of France between 1234 and 1512, when it was gained for King Ferdinand by the Duke of Alba and integrated with Castile. The pilgrim route to the shrine at Santiago de Compostela went through Navarra and as a result there was a great flowering of Romanesque art all along the 'Way of St James'.

The little village of Aguero set amongst lush fields under the harsh rocks of the Pyrenees

Many traditions in Navarra are rooted in Basque culture. The lively *jota* is danced in Navarra and Aragon, and one of Spain's most famous celebrations is Pamplona's riotous festival of 'Sanfermines'

Tour 13

Southern Aragon is an area of arid plains, windswept plateaux and wild rugged mountains. While it may not appear to be the most hospitable of regions at first glance, there is some magnificent scenery. A visit to an oasis surrounding an old monastery, however, does provide a change. Stops are included at several interesting little towns and villages, built from the stone of the region and barely distinguishable from the surrounding landscape. The area is rich in Mudejar art (work of the Moorish people under Christian rule), and many fine examples of this intricate style of decoration can be seen along the route. South of Zaragoza is the most important wine-growing region of the province, labelled the 'wine route'.

Tour 14

Leaving the plains of Huesca, the route turns north and follows the course of the rivers to one of the important staging points of the Pilgrim's Way to Santiago. The landscapes change continuously with great panoramas of mountain peaks, eroded gorges and wooded valleys, fresh green forests and clear sparkling streams. All along the route are delightful Pyrenean villages, walled towns and castles, which bear traces of their medieval past. Many consist of a cluster of semi-detached houses rising up a steep hill to form a protective enclave. Here you will find much evidence of the Mozarabic-Romanesque style that is characteristic of the region. A visit to an old fortress – ancient stronghold of King Sancho Ramirez of Aragon – is also included. Another attraction is a visit to one of Spain's most impressive national parks.

Tour 15

On this tour you will see a variety of landscapes, from the plains of the south, characterised by the rich reddish-brown colour of the terrain, to the fertile regions and mountains of La Rioja. This little piece of land lying on the western side of the Ebro Valley is one of Spain's important wine regions. The route passes through medieval walled towns and castles, a number of which were built in strategic positions on hilltops overlooking the neighbouring provinces of Aragon and Castile, separate kingdoms at the time.

You will find fine examples of Moorish, Romanesque and Gothic art in the churches and buildings, with some special historic interest provided by one of the staging points along the 'Way to Santiago'.

Steep winding streets and alleys crowd the centre of Albarracín, a typical village of southern Aragon

The Ancient
Kingdom of Aragon

2/3 DAYS • 635KM • 394 MILES

Zaragoza is a busy commercial town, midway between Madrid and Barcelona. The Old Cathedral with Gothic and Mudejar influences, the Renaissance-inspired La Lonja and the 11th-century Aljafería, built by the Moors, are important buildings.

ITINERARY		
ZARAGOZA	▶	**Calatayud (87km-54m)**
CALATAYUD	▶	**Monasterio de Piedra**
		(28km-17m)
MONASTERIO DE PIEDRA	▶	**Daroca (68km-42m)**
DAROCA	▶	**Calamocha (26km-16m)**
CALAMOCHA	▶	**Orihuela del Tremedal**
		(80km-50m)
ORIHUELA DEL		
TREMEDAL	▶	**Albarracin (47km-29m)**
ALBARRACIN	▶	**Teruel (47km-29m)**
TERUEL	▶	**Alcañiz (158km-98m)**
ALCAÑIZ	▶	**Zaragoza (101km-63m)**

ⓘ Torreón de la Zuda, Glorieta Pi
XII s/n

▶ Take the NII southwest for
87km (54 miles) to
Calatayud.

❶ **Calatayud,** Zaragoza
The history of Calatayud goes
back to the time of the Moors
and its name is derived from
Kalat-Ayub, who founded the
old castle, now in ruins, in the
8th century. The town is on a
hillside, merging with its
surroundings. The Iglesia de
Santa María la Mayor has an
elegant Renaissance doorway
and the Iglesia de San Sepulcro
(12th–17th century) was once
the centre of the Knights
Templars of Spain. A number of
other churches in the town
show attractive examples of the
Mudejar style of art.

ⓘ Plaza del Fuerte

▶ Take the C202 southwest to
the Monasterio de Piedra
(Monastery of Stone).

❷ **Monasterio de Piedra,**
Zaragoza
The beautiful oasis that
surrounds the Monasterio de
Piedra makes a welcome change
from the surrounding arid land,
and a tour of the gardens will
probably be as much of an
attraction as a visit to the
monastery itself. They have
been turned into a lovely parkland of grottoes, pools and
cascades sloping down to the
banks of the River Piedra. Look
out for the Cola de Caballo
waterfall, which tumbles down
from a considerable height and
is most impressive. You can look
down on it from a lookout point,

SCENIC ROUTES

The route runs through areas
of rugged mountains, barren
land and forests, and some
spectacular scenery, especially
around La Muela between
Zaragoza and Calatayud (NII);
and past La Almunia de Doña
Godina to Calatayud (NII). The
area around the Monastery of
Piedra is lush with forests and
waterfalls. The N234 from
Calatayud to Daroca offers
dramatic scenery. The road
from Calamocha to Orihuela
del Tremedal and on to
Albarracín through the mountains of the Montes
Universales is very attractive.

One of the waterfalls near the
Monasterio de Piedra

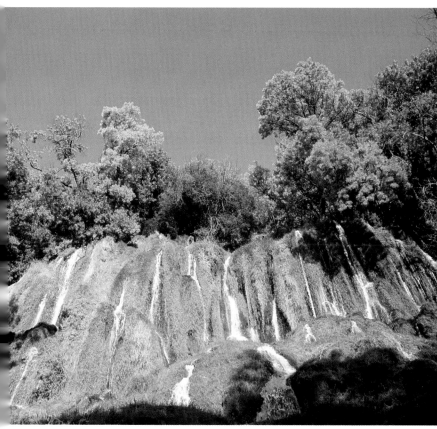

FOR HISTORY BUFFS

The village of Fuendetodos is the birthplace of the great Spanish painter, Francisco Goya. It lies about 24km (15 miles) east of Cariñena, which is on the N330 between Zaragoza and Daroca. You can see the modest house where he was born in 1746 and visit the small museum which contains relics and a collection of transparencies of his works.

while a splendid view can be had from the Iris Grotto. On the way to the monastery you will see two beautiful little lakes known as the Baño de Diana and the Lago del Espejo lying between two tall rocks.

The monastery was founded as a Cistercian house in 1194 and the oldest parts are the keep, chapter house and refectory. The attractive cloister was built in the 13th-century, and the elegant staircase with an impressive vault dates from the 14th and 15th centuries.

▶ *Take the C202 back to Calatayud and join the N234 (direction Teruel) to Daroca.*

❸ Daroca, Zaragoza
Daroca is a true medieval delight. It lies tucked away in a gorge on the River Jiloca, surrounded by hills. The walls date back to the 13th century and extend for some 3km (2 miles), with over 100 towers still remaining from the past. The Colegiata de Santa María was built between the 13th and 15th centuries and in the Chapel of the Holy Relics a shrine holds holy altar-cloths said to have been used to wrap the consecrated hosts during an attack by the Moors in the course of morning mass in 1239. The cloths were later found stained with blood and proclaimed sacred relics.

▶ *Continue on the N234 for 26km (16 miles) to Calamocha.*

❹ Calamocha, Zaragoza
Calamocha is a picturesque little village with narrow streets, squares and some fine, well-preserved mansions. It features an old Moorish bridge and

BACK TO NATURE

Birdwatchers will be in their element at the Laguna de Gallocanta, southwest of Daroca, Spain's largest inland lake. Among its inhabitants are red-crested pochards, larks and harriers. Little and great bustards can be found in the surrounding countryside and cranes are winter visitors.

tower, and has an attractive baroque-style parish church.

▶ *Continue south on the N234. Turn right to Santa Eulalia then continue west to Orihuela del Tremedal.*

❺ Orihuela del Tremedal, Teruel
The tour goes through some lovely mountain scenery to Orihuela del Tremedal, set among the pine-clad slopes of the Sierra de Albarracín. The parish church is an impressive baroque building and there is a fine 16th-century Ayuntamiento.

▶ *Take a winding regional road southeast to Albarracín.*

The castle walls of Albarracín stand in contrast with the narrow streets and arches of the village below, *left*.

6 Albarracín, Teruel

Cave paintings discovered in the area show that the mountains of Albarracín were inhabited in prehistoric times. Designated a National Monument, the town is very picturesque, with steep winding streets, old archways and timbered houses. Many have overhanging storeys, with wooden balconies and lovely wrought-iron grilles. The cathedral, rebuilt in the 16th century, features a large square belfry topped by a lantern. The chapter house contains a collection

RECOMMENDED WALKS

The Montes Universales to the south of Albarracín has a National Game Reserve and offers splendid walks among its wild landscapes of barren rocks and mountains with strange rock formations.

BACK TO NATURE

Northwest of Albarracín is the Sierra de Albarracín. If you are lucky you might spot a red deer, while birds of prey such as griffon vultures, goshawks and red kites soar overhead. Botanists will be intrigued by the plant life, with birthwort, dense-flowered orchids and gromwells being among the species to look for. Butterflies include the Camberwell Beauty.

The Old Cathedral at Zaragoza with its 17th-century belfry. Above: detail from the Moorish Aljafera.

of valuable 16th-century tapestries from Brussels.

Important prehistoric rock paintings can be seen in the caves of El Callejón de Plou and El Navazco, located a short distance to the south.

▶ *Take the regional road southeast to join the N234. Turn right to Teruel.*

7 Teruel, Teruel

Teruel, capital of its own province, stands high on a plateau surrounded by a deep moat, through which the River Turia flows. The original town of Turba was Iberian. In 218BC it was sacked by the Romans. It was then under Moorish domination for several centuries before being retaken by the Christians. A large number of Moors remained here, however, and were known as Moriscos, and were renowned for their skills in masonry and ceramics.

The town has five Torres Mudejares (Mudejar towers) built between the 12th and 16th centuries. These have square belfries on top adorned with ceramic tiles. The base of each structure has an arched opening, which gives access to the street, and the façade is richly decorated with brickwork and tiles. The ornate towers of the churches of San Martín and El Salvador are considered among the finest examples of their kind. Built in the 12th century, almost side by side, the 'twin towers' are a handsome landmark of Teruel.

The original stucture of the cathedral dates back to the 12th century and was recognised as a cathedral only in the 16th century. It is noted for its tall, slender tower and cupola, which was built in 1538 and is covered with colourful tile decorations. The 13th-century Iglesia de San Pedro shows Mudejar influence.

Remains of the fortifications include the solid tower, Torre Lombardara, and the gates of La Traición and La Andaquilla also

SPECIAL TO...

The legend of the Lovers of Teruel dates back to the early 13th century and tells of a love affair between Diego de Marcilla and Isabel de Segura, two young people from Teruel. An enforced separation ended tragically in Romeo-and-Juliet style. The bodies of the couple lie in a mausoleum adjoining the church of San Pedro. This romantic story is popular all over Spain, and has been told in many poems and dramas.

belonged to the old battlements. A prominent feature of Teruel is the Acueducto de los Arcos (Aqueduct of the Arches), which was constructed in 1558 by the French architect Pierre Vedel along Roman lines.

ⓘ *Tomás Nogués 1*

▶ *Take the N420 northeast. At Montalbán take N211 east to Alcañiz, 158km (98 miles).*

8 Alcañiz, Teruel

The ancient town of Alcañiz is built up a hillside, surrounded by orchards and olive groves. This fertile area is noted for the production of high-quality olive oil, and for *almendrados*, a sweet paste made from almonds.

The town is crowned by the 12th-century Castillo de los Calatravos, once the seat of the military Order of Calatrava in Aragon. Parts are Romanesque in style, from the 12th century, others are in Gothic style. The castle is now a parador.

One of Alcañiz's most impressive buildings is the Colegiata de Santa María la Mayor. Built in 1736, it is very tall with a magnificent portico. Among the town's most delightful features is the Plaza de España a large square with the attractive La Lonja, whose tall, elegant portals were once the meeting place of the market. Adjoining is the handsome Renaissance Ayuntamiento.

At Valdealgorfa, 12km (7½ miles) away, is the Cueva del Charco del Agua, where there are prehistoric rock paintings.

ⓘ *Plaza de España 1, Alcañiz*

▶ *.Return to Zaragoza on N232.*

Pyrenean Landscapes
of Upper Aragon

Huesca is a typical Pyrenean town, built above the River Isuela. A Gothic cathedral, a Renaissance Ayuntamiento, and a Romanesque former monastery, San Pedro el Viejo, are the most important places to see.

2/3 DAYS • 408KM • 253 MILES

ITINERARY	
HUESCA	▶ **Castillo de Loarre**
	(30km-19m)
CASTILLO DE LOARRE	▶ **Ayerbe (8km-5m)**
AYERBE	▶ **Berdún (54km-34m)**
BERDÚN	▶ **San Juan de**
	la Peña (29km-18m) ▶
SAN JUAN DE LA PEÑA	▶ **Jaca (21km-13m)**
JACA	▶ **Sabiñanigo (18km-11m)**
SABIÑANIGO	▶ **Biescas (15km-9m)**
BIESCAS	▶ **Torla(24km-11m)**
TORLA	▶ **Parque Nacional de**
	Ordesa (8km-5m)
PARQUE NACIONAL DE ORDESA	▶ **Ainsa (49km-30m)**
AINSA	▶ **Barbastro (68km-42m)**
BARBASTRO	▶ **Alquézar (23km-14m)**
ALQUÉZAR	▶ **Huesca (61km-38m)**

ℹ️ *Coso Alto 23 – Bajos*

▶ *Take the A132 northwest. At Esquedas turn right and take the regional road to Loarre. Branch off right before the village to Castillo de Loarre.*

❶ Castillo de Loarre, Huesca
The last part of this journey takes you through some stunning scenery to the impressive Castillo de Loarre, which towers majestically over the Ebro Valley beneath the Sierra de Loarre.

Originally built as a fortress, it was in use as a monastery in the 12th century, even though the area was under Moorish domination at the time. The building is encircled by massive walls with cylindrical towers and two entrance gates, from which there are magnificent views of the surrounding landscape. The church was completed in the 12th century and features a tall nave and a cupola in Romanesque style.

▶ *Return to the regional road and turn right through the village of Loarre to Ayerbe, 8km (5 miles).*

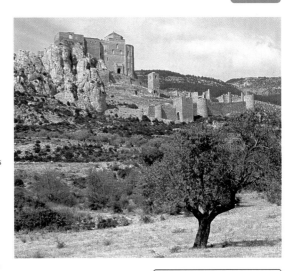

The fortress-monastery looking out from the hilltop at Loarre

❷ Ayerbe, Huesca
Make a brief stop here, where two buildings are worth a visit. The Ayuntamiento, housed in the Palacio del Marqués de Ayerbe is a fine old building from the 15th century. The Torre de San Pedro dates back to the 12th century.

▶ *Take the A132 north to join the N240 to Berdún.*

❸ Berdún, Huesca
Berdún is a cluster of houses huddled together up the hillside. This village forms an excellent base for excursions north into the Valle de Ansó, which offers some spectacular scenery of deep gorges and green valleys, together with some charming little villages.

▶ *Return to and continue along the N240, then turn left on to the C134. Turn right on to a regional road to San Juan de la Peña.*

❹ San Juan de la Peña, Huesca
Tucked away under a great rock is the ancient Monasterio de San Juan de la Peña (St John of the Crag). It has a magnificent

FOR HISTORY BUFFS

From Berdún a road leads north through some magnificent scenery to the small town of Ansó. Inscribed on a wall in the Museum of Costume is a list of names of those who were killed in the Spanish Civil War (1936–9). Heading the list is José Primo de Rivera, son of General Primo de Rivera, who had served as prime minister under the former monarch and was the founder of the Falangists. José was shot in prison in Alicante in 1936, shortly after war broke out.

SPECIAL TO...

Aragon has a traditional dance called the *jota*, which dates back to the 18th century. It is a lively affair involving great bounding steps and is accompanied by guitars or a small version of the guitar known as the *bandurrias*. The dance is performed at festival times, when the men wear the traditional costume of black velvet jacket over a blouse with slashed sleeves, black knee breeches, a colourful cummerbund and a bright handkerchief on the head.

setting overlooking a Pyrenean valley with a beautiful view of snow-capped mountains to the north.

The original monastery was founded in the 9th century by a monk called Juan, who is said to have decided to end his wanderings on this spot. Additions were made later to the original structure, which was built from the rock, and the Benedictine monastery of San Juan de la Peña was then formally founded by Sancho Ramírez, son of King Ramiro I. The monastery is associated with the legend of the elusive Holy Grail, claimed to have been passed on to the monks here for safekeeping by King Ramiro.

The cloister was built in the 12th century and is a superb example of Romanesque art, with beautiful carved capitals showing scenes from the Bible. Tombs of noblemen are in the Pantheon of Nobility and the Pantheon of the Kings. Don't miss the delightful Gothic-style Capilla de San Vicente .

▶ Rejoin N240 and go east to Jaca, 21km (13 miles).

BACK TO NATURE

The solitude of San Juan de la Peña and its surroundings provides ideal conditions for bird-watching. Look out for such species as griffon vultures who come to roost in the high cliffs that surround the monastery. Kestrels, golden eagles and rock thrushes may also be spotted here.

FOR CHILDREN

There are a number of festivals that would appeal to children. On the first Friday in May a pilgrimage takes place in Jaca to commemorate the Christian victory over the Moors. This is a colourful festival, with mock fights between the warring forces, music and dancing. On 25 June is the feast of Santa Oroisa, which is celebrated with processions and traditional dances performed by dancers from Yebra de Basa.

A Spanish version of bowls/boules under the trees at Jaca

5 Jaca, Huesca

Jaca is one of the major stages on the Way to Santiago, the pilgrimage route to Santiago de Compostela in Galicia that was established after the supposed tomb of the Apostle James the Great was discovered there in the 9th century. The great days of the pilgrimages were in the 11th and 12th centuries and pilgrims came from all over Europe.

The cathedral of Jaca is an outstanding example of what is known as the Romanesque style of the Pilgrim's Way, developed between the Pyrenees and Galicia. Notable are the chapels of San Miguel, the 16th-century Trinidad (Trinity), with a Romanesque grille, and the Capillo de San Jerónimo, a fine example of baroque art.

The Benedictine monastery is another interesting building in Jaca. It contains the sarcophagus of the Infanta Sancha. The Ayuntamiento, built between 1544 and 1546 has lovely wrought-iron grilles and is a good example of Aragonese-Plateresque style. The impressive moat of the Ciudadela (Citadel) dates back to the time of Philip II. In contrast, take a look at the modern style of architecture of the Palacio de Congresos (Congress Palace) and the Palacio de Hielo (Ice Palace).

i Avenida Regimiento de Galicia 2

▶ *Continue southeast on the N330 to Sabiñanigo.*

6 Sabiñanigo, Huesca
This small mountain town in beautiful surroundings has an interesting Museo Etnológico de Artes Populares, featuring items of regional art. Near by are several churches of Moorish-

At Jaca, the Ciudadela's moat must have been a formidable defence

SCENIC ROUTES

An interesting detour can be made by taking the N330 north through a beautiful mountainous route to Canfranc, a frontier town with France. Built high up on a hill overlooked by a castle, this old town has changed little with the passage of time. The international railway station is a fascinating relic of the past.

Romanesque style, such as those in Larrede, Oros Bajo, Satue and San Juan de Busa.

▶ *Take N260 north to Biescas.*

7 Biescas, Huesca
Biescas is a pretty little summer resort with neat white houses and red-tiled roofs. The parish church was erected by the

Knights Templar. Look out for the Ermita de Santa Elena on the outskirts of town, perched on top of a steep rock.

If you have time, visit the picturesque little villages of Panticosa (with a spa and lake) and Sallent de Gallego, a good fishing and mountaineering centre (north on the C136).

▶ *Take N260 east to Torla.*

8 Torla, Huesca
The drive continues through typical Pyrenean scenery to the picturesque little mountain village of Torla, with its narrow, winding streets and hidden corners. Torla serves as the entrance to the Parque Nacional de Ordesa.

▶ *Take the road for a short distance into the Parque Nacional de Ordesa y Monte Perdido.*

9 Parque Nacional de Ordesa, Huesca
This is an area of exceptional beauty and great geological interest, covering a vast expanse of mountains, valleys and forests. It was designated a National Park in 1918 to protect the rich flora and fauna and the natural surroundings and has been increased in size over the years. A deep canyon through ridges of limestone has created gigantic rock formations in magnificent shades of grey, red and ochre. Weather conditions normally allow access by car between May and September. The park has marked pathways, which take you to caves, pools

RECOMMENDED WALKS

There are endless possibilities for walking in the mountains and valleys of the Aragonese Pyrenees. Torla is a good base for walks into the Ordesa National Park, offering superb scenery. Trails are marked and there is an information office.

and waterfalls, and a number of lookout points offering magnificent views. Among the numerous beauty spots don't miss the Tamborrotera Waterfall, which can be viewed from a lookout point near the park's entrance.

▶ *Return to Torla and take the N260 south to Ainsa.*

BACK TO NATURE

The Ordesa National Park is home to mammals such as ibex, chamois, mountain goat, polecat, badger and wild boar and a great number of different species of birds, including some rare ones such as the golden eagle and bearded vulture.

Torla, a typical mountain village, overpowered by the dramatic cliffs of the Pyrenees

10 Ainsa, Huesca
The old walled town of Ainsa is built on a promontory overlooking the junction of the rivers Cinca and Ara. In the 11th century it was the capital of a small kingdom formed by García Jiménez after his victorious battles against the Moors. The town is picturesque, with old stone houses and a pretty main square, the Plaza Mayor, bordered by attractive arcades. The Romanesque parish church features an interesting bell-tower and an elegant cloister.

▶ *Take the C138 south and join the N123 to Barbastro.*

11 Barbastro, Huesca
Barbastro is a city with ancient roots. The original town was devastated by Pompey and received the name of Brutina, after Decius Brutus. Occupied by the Moors it was retaken by the Christians in 1064. The cathedral is a fine building in the late Gothic style. It has an elegant interior, with lovely stellar vaults and altarpieces by Damian Forment and his pupils. The Palacio de los Argensolas, built in the late 15th century, is now the Ayuntamiento.

▶ *Take the regional road northeast for 23km (14 miles) to Alquézar.*

12 Alquézar, Huesca
A drive through rugged terrain takes you to this fascinating little village straggling up the slopes of a rock, overshadowed by a large castle. The town has a Moorish appearance, with reddish-brown buildings that merge in with the natural colours of the surroundings. Leave your car in a parking area at the entrance to the village and proceed on foot, through narrow streets lined with large arcades, eaves and galleries. Up the hill is the castle, built in the 12th century. The Colegiata inside the castle has the remains of an elegant Romanesque cloister and a small museum, which contains a beautiful Gothic statue of Christ.

▶ *Take the regional road southwest and join the N240 back to Huesca, 61km (38 miles).*

RECOMMENDED WALKS

From Alquézar there is an interesting walk to the Grotto of Villacantal which is believed to date back to prehistoric times. Near by is another cave where animal paintings, thought to be some 4,000 years old, can be seen from the outside.

Navarra &
Wine Country

ITINERARY

PAMPLONA	▸ Artajona (32km-19m)
ARTAJONA	▸ Tafalla (11km-7m)
TAFALLA	▸ Ujué (19km-12m)
UJUÉ	▸ Olite (19km-12m)
OLITE	▸ Tudela (53km-33m)
TUDELA	▸ Tarazona(23km-14m)
TARAZONA	▸ Agreda(20km-12m)
AGREDA	▸ Soria(50km-31m)
SORIA	▸ Logroño(107km-66m)
LOGROÑO	▸ Estella (48km-30m)
ESTELLA	▸ Pamplona (43km-27m)

2 DAYS • 425KM • 263 MILES Pamplona (Iruñea), the Roman city of Pompey, is famous for the festival of *Sanfermines*, the running of the bulls, held in July. Once capital of the kingdom of Navarra, today it has to be content with a province. A maze of narrow streets surrounds the massive cathedral with its 14th-century cloister, an architectural gem. The town's focal point is the Plaza del Castillo, partly encircled by old ramparts.

The glassed-in balcony, offering protection from inclement weather, is found in many parts of Northern Spain; here in Pamplona.

[i] Duque de Ahumada 3

SPECIAL TO...

The *Sanfermines*, described in Hemingway's novel *The Sun also Rises*, is one long round of music, dancing and drinking. Early each morning the bulls selected to fight later in the day are let loose to run through the streets, and the men of the town show their courage by racing in front.

▶ Take the N121 south. Branch off right and take the regional road southwest to Artajona

❶ Artajona, Navarra
From quite a distance you can spot the fortifications that surround the medieval town of Artajona. Known as El Cerco de Artajona, this conclave of solid ramparts and square towers is a very impressive sight. On the summit stands the fortified Iglesia de San Saturnino. Dating back to the 13th century, it is noted for its finely sculpted façade and 15th-century retable.

▶ Take the regional road south-east for 11km (7 miles) to Tafalla.

FOR HISTORY BUFFS

A drive north of Pamplona for some 48km (30 miles) brings you to the mountain pass of Roncesvalles. This was the scene of a battle in 778 between the forces of Charlemagne, trying to withdraw to France, and the Basques of Navarre. The hero Roland, a commander of Charlemagne's army, was killed during the fighting, and a monument commemorates the event. Near by is the town of Roncesvalles, which contains an impressive 12th-century Augustinian abbey

---

RECOMMENDED
WALKS

One of the most pleasant areas for walking on this tour is around Roncesvalles, which offers beautiful surroundings of meadows, woods and valleys, with little villages dotted about the countryside. If you enjoy walking in woods, try the forest of Garralda, which is in the vicinity and famous for its magnificent oaks.

SCENIC ROUTES

On the N121 Olite to Tudela road, there is a scenic stretch between Caparroso and Arguedas. Sections of the drive after Tarazona to Agreda on the N122 also offer some impressive scenery. The desolate red-brown landscapes around Soria gradually give way to twisting mountain roads around Puerto de Piqueres and enter the wine-growing region of La Rioja, where the fertile plains of the southern part lead to the mountainous areas of the north.

▷ *Take the C132 east and branch off southeast to Ujué, just after San Martín de Unx.*

3 Ujué, Navarra

The last bend in the road reveals the sight of this quaint hilltop village, dominated by a huge fortified church. A walk through its tiny winding streets and alleys and up narrow steps is a journey back into the Middle Ages. The Iglesia de Santa María dates back mostly to the late 11th century, with 14th-century additions. In the central chapel is a statue of Santa María la Blanca. The church is surrounded by the massive towers of the old fortifications with fine views of the Pyrenees.

▷ *Return to San Martín de Unx and take the regional road southwest to Olite, 19km (12 miles).*

4 Olite, Navarra

The medieval castle of Olite gives the appearance of a whole city in itself. It was once the seat of the Court of Navarra and has been excellently preserved. The castle was built in the 13th and 15th centuries and restored in 1940. It is an imposing structure of massive walls and tall square towers, part of which has now been turned into a parador. Below lies the little town of

The tower and turret, with arrow-slit window, add a fortress-like element to this church at Olite

Olite. The Iglesia de Santa María la Real is noted for its 14th-century Gothic portal. The Iglesia de San Pedro and the convents of San Francisco and Santa Clara all date from the Middle Ages.

ⓘ *Plaza de Carlos III s/n*

▷ *Take N121 south to Tudela.*

5 Tudela, Navarra

Tudela is an old episcopal town as well as the second city of Navarra. It lies on the banks of the River Ebro, and is the centre of a rich agricultural area. It was taken from the Moors in

2 Tafalla, Navarra

The ancient town of Tafalla lies on the banks of the River Cidacos, overlooked by the 14th-century fortress of Santa Lucia. The old part of town is around the main church and here you will find the attractive Plaza de los Fueros, together with a network of little streets and handsome mansions with elegant façades. The Romanesque Iglesia de Santa María is noted for the large 16th-century Renaissance altarpiece by the Basque sculptor, Juan de Ancheta. Of interest, too, is the 16th-century retable from La Oliva by the Flemish artist, Roland de Moys, in the Convento de la Concepción.

1119, but retained Moorish influences for centuries. This is clear in the old Moorish quarter and the Mudejar-style architecture of many of the houses, which were built of brick.

The cathedral is an imposing monument, built between the 12th and 13th centuries. An outstanding feature is the Gothic entrance, known as the Puerta del Judicio (Doorway of the Last Judgement). A wide archway over the door is decorated with sculpted figures portraying the Last Judgement. Inside, the church has many notable works of art from the Gothic period. The 18th-century Capilla de Santa Ana is noted for its rich interior and fine baroque altarpiece. The Romanesque cloister, with finely carved capitals, contains the tomb of Don Fernando, son of King Sancho El Fuerte (The Strong One) whose tomb is in the nearby Iglesia de San Nicolás. He died in 1234 and lay here in Tudela until he was reburied in Roncesvalles.

Other buildings of interest include the Ayuntamiento, with notable archives, the Renaissance Casa del Almirante (House of the Admiral) and the Iglesia de la Magdalena, which has a Romanesque tower and finely sculpted door. The Plaza Nueva was 'New' in the 18th century.

ⓘ *Plaza de los Fueros s/n*

▶ *Continue on the N121 southwest to Tarazona.*

6 **Tarazona,** Zaragoza
The present town of Tarazona was built on the site of the Celtiberian city of Turiaso. It was occupied first by the Romans, then by the Moors, and was recaptured in 1118 by the Christian King Alfonso I of Aragon. It continued as a royal residence until the 15th century. The town is noted for the number of Mudejar-style

buildings and is often referred to as the 'Aragonese Toledo'.

The cathedral, begun in the 12th century, shows a combination of styles, mainly Mudejar and Gothic, with influences of baroque and Plateresque art. The Iglesia de la Magdalena has an impressive Mudejar tower, and the Guildhall façade has reliefs of the legends of Hercules. The 14th- and 15th-century Palacio Episcopal was once the residence of the Kings of Aragon. The 16th-century Ayuntamiento has a frieze around the building depicting the capture of Granada.

ⓘ *Iglesias 5*

▶ *Take the N122 southwest for 20km (12 miles) to Agreda.*

7 **Agreda,** Soria
Perched high on a rock is Agreda, once an important frontier town overlooking the kingdoms of Aragon and Castile. Dominating the town is the Castillo de la Muela, which still shows traces of old Moorish ramparts. Buildings of interest include the Iglesia de San

Miguel; the Iglesia de Nuestra Señora de la Peña, with panel paintings from the Gothic period; and the Convento de la Concepción, which contains the tomb of Sister María de Agreda (1602–65), mystic and religious advisor to Philip IV of Spain.

Agreda is a good base for trips into the Sierra del Moncayo, which can be explored by car or on horseback.

▶ *Continue southwest on the N122 to Soria.*

8 **Soria,** Soria
Soria has inspired many Spanish poets. One of the most famous was the Sevillian poet, Antonio Machado (1875–1939), who lived here for a time. Outstanding among its many fine edifices is San Juan de Duero, a 12th-century monastery just outside the centre. At one time it belonged to the Knights Templars and features a beautiful cloister. The Palacio de los Condes de Gómara is a majestic building, built in the 16th century and dominated by an impressive tower. The Catedral de San Pedro (12th–16th

Terraced gardens at Agreda, once a stronghold on the frontier between Castile and Aragon centuries) is noted for its elegant doorway and Romanesque cloister. The 12th-century Iglesia de Santo Domingo has a richly decorated Romanesque façade, and the colonnades of the Iglesia de San Juan de Rabanera, preserved from the original cloister, have an unusual Romanesque-Oriental design.

About 8km (5 miles) north of the town are the remains of Numancia, an old Celtiberian fort renowned for its resistance to a siege by the Romans, until it fell in 133BC. The Romans built over the old city and many objects of significance were discovered during 20th-century excavations; some are in the Museo Numantino in Soria..

ℹ️ *Plaza Ramón y Cajal s/n*

➤ *Take NIII north to Logroño.*

9 Logroño, La Rioja
Logroño, capital of the region of La Rioja, stands on the banks of the Ebro. Its tower and the town's outline form a graceful silhouette, centred around the Iglesia de Santa María la Redonda with its impressive baroque towers. The Imperial Church of Santa María de Palacio was founded in the 11th century and has a lofty pyramid-shaped tower built in the 13th century. The 15th-century cathedral has a baroque façade from the 18th century, and the 13th-century Iglesia de San Bartolmé is noted for its Romanesque-Gothic doorway.

SPECIAL TO...

La Rioja is famous for its wines. The best-known is the full-bodied *tinto*, a high-quality red wine. It also produces the *claretes*, which are light red wines and the golden *blancos* which are dry and aromatic. In late September there is a Wine Festival in Logroño, with bullfights, parades and poetry competitions.

Watching the world go by in the quiet town of Soria

An historic stone bridge used by the pilgrims on their journey to Santiago de Compostela spans the River Ebro.

ℹ️ *Miguel Villanueva 10*

➤ *Take the NIII north to Estella.*

10 Estella, Navarra
The old town of Estella lies on the banks of the River Ega. During the Middle Ages it was the residence of the Kings of Navarra and also a staging point for the pilgrims. The 12th-century Iglesia de San Pedro de la Rua has a fine façade and Romanesque cloister. The Iglesia de Santo Sepulcro stands on the pilgrim route while three palaces feature among its many old mansions.

ℹ️ *San Nicolás 2*

➤ *Return to Pamplona on NIII.*

FOR CHILDREN

Children should enjoy a festival that takes place in Anguiano (southwest of Logroño) on 21 and 22 July in honour of Mary Magdalene. The celebrations centre around the Danza de los Zancos, or Stilt Dance, when a troupe of dancers descend the steps of the church on stilts and then proceed down the hill at great speed. They wear colourful costumes and are an unusual demonstration of folklore. A detour of some 49km (30 miles) southeast of Logroño, on the N232, takes you to Calahorra where there is a zoo, at Término del Vadillo.

CENTRAL SPAIN &
THE WEST

A vast part of Spain is the great central plain known as the Meseta, or tableland, ringed by hills and bordering Portugal. In the centre lies Madrid, capital of Spain and the highest capital in Europe, at an altitude of 646m (2,120 feet). To the north is Castile-Leon, while south contains Madrid and Castilla-La Mancha. In the southwestern section is Extremadura which is also part of the Meseta

The main central Cordillera sweeps down the Castilian plain from northeast to southwest, and is divided into the Sierra de Guadarrama, Sierra de Gredos and the Peña de Francia. The dry, barren Toledo mountains dominate the landscape south of Madrid while to the east the wild Serranía de Cuenca. The Duero Tajo, Guadiana and Guadalimar are four important rivers that rise in the heartlands of the region and flow down to the Atlantic. Dramatic changes of scenery and climatic differences are contained within the region, where wild eroded landscapes contrast with green forests and the dry flatlands of the south.

Castile is derived from the word *castillo*, meaning castle. This was a land of castles built to defend its borders during the conflicts between the Moors and Christians. Later, further fortifications were erected between the kingdoms of Castile and Aragon. The marriage of Isabella of Castile and Ferdinand II of Aragon in 1469 joined these two kingdoms and unified Spain.

La Mancha is a vast plain, where windmills and castles serve as a reminder that this is Don Quixote land. Extremadura has played an important role in history as the birthplace of many of the great explorers. It presents a panorama of dry, rocky moorlands, with irrigated areas around the Alagón and Tajo.

Among the crafts still practised in Castile are the traditional blue-and-yellow ceramics from Talavera and pottery in La Mancha.

A profusion of pinnacles decorates Segovia's late-Gothic cathedral

Tour 16

Art is the essence of this tour. Admirers of El Greco can see his greatest masterpieces in the best possible setting – Toledo. This jewel of a town is one of Spain's major attractions, renowned for its spectacular setting as well as for the treasures to be seen here. Another highlight is a visit to one of the famous Royal Palaces, with their lavishly decorated rooms and elegant gardens. A drive south through the plains of south Meseta is rewarded by a glimpse of La Mancha country.

Tour 17

This eastern section of Castilla-La Mancha offers an unusual itinerary with terrific scenery. The route takes in some of the splendid old fortified towns that once protected the borders between warring kingdoms. A total contrast is provided by a visit to the fascinating 'hanging houses', and a drive through some spectacular scenery to an area of extraordinary rock formations. The journey picks up the trail of Don Quixote, which leads down to the great plains and windmills of La Mancha.

Tour 18

The first part of this tour travels west through the Central Cordillera, with the magnificent scenery of the Guadarrama Mountains to the north and the southern peaks of the Sierra de Gredos. In the mountains are two special monuments: a great monastery and a memorial to the fallen of the Civil War, close in geography but centuries apart. A walled city in a dramatic setting and an ancient monastery are combined with visits to some fine churches and a crafts centre.

Tour 19

Royal palaces and ancient castles form the basis of this tour, with the focus on a beautiful golden city, where the famous Alcázar and Aqueduct rate high among Spain's many attractions. A number of palaces in this area were originally built as Royal hunting lodges. The circular tour to the northwest of Madrid passes through the magnificent forests and lush green valleys found around the Guadarrama Mountains.

Tour 20

This tour explores a lesser known area of Spain. Extremadura is a sparsely populated region in the extreme west of the country, sharing an extensive border with Portugal. The fascination of the area lies in its very remoteness and the desolation of its landscapes, some of which are magnificent. Cortés and Pizarro were born here, as were many other great explorers.

Tour 21

This tour covers an area northwest of Madrid. The region has close associations with Spain's great hero, El Cid, the valiant conqueror of the Moors. A dominant feature of the tour is one of the country's most famous cathedrals, which is known for its impressive interior, where you can see the tomb of El Cid.

Plaza Mayor, the centre of old Madrid, is a great place to relax

Art Treasures of
Castilla-La Mancha

ITINERARY

MADRID	▶	**Illescas (36km-22m)**
ILLESCAS	▶	Toledo (34km-21m)
TOLEDO	▶	Consuegra(63km-39m)
CONSUEGRA	▶	Aranjuez (78km-48m)
ARANJUEZ	▶	Chinchón(22km-14m)
CHINCHÓN	▶	Ciempozuelos (19km-12m)
CIEMPOZUELOS	▶	Valdemoro (7km-4m)
VALDEMORO	▶	Pinto (6km-4m)
PINTO	▶	Getafe (10km-6m)
GETAFE	▶	Madrid (18km-11m)

2 DAYS • 293KM • 181 MILES

Busy, modern Madrid, capital of Spain, still embraces the medieval city's narrow streets crowding the Calle Mayor which runs from Puerta del Sol, Madrid's focal point.

Plaza Mayor 3

The richly carved alterpiece in Toledo Cathedral, one of the finest Gothic cathedrals in Spain

---

FOR CHILDREN

Between May and September children can enjoy a 'Tren de la Fresa' ride on the Strawberry Train, which runs from Madrid to Aranjuez at weekends. Wooden carriages are drawn by a steam engine and the name stems from when the service was used to transport strawberries during the last century. Today, strawberries are distributed among the passengers by hostesses in period costumes. The journey takes about an hour

---

▶ *From Madrid take the N401 southwest to Illescas*

Illescas, Toledo

Those with a special interest in art will want to stop here to look at paintings by El Greco. A collection of five works by the great master himself are to be seen in the church of the Hospital de la Caridad, featur-ing paintings from 1600 to 1604. While here, take a look at the 13th-century parish church of Santa María, which dates back to the 16th century and has a fine Mudejar tower.

▶ *Continue on the N401 to Toledo.*

2 Toledo, Toledo

Toledo is indisputedly one of Spain's finest jewels. It is rich in art and treasures, combined with a great deal of historical interest. Once the capital of an Iberian tribe, it was taken over by the Romans in 192BC and called Toletum. In 1085 the city was captured from the occupying Moors by King Alfonso VI of Castile and it became the residence of the kings of Castile, continuing to flourish as a centre of art and learning. It reached the height of its splendour at the end of the 15th and first half of the 16th centuries. When King Philip II transferred the capital to Madrid in 1561, however, Toledo lost its status.

The cathedral stands majestically on the Plaza Mayor (main square). Built between 1227 and 1493 on the site of the Great Mosque, it is widely regarded as the finest Gothic cathedral in Spain after Burgos, with influences of the Mudejar style to be seen in some parts. Its elegant tower looks over the city. The sanctuary is the most richly decorated area of the interior. Expanded in the 16th century, it is noted for the retable depicting the Life of

---

FOR HISTORY BUFFS

Eight kilometres (5 miles) east of Illescas is the small town of Esquivias, where Cervantes set up house after his marriage in 1548 to Catalina de Salazar y Palacios, said to have been the inspiration behind his poem *Galatea*. The records of his marriage can be seen in the registry of the church of Santa María.

The spectacular setting of Toledo, overlooking the River Tajo

Christ. The Chapter House is distinguished by its fine Mudejar ceiling and stucco doorways.

The Sacristy has an excellent collection of paintings by El Greco, Goya, Van Dyck and other famous artists. The Treasury Room boasts an elegant Plateresque door by Covarrubias and a fine Mudejar ceiling. Of particular interest, however, is the splendid 16th-century gold- and silver-gilt monstrance by Enrique de Arfe. It stands 3m (10 feet) high and weighs about 200kg (440 pounds) and is carried through the streets during the Corpus Christi processions.

Toledo has been an inspiration for many writers and poets, but mention Toledo and most people think of El Greco, the name Domenikos Theotokopoulos is usually known by, who came from Crete to Toledo around 1577. Here he remained and painted, producing many masterpieces. The Iglesia de Santo Tomé contains *The Burial of the Count of Orgaz*, one of his most famous paintings. The museum in the former hospital of La Santa Cruz has a collection of his work, including the notable *Assumption of Our Lady*. Other valuable works of art may also be seen here; more fine paintings can be seen in the Duquesa de Lerma (Museum of the Foundation). Enthusiasts will want to visit the Casa y Museo del Greco, which stands very close to the place where he lived from 1585 until his death in 1614. The famous *View of Toledo* features among the superb collection of his work to be seen in the museum.

The Alcázar (Citadel) stands in a prominent position on the highest point of the town. It was destroyed and rebuilt many

---

SPECIAL TO...

There is a long tradition of Arab-originated craftwork in Toledo, which is known for its damascene articles, metalwork and steel ornaments inlaid with gold or silver. Knives, jewellery and all sorts of adornments for the home make attractive, if somewhat overdone, souvenirs.

BACK TO NATURE

Situated in the wooded Montes de Toledo (Toledo mountains), in the southern part of the region, is the Coto Nacional de los Quintos de Mora (Quintos de Mora game reserve), which is the natural habitat of a wide variety of wildlife. Here you may spot any number of different animals, such as red deer, roe deer, boars, rabbits and hares. Birdlife includes partridges, wood pigeons, turtle doves, bee-eaters and quail. Also look for eyed and wall lizards among the rocks.

8 Consuegra, Toledo

This part of the itinerary takes you south to the flat desolate heartlands of La Mancha, immortalised by the pen of Miguel Cervantes in his classic tale of the adventures of Don Quixote and his faithful servant Sancho Panza. The very essence of La Mancha is conjured up here by the silhouette of an old ruined castle and 13 white windmills, many of which have been rebuilt and some of which are museums for pottery and wine. The village of Consuegra has a charming main square overlooked by a large tower. It was here that Don Diego died, the only son of Spain's great hero, El Cid.

SCENIC ROUTES

This route travels south to La Mancha through vast flat expanses of fields that stretch away to invisible horizons. Occasional trees, hills and hamlets relieve the landscape. Its very remoteness and the subtle colours have a definite appeal, a sentiment shared by Cervantes, who chose this setting for the travels of Don Quixote. No visit to La Mancha is complete without a glimpse of the famous windmills in the southern part of the region. You will see them around Consuegra, but for a good 'windmill run' take the C400 southeast from Consuegra to Campo de Criptana (southeast on the C400, then left on to the N420).

At Consuegra, one of the famous windmills on the La Mancha plain immortalised by Cervantes

times during the course of its history. In the 16th century Charles V had the fortress converted into a royal residence. It was damaged during the wars of the 18th and 19th centuries, and devastated by the siege in 1936 during the Civil War. The garrison, then a cadet school, was besieged by Republican forces. The inmates of the garrison, which included many women and children, held out heroically for some eight weeks until relief came. The reconstructed building is now a national monument.

ℹ️ *Puerta de Bisagra*

➤ *Leave by the N401/N400, turn right on to the N401, then left on to the C400 to Consuegra.*

Fountains refresh the gardens of the Palacio Real, Aranjuez

SPECIAL TO...

La Mancha is an important wine-growing region. Among the best known ones are the light red and white table wines from Valdepeñas in the south. A wine festival is held here early in September to celebrate the grape harvest.

▶ Take the C400 east to Madridejos and join the NIV north. Continue for 78km (48 miles) to Aranjuez, which lies 5km (3 miles) off this road.

4 Aranjuez, Madrid

The town is dominated by the famous Palacio Real (Royal Palace). Grand entrance gates lead to a large courtyard where you can admire the palace's lovely façade. It was built in the classical style, showing harmony and symmetry in its proportions. The central staircase is Italian in design, and the walls on either side are hung with tapestries from Belgium. The elegant salons include the Sala de la China, the Salon del Trono and el Arabe, which was built for Queen Isabella II and whose sumptuous decorations bear a resemblance to those of the Alhambra at Granada.

Close by is the Casa del Principe (Prince's House). This small palace was built in the neoclassical style by Charles IV for his son and is noted for the Pompeiian Gallery, which is filled with magnificent marbles and statues. Another important building is the Casa del Labrador (Labourer's House), which resembles the Petit Trianon at Versailles. Also neoclassical in style, it has an ornate interior decorated with silk hangings. Its collection of treasures includes Roman mosaics, porcelain clocks and a magnificent gallery of Greek statues.

Several gardens surround the palace. These are beautifully laid out with waterfalls and pools, graceful statues and attractive little pavilions. The gardens bear different names, including the Jardín del Rey (King's Garden), Jardín de la Reina (Queen's Garden), Jardín de la Isla (Island Garden), situated on a tiny man-made island between two sections of the river, with its avenue of plane trees, and the Jardín del Principe (Prince's Garden), which contains many exotic species of trees.

i Plaza San Antonio 9

➤ *Take the regional road (M305) northeast to Chinchón.*

5 Chinchón, Madrid
One of the most attractive features of this charming little village is the Plaza Mayor. The square is surrounded by three- and four-storey houses with wooden balconies, from which spectators used to watch the famous bullfights here in the old days. The parish church overlooking the square contains a painting of the Assumption, which has been attributed to Goya (whose brother was once the town's parish priest).

➤ *Take the M404/C404 west to Ciempozuelos.*

6 Ciempozuelos, Madrid
A brief stop here is suggested for those with a special interest in art and architecture. Two monuments are of note. The Sanatorium is a magnificent example of the neo-Mudejar style of architecture, and the

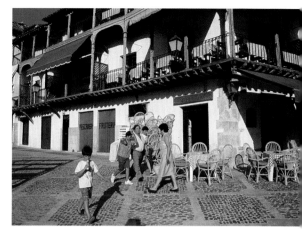

Houses in Chinchón's Playa Mayor have balconies, once grandstands for bullfights in the square below

small parish church contains the fine painting, *The Head of Mary Magdalena*, by Claudio Coello.

➤ *Carry on along this road, then turn right on meeting the NIV. Drive for a short distance north and turn left to Valdemoro.*

7 Valdemoro, Madrid
More works by the artist Claudio Coello can be seen in the little 16th-century parish church, along with paintings by Goya and by his brother-in-law, Francisco Bayeu.

➤ *Rejoin the NIV and continue north. Turn left to Pinto after a short distance.*

8 Pinto, Madrid
The major attraction of Pinto is the Castillo de los Duques de Frías, an imposing structure dating back to the 15th century, where the Princess of Eboli, notorious for her intrigues at the court of Philip II, was confined from 1578 to 1581. The parish church was built in the Gothic-Plateresque style and has some finely carved decorations.

➤ *Take the NIV north again and turn left on to the M406 to Getafe, 10km (6 miles).*

9 Getafe, Madrid
Getafe's most notable building is the Renaissance-style Iglesia de la Magdalena, with huge columns and a splendid retable. Inside there are paintings by two baroque artists, Claudio Coello and Alonso Cano.

Just beyond the junction of the M406 and the NIV, a turning to the right takes you to the Cerro de los Angeles (Hill of Angels). This conical hill is considered the geographical centre of Spain and is marked by the 'Corazón de Jesús' (Heart of Jesus) monument, which is topped by a figure of Christ and a church. There are superb views from here over the plains of Castile, the Guadarrama mountains and Madrid.

➤ *Take the road east to the NIV and return to Madrid.*

FOR HISTORY BUFFS

In the Valley of Jarama, north of Chinchón where the C300 joins the NIII, a tough battle was fought during the Spanish Civil War (1936–9). Americans were among the volunteers on the Republican side. You can still trace the old trenches.

RECOMMENDED WALKS

The hot, dry plains of La Mancha may not be conducive to much walking, but the fresh green gardens of the Palace of Aranjuez are most agreeable for a quiet stroll. Among the several gardens in the palace grounds, the Jardín del Principe has inspired many artists with its shady trees and graceful monuments.

Traces of
Don Quixote

3 DAYS • 668KM • 416 MILES

The Madrid of the Habsburgs is best seen in the magnificent Plaza Mayor, the Casa del Ayuntamiento and the Convento de las Descalzas Reales. The Palacio Real, with superb painted ceilings and many treasures, exemplifies the neoclassical architecture in favour under Spain's Bourbon kings.

ITINERARY		
MADRID	▶	**Alcalá de Henares** (33km-21m)
ALCALÁ DE HENARES	▶	**Guadalajara** (23km-14m)
GUADALAJARA	▶	**Sigüenza** (75km-47m)
SIGÜENZA	▶	**Cifuentes** (50km-31m)
CIFUENTES	▶	**Cuenca** (142km-88m)
CUENCA	▶	**La Ciudad Encantada** (35km-22m)
LA CIUDAD ENCANTADA	▶	**Belmonte** (123km-76m)
BELMONTE	▶	**Mota del Cuervo** (16km-10m)
MOTA DEL CUERVO	▶	**Ruinas de Segóbriga** (60km-37m)
RUINAS DE SEGÓBRIGA	▶	**Uclés** (14km-9m)
UCLÉS	▶	**Tarancón** (16km-10m)
TARANCÓN	▶	**Arganda** (54km-34m)
ARGANDA	▶	**Madrid** (27km-17m)

ℹ️ *Plaza Mayor 3*

▶ *From Madrid take the A2, which becomes the NII, northeast to Alcalá de Henares*

🄾 **Alcalá de Henares,** Madrid
Alcalá is known as the birthplace of Miguel Cervantes, author of *Don Quixote de La Mancha*, and for the founding of the Ildefonso University in 1508. The university developed into one of the most famous centres of culture and science in western Europe. When it was transferred to Madrid in 1837 the town lost its status and declined. The headquarters of the university were rebuilt between 1543 and 1583 by the great Rodrigo Gil de Hontañón and is the present Colegio Mayor de San Ildefonso. This elegant Renaissance building was damaged during the Spanish Civil War, but has been well restored.

The town's main square is called Plaza de Cervantes, after the author. The Calle Mayor, where Cervantes was born in 1547, leads off the square. The Casa de Cervantes was built near his birthplace and houses a small museum with interesting items relating to his life.

Cervantes had already written a number of works before he published the first part of *Don Quixote de La Mancha* in 1605 to instant acclaim.

ℹ️ *Callejón de Santa María*

▶ *Continue on the NII to Guadalajara.*

SPECIAL TO...

Alcalá de Henares is renowned for its wide variety of sweets and delicious cakes It is known especially for its *almendras garrapinadas* (caramelised almonds), which are produced by the nuns of the Convento de San Diego and can be bought at the door of the convent. Many different types of cakes, special to Alcalá, can also be found here, such as *rosquillas de Alcalá* (cakes in the form of a ring), *pestiños* (honey cakes) and *canutillos rellenos* (filled cakes in a tubular shape).

The 16th-century buildings of the College of St Ildefonso, originally the University, at Alcalá de Henares

2 Guadalajara, Guadalajara
The finest feature of
Guadalajara is the Palacio del
Infantado. Built between 1461
and 1492 by Mendoza, second
Duke of Infantado, the palace
was severely damaged by
bombs in 1936 during the
Spanish Civil War, but has been
restored. The pale façade has
diamond stonework decorations
and an intricately carved gallery
on top. Inside is a lovely two-
storey patio with notable
Isabelline arching (a type of
ornate decoration used in the
15th century during the reign of
Queen Isabella the Catholic).
Take a look, also, at the Roman
bridge over the River Henares.

i *Plaza Mayor 7*

▶ *Take the NII northeast then
turn left on the C204 to
Sigüenza.*

3 Sigüenza, Guadalajara
The castle was founded by the
Romans and rebuilt between

Erosion has sculpted the limestone
rocks at La Cuidad Encantada

SCENIC ROUTES

The most spectacular part of
the journey is between Cuenca
and La Ciudad Encantada. The
route follows a winding road
through firs and pines up to
the Serranía de Cuenca, with
superb views of the surrounding mountains, gorges and
plains. From a lookout point
called El Ventano del Diablo
(Devil's Window) you can see
for miles over the mountains
and plains. The route continues
through great eroded
landscapes to La Ciudad
Encantada.

the 12th and 15th centuries, to
become the residence of the
bishops until the middle of the
19th century. It has a formidable
fortress-like appearance, and
has now been converted into a
parador with magnificent views
of the surrounding landscapes.
The Plaza Mayor is overlooked
by the cathedral, a solid structure of great towers and
buttresses, built between the
12th and 14th centuries.
Adjoining the cathedral is the
Museo Episcopal, where you
can see some fine paintings by
El Greco and Zurbarán.

i *Cardenal Mendoza 2*

▶ *Return to the NII, turn right
for a little way, then left to
take the C204 to Cifuentes.*

4 Cifuentes, Guadalajara
The name of Cifuentes means
'a hundred fountains', and
indeed there are springs all over
the area. In La Provincia square
is the 12th- to 13th-century
Iglesia de El Salvador, with a
late Romanesque portal and a
Gothic rose window, as well as
the Convento de Santo
Domingo. The ruins of a large
14th-century castle top the hill.

▶ *Continue south on C204 and
just east of Sacedon turn left
on the N320, southeast to
Cuenca, 142km (88 miles).*

5 Cuenca, Cuenca
The little main square is dominated by the cathedral, an
imposing structure with an
attractive pale-coloured façade.
Built between the 12th and
13th centuries, it shows a
mixture of Gothic and
Renaissance styles. Features of
special note are the 18th-
century high altar and elaborate
16th-century grille before the
choir. Around the corner is the
Museo Episcopal, which
contains two fine El Greco
paintings, some beautiful tapestries and a collection of rich gold
religious crosses.
   A path along the southern
wall of the cathedral leads down
to the spectacular 'Casas
Colgadas', or Hanging Houses,
for which Cuenca is famous.
The buildings cling to the side
of the cliff with balconies that
protrude over the precipice.
Originally built in the 14th
century as a palace, they were

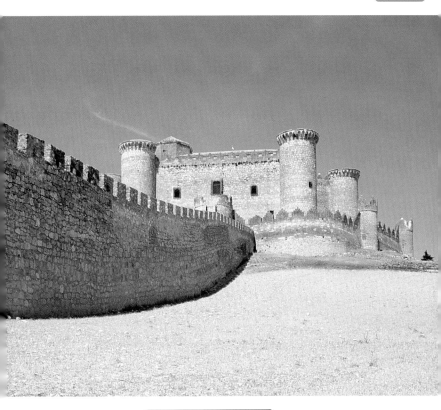

The walls and round towers of the 15th-century castle at Belmonte

later used as a town hall. By the 19th century they had fallen into decay but were restored in the early part of this century. One of the houses has been converted into a Museum of Modern Art and shows large, mainly abstract canvases against pure white walls.

i *Glorieta González Palencia 2–3°*

▶ *Take the regional road north. Soon after El Ventana del Diablo lookout point, turn right on to the minor road to La Ciudad Encantada (the Enchanted City).*

6 La Ciudad Encantada,
Cuenca

This is an extraordinary fantasy world of gigantic rock formations, the result of thousands of years of erosion. Nature really has had a go here, and the imagination runs riot with the sheer

---

RECOMMENDED WALKS

Serious walkers will be in their element among the wild rocky landscapes of the Serranía de Cuenca. Northeast of La Ciudad Encantada is a lovely area of rich vegetation and pine forests, offering some gentle walks. A major attraction here is the sight of the source of the River Cuervo (Nacimiento del Cuervo), which emerges partly out of a cave in a series of rippling cascades.

---

size and incredible shapes of the rocks, which resemble a Roman bridge, a giant mushroom, a human profile and even the 'lovers of Teruel' (see page 84, Special To). Arrows high up on the stones lead through a labyrinth of lost worlds.

▶ *Return to Cuenca by the alternative route, taking the regional road south, through Valdecabras. At Cuenca, take the N420 south to Belmonte (via La Almarcha).*

7 Belmonte, Cuenca

Make a brief stop here to see the old castle on top of the hill. It has circular towers and was built by Juan Fernández Pacheco, Marquis of Villena, in the 15th century as a means of defending his extensive territories. It was later abandoned, but was restored and rebuilt in the 19th century. The old Colegiata church has an impressive collection of altarpieces from the 15th to 17th centuries and some fine choir-stalls.

▶ *Continue on N420 south-west to Mota del Cuervo.*

The dramatic cliffs of Cuenca above the valley gardens

10 Uclés, Cuenca

The massive monastery, whose solemn appearance indicates a certain past importance, once belonged to the knightly Order of Santiago (St James). They were lords of the village from the 12th century, and the castle is sometimes referred to as the 'Escorial of La Mancha'. It has a magnificent Plateresque façade and an elegant 16th-century cloister. The two towers are impressive and parts of the old fortification walls still remain.

▶ *Return to the NIII and continue northwest to Tarancón.*

11 Tarancón, Cuenca

The church here has a fine Gothic façade and a notable retable. Another building of interest is the handsome mansion built by Queen María Christina after she married a guardsman, who she made the Duque de Riansares.

Continue on the NIII northwest to Arganda.

12 Arganda, Madrid

The splendid Renaissance Iglesia de San Juan Bautista, was built in 1525 and has notable altars in the Churrigueresque style. The Casa del Rey, a former country house in gardens, once belonged to the Spanish royal family, and there is a castle dating from 1400.

▶ *Return to Madrid on the NIII.*

8 Mota del Cuervo, Cuenca

Right in the heartland of La Mancha country is the little village of Mota del Cuervo, which offers the familiar sight of white windmills silhouetted against deep blue skies, with the parched plains of La Mancha stretching away into the far distance. Now you are well and truly on the Route of Don Quixote, and a look at the windmills, some of which have been restored to working order, explains why the gallant old knight saw them as huge giants and attacked them.

▶ *Take the N301 to Quintanar de la Orden. Turn right on to the regional road and travel northeast to the Ruinas de Segóbriga, just before the NIII, on the right.*

SPECIAL TO...

Mota del Cuervo produces some interesting pottery and is the only place in the region where 'turntable moulding' is done exclusively by women. It is known for its small polished jugs, called *tinajas*, which have a slim shape and flat handle.

---

9 Ruinas de Segóbriga, Cuenca

Once part of an important Roman town, the capital of Celtic Iberia, the ruins of Segóbriga include an amphitheatre and thermal baths. Traces can also be seen of an old wall and of the Hispano-Visigothic basilica.

▶ *Take the regional road to join the NIII. Turn left after 2km (1 mile) then right to Uclés.*

FOR HISTORY BUFFS

A short distance south of Quintanar de la Orden is the small village of El Toboso, which is claimed as the home of Dulcinea, legendary heroine of Cervantes' Don Quixote. The so-called Casa de Dulcinea contains a library relating to Cervantes. The village itself has one windmill and is charming, with little streets and patios, evoking scenes in the book.

Mountains &
Monuments

Madrid's Museo del Prado is a world-class museum, with paintings by El Greco, Velázquez, Goya, Murillo and Zurbarán, among the Spanish greats, and outstanding works from other nationalities. The Museo Nacional Centro de Arte Reina Sofia, home to Picasso's *Guernica,* and the Museo Thyssen–Bornemisza are are also outstanding.

2/3 DAYS • 585KM • 364 MILES

ITINERARY		
MADRID	▶	**Valle de los Caidos**
		(52km-32m)
VALLE DE LOS CAÍDOS	▶	**El Escorial (14km-9m)**
EL ESCORIAL	▶	**Ávila (63km-39m)**
ÁVILA	▶	**Piedrahita (56km-35m)**
PIEDRAHITA	▶	**El Barco de Ávila**
		(21km-13m)
EL BARCO DE ÁVILA	▶	**Béjar (30km-19m)**
BÉJAR	▶	**Plasencia(59km-37m)**
PLASENCIA	▶	**Monasterio deYuste**
		(47km-29m)
MONASTERIO DEYUSTE	▶	**Talavera de la Reina**
		(124km-77m)
TALAVERA DE LA REINA	▶	**Navalcarnero (86km-53m)**
NAVALCARNERO	▶	**Madrid (33km-21m)**

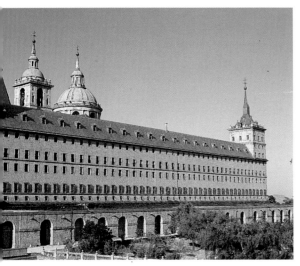

El Escorial, both monastery and palace, built for King Philip II

whose full title in Spanish is the Monasterio de San Lorenzo del Escorial, stands as a testimony to King Philip II. He had it built to commemorate his defeat of the French at the battle of San Quentin on 10 August (St Lawrence's Day), 1557, and also as a burial place for his father, the great Charles V. It was started in 1567 by Juan Bautista de Toledo, who had trained in Italy, and was completed by his assistant, Juan de Herrera, in 1584.

The building centres around the church, which has two tall towers and a dome. The main entrance is through a large courtyard known as La Lonja. This leads to the vestibule and follows through to the Patio de los Reyes (Courtyard of the Kings). A few steps take you to the entrance to the church, which marks the building's geometric centre. The Panteón

i *Plaza Mayor 3*

▶ *From Madrid take NVI then A6. At exit 2 turn off to the southwest on M600, then almost at once turn right to the Valle de los Caídos*

▶ *Rejoin the M600, turn right and continue to El Escorial.*

2 **El Escorial,** Madrid
The Monasterio del Escorial is one of the wonders of Spain. This great granite building,

1 **Valle de los Caídos,** Madrid
A tall cross rising in the distance from a rock mass marks the monument of the Valle de los Caídos, supposedly dedicated to all who were killed during the Civil War but actually to those on the Nationalist side only. At the base of the cross is the entrance to the basilica, a vast crypt cut out from the granite of the mountain. A flight of steps leads to the church. More steps lead to the crypt, covered by a vast underground dome, made up of several million mosaic pieces depicting saints, personalities and symbols of the Civil War. On opposite sides of the altar are the tombs of General Franco, who died in 1975 and José Antonio Primo de Rivera, who died in 1936. Behind the altar is the choir, with stalls for the Benedictine monks from the adjoining monastery.

You can also take a funicular up to the Cross from where there is a magnificent view of the surrounding landscape.

FOR HISTORY BUFFS

A short drive south of El Escorial brings you to a spot known as the Silla de Felipe II (Philip II's seat). On the summit of a small hill among some boulders you will see what appear to be four seats carved from the rock. It is said that the king used to come here and meditate, while keeping a watchful eye on the progress of the construction of the monastery. There is a magnificent view from here of the monastery and the whole panorama.

de los Reyes (Royal Pantheon) contains the sarcophagi of most of the Spanish kings since Charles I. A few still remain unoccupied. King Philip and his successors lived in the richly decorated Palacio Real. The Biblioteca de Impresos is sumptuously decorated with tapestries and frescos by many painters. It contains some 40,000 volumes and hundreds of ancient manuscripts, codices and bibles. Two priceless items are the illuminated *Codex Aureus* made for the German Emperor Conrad II (completed in 1039) and the diary of St Theresa of Ávila.

The Arts Museum has a superb collection of paintings by famous masters. One of these is *The Martyrdom of St Maurice and the Theban Legionary* by El Greco. The Architectural Museum has a fascinating display of documents and plans relating to the construction of the monastery.

Of great interest, too, is the Habitación de Felipe II (Philip II's cell), where he spent the last years of his life in spartan conditions and troubled by pain. He died in an adjoining alcove in 1598. The Casita del Príncipe lies in lovely gardens to the east of the monastery. It was built by Charles IV, and contains elegant furniture and fine paintings.

[i] *Floridablanca 10*

▶ *Take the M505 northwest for 63km (39 miles) to Ávila.*

8 Ávila, Ávila

The medieval walls of Ávila are a familiar landmark in the area and can be seen for miles around. With 88 round towers and nine gates, they extend for 2,526m (2,763 yards), encircling the town. The Catedral de San Salvador forms part of the wall and has a rather fortress-like appearance. It was built between the 11th and 13th centuries and combines Romanesque and baroque styles. Of special note inside are the 16th-century stained-glass windows, the painted altarpiece and the alabaster tomb of Cardinal Alonso de Madrigal, who was Bishop of Ávila and died in 1455. The Basílica de San Vicente is noted for its 14th-century façade and portal.

Avila within its medieval walls

The Romanesque Iglesia de San Pedro (12th–13th century) has a lovely rose window and fine high altar. The 15th-century Convento de Santo Tomás features beautifully carved choirstalls and a fine retable by Pedro Berruguete. In the mausoleum is the tomb of Prince Juan, only son of the Catholic monarchs Ferdinand and Isabella, who died in 1497 when only 19. When you leave the cathedral by the other door you will find yourself within the walls of the old town. On this square stands the former Convento de Santa Teresa, which contains a chapel built in 1638 on the site of her birth-place. Inside you can see writings of the saint and relics – including her well-preserved ring finger. Facing the convent is the old palace of the former Viceroy of Peru. For more insight into St Theresa's life, look out for the Convento de la Encarnación, where she first took orders and spent some 30 years of her life, latterly as prioress. St Theresa was an exceptional person, remembered for her mystical writing and autobiography. Founder of a number of convents, she was canonised in 1622.

SCENIC ROUTES

West of Madrid the impressive mountain panoramas of the Sierra de Guadarrama give way to the brown windswept plateau and strange boulders to be found around Ávila. Beyond Ávila the route enters the Sierra de Gredos, an area of dramatic mountain ranges and high peaks. The stretch between El Barco de Ávila and Plasencia on the N110 passes through some spectacular scenery of mountains, valleys and pine forests. The drive from Plasencia to the Monasterio de Yuste and beyond Arenas de San Pedro (C501) also offers some outstanding scenery of heavily forested mountains.

BACK TO NATURE

The great mountain range of the Sierra de Gredos, which dominates the region to the west of Madrid, is an important habitat for birds of prey, and among the species that can be seen here are short-toed and booted eagles, red kites and the goshawk, as well as the occasional black stork. Among the many flowers, you can find lupins, peonies and lilies-of-the-valley. The Spanish argus butterfly is special to the area. In the centre of this region is a national park, Coto Nacional de Gredos, where ibex live high up among the crags.

---

[i] *Plaza de la Catedral 4*

▶ *Take the N110 southwest to Piedrahita.*

4 Piedrahita, Ávila
The summer resort of Piedrahita was the birthplace of the Grand Duke of Alba, general of the army of King Philip II. Goya spent some time at the duke's palace here and it is said that there was a love affair between the painter and the Duchess of Alba, who was the model for his well known paintings of *La Maja*.

▶ *Continue on the N110 to El Barco de Ávila.*

5 El Barco de Ávila, Ávila
A drive through magnificent mountain scenery brings you to the town of El Barco de Ávila, where a brief stop will enable you to visit the 14th-century Castillo de Valdecorneja and the Gothic parish church, which contains some fine paintings. Spare a glance, too, for the old bridge over the River Tormes.

▶ *Take the C500 west to Béjar.*

6 Béjar, Salamanca
The Palacio Ducal, an elegant 16th-century palace with a Renaissance courtyard, houses the Museo Municipal. The Ayuntamiento is noted for its attractive arcades. In the Iglesia de San Gil is a museum housing the works of the great sculptor Mateo Hernández, renowned for his animal figures sculpted from hard stone.

[i] *Paseo de Cervantes 6*

▶ *Take the N630 to Plasencia.*

7 Plasencia, Cáceres
The cathedral, started in the 13th century and never completely finished, is a splendid structure with an attractive Plateresque north doorway. Inside, notice the finely sculpted statues by Gregorio Hernández (17th century) on the altarpiece, a 15th-century retable by Hernández in the Capilla Mayor and a graceful 15th-century cloister. The old quarters around the cathedral contain narrow streets, fine façades and houses with attractive wrought-iron balconies. Stepped streets lead up to the old ramparts, where you can walk and enjoy the fine views.

▶ *Take the C501 east for some 45km (27 miles). Turn off north to the Monasterio de Yuste.*

8 Monasterio de Yuste, Cáceres
Set deep in the woods is the old Monasterio de Yuste. It was founded by Hieronymite monks in 1404 and severely damaged by the French in 1809 during the Peninsular War. It fell into decay for a long period until its recent restoration. This was where Emperor Charles V retired to in 1556 after his abdication, leaving the throne to his son Philip II. You can see the royal chambers where Charles lived until his death in 1558, including his bedroom from where he could hear mass. A path leads up to a terrace from which there are good views of the surrounding plains.

[i] *Trujillo 1*

Madrid's 18th century Cibeles fountain shows the Greek goddess of fertility riding her chariot

> Join and take the NV east-wards. Branch off left for a short distance to Navalcarnero.

RECOMMENDED WALKS

The region of Gredos offers countless walks, and there are a few marked paths. There is a very pleasant walk from the Club Alpino to the lake (Laguna de Gredos) at the foot of the Almanzor peak. Other walks include a route along the Gargantas de Gredos del Pinar and the Garganta de Chilla, from El Raso.

> Return to and continue east on the C501. Join the N502 after Arenas de San Pedro and continue south to Talavera de la Reina.

Talavera de la Reina,
Toledo

Talavera de la Reina is famous for its attractive blue-and-yellow tiles, or azulejos, which have been produced since the 15th century. The tiles have been used over the centuries to adorn palaces, mansions, churches and other buildings. Craftsmen took their skills to Mexico after the Conquest in 1521 and the traditional craft continued. The Museo Ruiz de Luna displays potteryware from the 15th to 19th centuries. Places of interest in the town include the 13th-century Romanesque Iglesia de San Salvador, the Gothic Colegiata de Santa María la Mayor (13th–15th centuries), the Mudejar-style parish church of Santiago and the Capilla de Nuestra Señora del Prado, which is adorned with beautiful glazed tiles dating back to the 16th and 18th centuries.

i Ayuntamiento, General Primo de Rivera

SPECIAL TO...

El Puente del Arzobispo, southwest of Talavera de la Reina, is an important pottery centre and produces a variety of attractively decorated ceramics. Embroidery is also a popular craft in Spain and is often undertaken by families in rural areas.

10 Navalcarnero, Madrid
Make a brief stop here to take a look at the delightful little porticoed square and the parish church, which houses a notable retable and a fine work depicting the Apostles. In 1649 Philip IV was married to Anne of Austria here.

FOR CHILDREN

A few miles northwest of Navalcarnero is the small town of Aleda del Fresno, where you will find an excellent Safari Park. A swimming pool, lively fairground, mini golf and horse riding feature among the attractions it offers.

> Rejoin the NV and return to Madrid, 33km (21 miles).

The Route of
the Royal Palaces

The Puerta del Sol is the nerve centre of Madrid, an area for shopping enthusiasts with two large department stores. Even more elegant is the part to the northwest, around Serrano, Goya and Conde of Peñalver. On Sunday, visit El Rastro (the flea market), south of Calle Mayor with its colourful stalls, stirring gypsy music and lively crowds.

2/3 DAYS • 364KM • 226 MILES

ITINERARY

MADRID	►	El Pardo (13km-8m)
EL PARDO	►	Colmenar Viejo (29km-18m)
COLMENAR VIEJO	►	Manzanares el Real (16km-10m)
MANZANARES EL REAL	►	Miraflores de la Sierra (16km-10m)
MIRAFLORES DE LA SIERRA	►	El Paular (27km-17m)
EL PAULAR	►	La Granja (38km-24m)
LA GRANJA	►	Segovia (11km-7m)
SEGOVIA	►	Pedraza (44km-27m)
PEDRAZA	►	Sepúlveda (25km-16m)
SEPÚLVEDA	►	Riaza (24km-15m)
RIAZA	►	Buitrago (41km-25m)
BUITRAGO	►	Torrelaguna (25km-15m)
TORRELAGUNA	►	Madrid (55km-34m)

ℹ️ *Plaza Mayor 3*

➤ *From Madrid take the NVI northwest. At Puerte de Hierro take the C601 north to El Pardo.*

0 El Pardo, Madrid

The way to El Pardo is through the Bosque del Pardo, delightful wooded parkland where you might glimpse deer, wild boar or an eagle soaring above. These were old royal hunting grounds dating back to the 14th century. In the middle of this lush greenery lies the little town of El Pardo and the Palacio de El Pardo. The palace was built by Philip III over an earlier palace (built by Philip II and subsequently destroyed by fire), and was enlarged in the 18th century. General Franco resided here for 35 years until his death in 1975.

Elegant reception rooms and private apartments are lavishly furnished with ornate clocks, mirrors, lamps and candelabra, as well as Sèvres' porcelain and a collection of 360 tapestries. Also on show are General Franco's Great Dining Room, where cabinet meetings took place, and his private office, which contains a notable portrait of Queen Isabella.

In the town across the river is the Convento de Capuchinos (Capuchin Convent), which contains a remarkable sculpture, the *Christ of El Pardo*, by Gregorio Fernández.

➤ *Head east to join the M607/C607. Turn left and go north to Colmenar Viejo.*

SCENIC ROUTES

The most scenic parts of this route are to be found in the Sierra de Guadarrama, with its forested mountains and valleys. The road continues through hills and pine forest, and the land becomes lush and green near La Granja. From La Granja to Segovia it passes through rolling hills and plains, which become an ochre colour around Segovia. On the way back there are winding roads and sweeping views of the Sierras as you travel from Pedraza through Sepúlveda and Riaza to Buitrago.

King Phillip IV rides out in front of Madrid's neoclassical Royal Palace

2 Colmenar Viejo, Madrid
A drive past the old royal deer park takes you to the pleasant little town of Colmenar Viejo, where the main attraction is the Gothic parish church. It was built in the 14th century and has an impressive entrance door. Inside is a fine 16th-century Plateresque retable.

▶ Continue north to rejoin the M607/C607. Go straight across this road, however, and continue north on the M611. Take a left turn, then left again on to the M608 to Manzanares el Real.

3 Manzanares el Real, Madrid
The 15th-century castle was once the property of the Marquis of Santillana, a famous poet at the court of King Juan II in the Middle Ages. It now belongs to the Dukes of El Infantada and has been passed to the state for restoration.

▶ Turn northeast on the M608. Turn left at Soto de Real on to the M611 and continue north to Miraflores de la Sierra.

RECOMMENDED WALKS

South of the castle at Manzanares el Real is the man-made lake, Embalse de Santillana, where you can take a pleasant stroll along the shores.

An 18th-century Sphinx in the gardens at La Granja

FOR CHILDREN

Children will enjoy a visit to the Parque de Riofrío. Situated in the foothills of the Sierra de Guadarrama, 11km (7 miles) southwest of La Granja, these were old hunting grounds surrounding the Riofrío Palace, which stands in the middle of the park. Fallow deer and stags roam freely in this beautiful expanse of grasslands and evergreen oak woods.

---

4 Miraflores de la Sierra, Madrid
A lookout point on the outskirts of this picturesque town offers a magnificent view of the mighty mountains of the Sierra de Guadarrama. You can also see the source of the River Manzanares.

▶ Continue northwest on the same road. Turn left on joining the M604 to El Paular.

5 El Paular, Madrid
The old Carthusian Monasterio del Paular lies in the valley of the River Lozoya. It dates back to 1390 and was the first Carthusian monastery in Castile. It was abandoned in the 19th

century and fell into decay. However, it is now under restoration and inhabited by Benedictine monks. An impressive Gothic door leads to the interior of the church. Its main features are a fine screen and a retable, an outstanding work, with rich sculptures and exquisite filigree work. Do not miss the splendid Gothic cloister with its four sets of vaults.

▶ Take the M604 southwest and join the N601 north to La Granja.

6 La Granja, Segovia
La Granja de San Ildefonso, to give it its full name, is famous for its magnificent French-style palace. The present palace was commissioned by Philip V (grandson of Louis XIV) and was completed in 1723. A few years later it was remodelled and turned into a minature of Versailles. The main façade of the palace faces the gardens. Inside are a series of elegant rooms and galleries decorated in the rococo style. On the first floor are the sumptuous Throne Room and the Royal Bedroom. Outstanding is the magnificent collection of Spanish and Flemish tapestries.
The gardens cover an area of 145 hectares (358 acres). The lower part is famed for its beautiful fountains. The upper gardens have not been tended and are inhabited by deer.

▶ Continue on the N601 to Segovia.

7 Segovia, Segovia
The aqueduct was built by the Romans in the 1st century AD, and is still used for conveying water from the neighbouring sierras to the town. It is considered one of the most impressive monuments of its kind and is a prominent landmark of Segovia. It consists of huge granite blocks held together by butterfly

ies formed by molten lead, and features 118 arches, 43 of which are double-tiered.

Segovia is also famous for the view of its magnificent Alcázar. This was first built in the 12th century and remodelled later. A pathway leading down to the aqueduct offers wonderful views of the Alcázar silhouetted against the sky, and further views over the countryside. Within the Roman walls are the old quarters, with a small main square, picturesque streets and elegant façades.

On the highest point of the town is the cathedral, an elegant structure built in the same mellow-coloured stone, with a tall square tower and pinnacles. It was built between 1525 and 1593 and is a fine example of late-Gothic art. Its large interior is noted for its brilliant stained-glass windows, impressive

Like something from a fairytale, the Alcázar at Segovia stands silhouetted above the town

sculptures and finely decorated altars. The 15th-century cloister was part of the original cathedral, which was destroyed in the 16th century but was reconstructed at a later date. A collection of 17th-century Flemish tapestries is housed in the chapter house. Other places to visit are the Capilla de Vera Cruz, the Monasterio El Parral and the 12th-century Iglesia de San Martín, in the charming Plaza San Martín.

ℹ️ *Plaza Mayor 10*

➤ *Take the N110 northeast. At Matabuena take the unclassified road left to Pedraza.*

Ordinary life continues beneath the Roman aqueduct at Segovia

8 Pedraza, Segovia

Entry to this old walled village is through the Puerta de la Villa (town gate), which leads straight to the delightful Plaza Major. A stroll through its quaint narrow streets and hidden corners will take you past many fine build-

---

SPECIAL TO...

A speciality of Segovia is suckling pig (known here as *tostón*). Although this dish can be enjoyed all over the country, there is nothing quite like sampling it right here in its home town.

BACK TO NATURE

The Sierra de Guadarrama forms the northern part of the great Central Cordillera, which sweeps across the Castilean plains west of Madrid. This is a beautiful area of wooded mountains, valleys and rivers, with several tributaries of the Tajo and the Duero rising in the north-eastern peaks. The area serves as nesting grounds for a number of birds of prey, including imperial eagles, griffon and black vultures, goshawks, red kites and buzzards. Much of the region is covered with pine forests, among which you may find plants such as Pyrenean broom, bluebells, and woodrushes.

9 Sepúlveda, Segovia

This attractive old town still has the remains of Roman fortifications. The focal point is the pleasant Plaza Major, which is overlooked by the old Ayuntamiento. Behind are the ruins of a castle. A walk around town reveals a number of interesting buildings in what is known as the Sepúlveda-Romanesque style. Up the hill is the ancient Iglesia del Salvador. Dating back to the 11th century, it features a galleried portico and separate belfry.

RECOMMENDED WALKS

You can do a lot of walking in the region of the Sierra de Guadarrama. The Valle de la Acebeda, in particular, offers a number of attractive walks.

▷ *Take the regional road east across the NI to join the NI10. Turn left on this road to Riaza, 24km (15 miles).*

10 Riaza, Segovia

Riaza is a picturesque little summer resort with ancient walls, old streets, arcades and elegant mansions, which centre around its attractive main square. In the parish church is a notable pietà.

▷ *Take the NI10 southwest to join the NI. Turn left and continue south to Buitrago.*

11 Buitrago del Lozoya, Madrid

The small medieval town of Buitrago was once the domain of the noble Mendoza family, who wielded much power in Spain in former times. Access to the old town of narrow streets is through a gate in the ancient walls that surround it. To one side of the town is the castle.

▷ *Continue south on the NI. At Lozoyuela take a left turn on to the M131 to Torrelaguna.*

FOR HISTORY BUFFS

Between Riaza and Buitrago the road climbs up to Puerto de Somosierra. Here in 1808, Spaniards defending the pass were defeated by a force of Polish lancers under Napoleon, thus clearing the way for his troops, who were able to advance to Madrid, which they entered five days later.

12 Torrelaguna, Madrid

Torrelaguna was the birthplace of the wife of San Isidro Labrador, patron saint of Madrid, and of Cardinal Cisneros, founder of the University of Alcalá de Henares, which was later moved to Madrid. Around the arcaded Plaza Mayor are the elegant Ayuntamiento and some fine palaces and mansions. An outstanding monument is the beautiful Gothic Iglesia de Santa María Magdalena.

▷ *Continue south on the M131. Turn right on to the M129, then rejoin the NI and return south to Madrid, 55km (34 miles).*

...gs bearing coats of arms from ...ygone days. In the 16th ...entury François I, King of ...rance, and his son were ...nprisoned in the huge castle ...anding atop a massive rock.

▷ *Leave Pedraza to the northwest. At La Velilla turn right and take the regional road northeast to Sepúlveda.*

Remote Lands
of the West

Cáceres is one of Spain's hidden secrets, yet it has much to offer. The Celts, Romans and Visigoths have all been here and left their mark. The Plaza Santa María is a lovely square, lined with the golden façades of fine buildings and the old quarters hold a wealth of treasures.

2/3 DAYS • 516KM • 321 MILES

ITINERARY	
CÁCERES	▶ **Trujillo (47km-29m)**
TRUJILLO	▶ **Guadalupe (83km-52m)**
GUADALUPE	▶ **Mérida (132km-82m)**
MÉRIDA	▶ **Badajoz (62km-39m)**
BADAJOZ	▶ **Alburquerque (45km-28m)**
ALBURQUERQUE	▶ **Valencia de Alcántara (35km-22m)**
VALANCIA DE ALCÁNTARA	▶ **Arroyo de la Luz (92km-57m)**
ARROYO DE LA LUZ	▶ **Cáceres (20km-12m)**

South-western Spain's hot climate makes eating at an outdoor café part of every holiday

ⓘ *Plaza Mayor 10*

▶ *Take the N521 east to Trujillo.*

❿ **Trujillo,** Cáceres

The old town of Trujillo is of great historical interest and has strong associations with the discoveries and conquests of the New World. It is sometimes referred to as the 'Cradle of the Conquistadores', as a number of leading explorers and conquistadores were born here. The most famous was Francisco Pizarro (1475–1541), who overthrew the mighty empire of the Incas and conquered Peru (1531–34), bringing untold wealth to Spain. He married an Inca princess, but was in the end killed in his own palace by compatriots.

Other natives of Trujillo who have their place in history include Alonso de Monroy, known for his exploits in Chile; Francisco de Orellana (who departed in 1542 to explore the jungles of the Amazon); Diego de Paredes (nicknamed the 'Samson of Extremadura' for his physique), whose involvement was with Venezuela; and Hernando de Alarcón, who explored California. The discovery of the Americas in 1492 and subsequent explorations put Trujillo on the map, and the town flourished during the Golden Age of Spain.

The main square, Plaza Mayor, is one of Trujillo's most attractive features. A splendid equestrian statue pays tribute to Pizarro. The monument in bronze (erected in 1927) is the work of the American sculptors Charles Runse and Mary Harriman. The square is built on different levels, connected by broad steps and lined with beautiful portals and façades. Of special interest is the Palacio de los Marqueses de la Conquista. This was built by Hernando Pizarro, brother of the Conquistador, who also went to seek his fortune in Peru, but later returned to his native lands. It is a magnificent palace built in the Plateresque style and noted for its elaborate window grilles and beautiful corner balcony.

Other fine buildings include the Palacio de los Duques de San Carlos (see the two-storeyed patio linked by a projecting staircase), the 16th-century Palacio del Marquis de Piedras Albas with a Renaissance loggia, the former 16th-century Ayuntamiento and the Palace of Justice.

The old part of town is a fascinating jumble of streets and alleyways, lined with many elegant mansions bearing coats of arms. A walk up narrow cobblestoned streets leads to the lovely 15th-century Gothic Iglesia de Santa María la Mayor. It features a Romanesque bell tower and has an attractive interior, which contains the tomb of Diego García de Paredes, born here in 1466. A Romanesque figure of the Virgin of La Coronada may be seen in the 13th-century Iglesia de Santiago. At the top of the town is the old castle, which was built by the Moors on Roman foundations. A wall shrine with the figure of the patron saint, Nuestra Señora de las Victorias, lies above the main gate, known as El Triunfo (The Triumph). There are wonderful panoramic views from the castle of the surrounding landscapes of the Extremadura.

ⓘ *Plaza Mayor s/n*

BACK TO NATURE

The Parque Natural de Monfragüe lies to the northeast of Cáceres, and is a vast area of great rugged peaks, deep gorges and forests, watered by the River Tagus, which cuts right through it. The area is rich in flora and fauna and is a breeding ground for a great variety of birds. Among the many birds of prey that make their home here are the imperial eagle, black vulture, peregrine and several species of owl. Many animals, including deer, wild boar, moufflon and even the elusive Spanish lynx, live in the area.

FOR CHILDREN

Children can enjoy boating on the lakes in the region. A good choice would be the Embalse de Alcántara, which is northeast of Cáceres and provides facilities for various water sports.

RECOMMENDED WALKS

The country north of Cáceres and Trujillo, a somewhat isolated area, offers interesting scenery. There are pleasant spots for walking along the shores of the reservoirs to be found here, and also by the banks of the River Tagus.

▷ *Take the C524 southeast. At Zorita take the C401 east, then turn left to Guadalupe.*

2 Guadalupe, Cáceres
The main attraction of Guadalupe is the monastery, a fortress-like structure of battlements and turrets in mellow stone lying high up above the little village of Guadalupe. The monastery was built by Alfonso XI for the Hieronymites, who lived here between the 14th and 19th centuries. Since 1928 it has been occupied by monks of the Franciscan order. The church contains the much-venerated statue of the Black Virgin, known as La Virgen Morena, whose headdress is richly encrusted with gems. The sanctuary has long been an important pilgrimage centre, and religious festivals take place here on 8 and 30 September and 12 October, the day of La Hispanidad (Day of the Discovery of the Americas).

i Plaza Mayor

▷ *Rejoin the C401 and take the NV from Miajadas south to Mérida.*

3 Mérida, Badajoz
Important Roman remains are the major attraction of Mérida. The original town of Augusta Emerita dates back to the 2nd century AD and was named after its founder, the governor of Augustus. It flourished under the Romans and was then ruled

The Roman theatre at Mérida is still used for performances

by the Moors between 713 and 1229, when it was taken by the Catholic King Alfonso IX.

The Teatro Romano is most impressive. The original theatre was built by Agrippa, son-in-law of Augustus, and rebuilt in the 2nd century BC, after it had been destroyed by fire, with a seating capacity for some 6,000 spectators. The theatre provides a magnificent setting, and plays are staged here in the summer. The arena dates back to the 1st century BC and it is believed the chariot races that took place here were watched by up to 14,000 people. Below the arena are traces of the Casa Romana del Anfiteatro (Patrician Villa), with faintly visible signs of the old pavements and parts of the walls, showing mosaic decorations. The Museum of Roman Art houses a fine collection of Roman, Gothic and Moorish objects, along with Roman sculptures, mosaics, coins and pottery.

The Alcazába was built by the Moors in the 9th century on an original Visigoth building. Later it was converted into a monastery.

Spanning the River Guadiana, the Puente Romano

FOR HISTORY BUFFS

A drive along the N430 east of Mérida, followed by a right turn on to the C520, leads to Medellín, where Hernán Cortés, conqueror of Mexico was born in 1485. Cortés landed in Mexico in 1519 with a small band of men and advanced to Tenochtitlan, capital of the Aztec Empire, where he was received by the Emperor Montezuma. By 1521 he had overthrown the Aztec Empire, and he built a new capital. Later Cortés fell from favour and returned to Spain, where he died in 1547, disillusioned and forgotten. A statue of the conqueror stands on the 17th-century bridge over the River Guadiana.

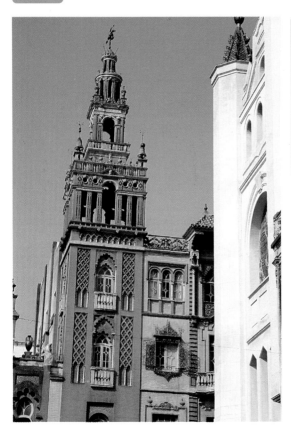

The Plaza de la Soledad in Badajoz, a frontier town which has endured battles and sieges in many wars

SPECIAL TO...

Mérida is the scene of an important cultural festival which takes place in the summer during June, July and August. Plays are staged in the open in the elegant Roman theatre and amphitheatre. There are also ballet performances, exhibitions and other events.

is an impressive structure extending for 792m (866 yards) with 64 arches. The bridge is an important feature of Mérida, along with the Acueducto Romano, which is another outstanding structure. The bridge over the small River Albarregas is also Roman.

The little town of Mérida has a pretty main square, the Plaza de España, which is lined with arcades and overlooked by the Iglesia de Santa María (13th–15th century). To the northwest is the Arco de Trajano, a Roman triumphal arch. This imposing monument is almost 13m (43 feet) high and was once the town's north gate.

i Pedro M Plano s/n

▶ Continue on the NV west for 62km (39 miles) to Badajoz.

4 Badajoz, Badajoz
The town of Badajoz is situated on the banks of the River Guadiana, not far from the Portuguese border. It is the capital of the province of Badajoz and a bishopric. The town was called Colonia Pacensis by the Romans and received its present name from the Moors. A small Moorish kingdom was established here, until it fell to the Catholic King

FOR CHILDREN

One particular attraction for children is the zoo in Almendralejo, some 26km (16 miles) south of Mérida on the N630.

Alfonso IX of Leon in 1229. Over the years its strategic position, so close to Portugal, caused the town to be involved in many bitter battles during the various European wars.

The focal point of the town is the Plaza de España, which is overlooked by the 13th-century Gothic Catedral de San Juan (St John). It has a fortress-like tower and a 17th-century Renaissance façade and doorway. There are some fine old tapestries in the sacristy and a small Diocesan museum in the chapter house. The Palacio de la Diputación houses the Museo Provincial, which features paintings by artists from the region. The Puente de Palmas is an impressive 16th-century granite bridge with 32 arches over the River Guadiana.

The town is overlooked by the old Moorish Alcazába, from which there are good views.

i Plaza de la Libertad 3

▶ Take the N523 north. Branch off on the C530 and travel north to Alburquerque.

5 Alburquerque, Badajoz
A drive over the mountain pass of Los Conejeros will bring you to the village of Alburquerque, which is dominated by the remains of a massive 13th-century castle, once the scene of fierce fighting between the Portuguese and the Moors. A climb up to the castle ruins offers, as you would expect, fine views of the surrounding countryside. The village down below

is surrounded by ancient walls and well worth strolling around. It has two interesting churches: the 13th-century Gothic Iglesia de Santa María del Mercado and the parish church of San Mateo, in the Gothic-Renaissance style.

▷ *Continue on the C530 and take a left turn to Valencia de Alcántara.*

6 Valencia de Alcántara,
Cáceres

The little frontier town of Valencia de Alcántara serves as a customs post for travellers to and from Portugal, 14km (8½ miles) away. It is a very pleasant town, with old walls and the ruins of a 13th-century Moorish castle. Two churches of special interest are the 13th-century Iglesia de la Encarnación,which has a very fine Gothic façade, and the 16th-century Iglesia de

Nuestra Señora del Rocamador, whose Christ figure has been ascribed to the artist, Berruguete.

A number of dolmens have been discovered in the area, signifying the presence of prehistoric man.

▷ *Take the N521 east and turn left on the C523 to Arroyo de la Luz.*

7 Arroyo de la Luz, Cáceres

On the way here you might like to make a detour to the town of Alcántara, which features a famous Roman bridge over the gorge of the River Tajo. The bridge dates back to AD106 and is an impressive structure of huge dimensions.

The charming little town of Arroyo de la Luz is an important pottery centre for the region. Its main building of interest is the

The Plaza San Jorge, Cáceres, a town full of beautiful unspoilt Gothic and Renaissance buildings

Iglesia de la Asunción, which features a splendid Gothic portal and contains a notable carved retable inside, a work of the artist Luis Morales, a native of Badajoz.

▷ *Rejoin the N521 and return to Cáceres.*

SCENIC ROUTES

This region is an area of arid, brown-coloured lands, with bare rugged mountains and dry valleys, combined with fertile lands. One of the most scenically attractive areas is along the C530 from Alburquerque to Valencia de Alcántara.

Historical Cities
& Cathedrals

Salamanca has the oldest University in Spain and many lovely buildings of which those in the Plaza Mayor are perhaps the most attractive, topped by the Ayuntamiento. From the left bank of the River Tormes there is a splendid view of the town across the Roman bridge.

2/3 DAYS • 586KM • 365 MILES

ITINERARY

SALAMANCA	▶	**Villanueva de Cañedo** (28km-17m)
VILLANUEVA DE CAÑEDO	▶	**Zamora** (42km-26m)
ZAMORA	▶	**Valladolid** (96km-60m)
VALLADOLID	▶	**Palencia** (46km-29m)
PALENCIA	▶	**Burgos** (85km-53m)
BURGOS	▶	**Lerma** (37km-23m)
LERMA	▶	**Aranda de Duero** (43km-27m)
ARANDA DE DUERO	▶	**Peñafiel** (38km-24m)
PEÑAFIEL	▶	**Tordesillas** (85km-53m)
TORDESILLAS	▶	**Salamanca** (86km-53m)

0 Villanueva de Cañedo, Salamanca

The main attraction here is the 13th-century Castillo del Buen Amor, an old fortified palace with large circular towers. It has an impressive interior with a fine Mudejar coffered ceiling and an inner patio.

▶ *Rejoin the N630 and continue north to Zamora.*

2 Zamora, Zamora

Zamora was long under Moorish domination, and was the scene of many battles between the Moors and the Christians, during which 'El Cid', conqueror of the Moors, played an important role. The cathedral stands near the right bank of the River Duero. It was built between 1151 and 1174 and is largely Romanesque, with a square tower and an impressive Byzantine-style cupola. Some splendid sculptures adorn the Puerta del Obispo (Bishop's Door). Inside, the aisles are Romanesque-Gothic. In the Capilla Mayor (Main Chapel) is a notable

RECOMMENDED WALKS

There are some beautiful areas for walking in the Sierra Peña de Francia, to the south of Salamanca. It offers superb mountain scenery, together with woods, lush green valleys and picturesque little villages dotted about the countryside. Much of the route follows the course of the River Duero, where you can take some time off and stroll along its banks. Around Tordesillas there are pleasant pathways along the river shaded by poplars and other trees.

ⓘ *Casa de las Conchas, Rua Mayor*

▶ *From Salamanca take the N630 north towards Zamora. After Huelmos de Cañedo, take a right turn to Villanueva de Cañedo.*

Top: The Ayuntamiento at Salamanca looks out over the famous Plaza Mayor. *Right:* the tower of the new cathedral

15th-century altarpiece and several impressive tombs. The cloister houses a museum that among other exhibits has a collection of 15th- to 17th-century Flemish tapestries.

The little 12th-century Iglesia de Santa Magdalena is a particularly fine example of the Romanesque style of architecture that was most evident in Zamora in the 12th century. Other churches built in a similar style are those of Santo Tomás, Santiago de Burgos and Santa María de la Horta. The 12th-century Iglesia de San Cipriano is noted for its finely decorated façade.

Standing on the Plaza Mayor are the 17th-century Ayuntamiento and the Gothic Iglesia de San Juan, which has attractive paintings around the altar. There is a good view of the town from the Puente Viejo (old bridge).

SCENIC ROUTES

Much of this itinerary offers interesting rather than spectacular scenery. One of the most attractive sections of the drive is between Zamora and Toro on the N122, which follows the course of the River Duero, offering pleasant views.

[i] Calle Santa Clara 20

▶ Take the N122 east. Join the N620 at Tordesillas and continue northeast to Valladolid.

3 **Valladolid,** Valladolid
The busy industrial town of Valladolid lies in the heart of the 'Meseta Central' plateau, in an area of flat landscapes. In the centre, near the Plaza Mayor, is the cathedral. This was started in 1580 on a grand scale by the renowned architect Juan de Herrera. Building continued in the 18th century under Alberto Churriguera, but the cathedral was never completed. Of special note is an impressive

16th-century high altar by the sculptor Juan de Juni.

Adjoining the cathedral is the Museo Episcopal, which contains religious relics, jewellery and a magnificent silver monstrance in the shape of a temple, made by the great Toledo craftsman, Juan de Arfe.

The former Colegio de San Gregorio (St Gregory's College) was built between 1488 and 1496. It has an Isabelline-Gothic façade carved with elaborate decorations including coats of arms. The Museo Nacional de Escultura on the first floor has an impressive collection of Spanish sculptures, including works by several of Spain's prominent artists of the 16th and 17th centuries.

The town's Museo Arqueológico is housed in the old Renaissance Palacio de Fabio Nelli and displays Roman sculptures, 13th- and 15th-century frescos and tapestries. The 12th- to 14th-century Iglesia de Santa María la Antigua is the oldest church in Valladolid and features a fine Romanesque tower. The 13th-century Iglesia de San Pablo has a superbly decorated façade, flanked by two quite simple towers. Valladolid university, a venerable institution founded in the 14th century, has a fine building which delights in a magnificent 18th-century baroque façade.

FOR HISTORY BUFFS

Literary experts might be interested in making a special visit to the Casa de Cervantes in Valladolid, away from the centre of town, where the famous author of *Don Quixote* lived between 1603 and 1606. The house has been well preserved, and contains a small museum where you can visit the room thought to have been the writer's study and look at one of his manuscripts on display.

SPECIAL TO...

The town of Valladolid is surrounded by an important wine-growing region, which stretches south towards Salamanca and takes in part of the province of León to the north. The best-known wines are those of La Nava, Roa and Peñafiel, which can be either red or white and tend to be fairly strong, and the heavy red wines of Toro which are grown further west. During the month of October you can make a little tour of the area, following the traditional 'Routes of the Wine'.

[i] Plaza de Zorilla 3

▶ Continue on the N620. Branch off left on to the N611 to Palencia.

4 **Palencia,** Palencia
The Gothic cathedral stands on the small square called Plaza Santa, just off the Plaza Mayor. It was built between 1321 and 1516 on the ruins of a Romanesque chapel erected by Sancho the Great. The interior is decorated in a mixture of Gothic, Isabelline, Plateresque and Renaissance styles. Some fine sculptures include works by Gil de Siloé and Simon of Cologne. The Capilla Mayor (main chapel) contains a magnificent main altarpiece with paintings by Juan de Flanders. The Chapel of the Holy Sacrament, behind the main chapel, features a notable retable by Valmaseda. Among many valuable objects in the Treasury is a beautiful 16th-century silver custodia by Juan de Benavente. A museum in the cloister contains an El Greco painting, together with other fine works of art and some 15th-century sculptures.

The 13th-century Iglesia de San Francisco has a sacristy with fine Mudejar vaulting. The parish church of San Miguel (13th–14th century) is noted for

The 14th century Santa Mariá Arch, gateway to Burgos, with the spire of the cathedral beyond

ⓘ *Calle Mayor 105*

▶ *Leave southeast by the N610. Rejoin the N620 and continue northeast to Burgos.*

its Romanesque portal and impressive tower. In the 16th-century Convento de Santa Clara (Convent of St Clare) is a reclining figure of Christ. Of special interest is the Capilla de San Bernardo (Chapel of St Bernard), where El Cid's marriage took place.

🔟 Burgos, Burgos

Burgos is famed for its cathedral which is one of the largest and most impressive in Spain. The city was closely associated with the great Rodrigo Díaz de Vivar, better known as 'El Cid Campeador' (El Cid the champion). His body found a final resting place in the cathedral here in 1929.

The cathedral was founded by Ferdinand III in 1221, with a second phase of building in the 15th century, when its two tall pinnacles were added by John of Cologne. This imposing limestone structure has a richly decorated Gothic façade. In the transept is the tomb of El Cid.

His wife Ximena lies beside him. There is a fine 16th-century altarpiece in the Capilla Mayor and the finely carved choirstalls also date from the same century. The Capilla del Condestable (Constable Chapel) was designed by Simon de Cologne in 1482 in the Isabelline style. In the centre is an elaborately carved tomb of the Constable and his wife.

A number of beautifully designed chapels are placed around the interior of the cathedral. Of particular note are those of Santa Ana, whose magnificent retable includes the impressive Tree of Jesse, and the Capilla del Santo Christo, which contains a much venerated image of Christ. The 14th-century cloister contains an impressive figure of Christ at the Column by Diego de Siloé (16th-century). In the chapter house are some beautiful 15th- and 16th-century Flemish tapestries. Of special interest is the Capilla de Santa Caterina, which has some interesting historical documents, including the marriage contract of El Cid.

There are numerous monuments to visit in the city. The Santa María Arch, built in the 14th century, is a masssive entrance gate originally part of the city walls. The 14th-century Iglesia de San Gil is noted for its pietà sculpture and magnificent 13th- to 14th-century altarpiece. The Gothic Iglesia de San Estéban has an impressive doorway and the 15th-century Iglesia de San Nicolás features a notable high altar and lovely vaulting. In the Plaza del General de Primo de Rivera stands an equestrian statue of the hero El Cid, brandishing a sword.

The 15th-century Casa del Cordón is the place where Christopher Columbus was received in 1496 by the Catholic monarchs Ferdinand and Isabella after returning from his second voyage across the Atlantic. King Philip I died here in 1506.

About 4km (2½ miles) southeast is the Cartuja de Miraflores (Charter House of Miraflores). This lovely Carthusian house was founded by King John and rebuilt in the 15th century. It is still a monastery but visitors are allowed into the church where

Flowers along a little street in the village of Lerma

lie the resplendent tombs of King John, his second wife Isabella of Portugal and the Infante Alfonso, whose early

---

FOR CHILDREN

Obvious attractions for children are a little lacking on this tour. One particular aspect of Corpus Christi processions in Burgos, however, has a great appeal for children, judging by the reaction of the local ones at least! During the processions a huge silver monstrance is carried on a richly ornate cart that is manoeuvred by a man concealed underneath, giving the impression that the cart is moving mysteriously on its own.

8 Peñafiel, Valladolid

The splendid silhouette of the Castillo de Peñafiel rises high above the little village of the same name. Built in the 14th century, the castle has 12 round towers and an impressive keep. Other attractions in the village are the Plaza del Coso, where spectators at the bullfights used to watch from the balconies of the surrounding houses, and the 14th-century Iglesia de San Pablo (church of St Paul), which features some fine Mudejar architecture as well as Renaissance vaulting over the Capilla Infante (16th-century).

▷ *Continue west on the N122. At Valladolid take the N620 southwest to Tordesillas.*

9 Tordesillas, Valladolid

In the monastery here, Juana la Loca (the Mad One), daughter of Ferdinand and Isabella and mother of Emperor Charles V, locked herself away after the death in 1506 of her husband Philip the Fair. She died here in 1555. The monastery, built between the 14th and 18th centuries, has some patios with Mudejar decorations and a Gothic church with a 15th-century altar.

i *Ayuntamiento, Plaza Mayor 1*

▷ *Return to Salamanca on the N620.*

---

death in 1468 resulted in the succession to the throne of his sister, Queen Isabella the Catholic. Above the tombs of King John and Isabella rises a magnificent altarpiece by Gil de Siloé and Diego de la Cruz.

Plaza de Alonso Martínez 7

▷ *Take the NI south to Lerma.*

6 Lerma, Burgos

The 17th-century Palacio del Duque de Lerma (Ducal Palace) is one of several elegant mansions built during this period. Of interest is the tomb of Archbishop Cristóbal de Rojas of Sevilla which lies in the 17th-century Colegiata .

▷ *Continue on the NI south to Aranda de Duero.*

Pottery is one of the local crafts in Salamanca; this market offers shoppers a tremendous selection of different shapes and sizes

7 Aranda de Duero, Burgos

The main attraction in Aranda de Duero is the late-Gothic Iglesia de Santa María la Real. Founded in the 15th century by Ferdinand and Isabella, its chief splendour is the magnificent Isabelline doorway with rich gilded decorations. Take a look, too, at the attractive little 13th-century Iglesia de San Juan and the Capilla de le Virgin de las Vinas, which is a popular pilgrimage centre.

i *Ayuntamiento, Plaza Mayor 1*

▷ *Take the N122 west to Peñafiel.*

BACK TO NATURE

A regional road just after Lerma leads southeast to the ancient Monasterio de Santo Domingo de Silos, which offers an interesting visit. The monks here have made some highly successful recordings.
A few miles further on is the Garganta de la Yecla (Yecla Gorges), a fascinating wonder of nature, consisting of a deep gash in the rocks, very narrow in places, with a little stream flowing between. You can follow the course of the gorge.

GREEN SPAIN

This region in the north of Spain consists of the Basque country (Euskadi), Cantabria, Asturias and Galicia. Although there are historical, cultural and administrative divisions, the area shares some common geographical factors. Spain's Atlantic seaboard is wetter than any other part of Spain, resulting in fresh green landscapes. To the north the Bay of Biscay, or 'Mar Cantábrico', has a magnificent coastline of rugged cliffs, inlets and sandy beaches. The Basque mountains start where the western Pyrenees end and give way to the Cordillera Cantábrica, which sweeps across the north. The Cordillera includes the Picos de Europa, and rises to more than 2,500m (8,000 feet). Galicia to the west has a distinctive coastline of rugged cliffs and fiord-like inlets known as the 'Rías Altas' in the north and the 'Rías Bajas' down the west

The four areas have very different histories. The Basques were a strong, independant race, with a long history of seeking self-determination. Cantábria, further west, has a number of caves containing wall paintings that prove the presence of palaeolithic man. Asturias was once a separate kingdom, and played an essential part at the very beginning of the Reconquest. In Galicia which was occupied by the Celts as early as the 6th century BC. Santiago de Compostela, where the tomb of St James the Apostle (Santiago) was the goal of pilgrimages, led the development of the area from the 9th century. Galicians have their own language, Gallego, which bears some resemblance to Portuguese.

The Basque country has green pastures, maize-growing areas and fruit and walnut trees. Further south are vast plains with vineyards and cornfields. Cantábria is known for its dairy products, and Asturias is a cider-producing area. Fishing plays an important role in Galicia, and the region is famous for its seafood. In the Basque country many names are written first in Basque and then in Castilian. Galicia has a similar situation with its own language.

North and west Spain is green, the light is softer and old red-roofed houses line the village streets

Tour 22

Tucked away in the far north-western corner of Spain is Galicia, a little world of its own. Its jagged coastline of high cliffs and estuaries is reminiscent of the Norwegian fiords, and its countryside, climate and culture are far removed from the popular images of Spain. This tour is full of surprises, combining green hills, rivers and valleys, Roman towns and a spectacular coast interrupted by many picturesque fishing villages. The highlight is a visit to Spain's most important shrine, which has been the centre of pilgrimages for centuries. The town and its cathedral are among the most important and attractive monuments in the country.

Tour 23

This tour will delight anyone who enjoys spectacular mountain scenery. The route travels south from Oviedo into the Picos de Europa, making a stop in one of the major towns in the area, whose cathedral is known for its stained-glass windows. Following this are a number of visits to charming mountain towns. One of the most attractive parts of the tour is a trip to an important sanctuary in a secluded setting, surrounded by a magnificent panorama of green forested mountains. This is thought of as the birthplace of Christian Spain, as the first steps towards resistance to the Moorish occupation took root here. The tour rounds off with a drive along the northern coast and takes a look at the region's most important port.

Tour 24

Hills, valleys and remote rural villages form the background of this tour, which will appeal to those who love peace and quiet in beautiful surroundings. Exploration of the hinterland will take you through some isolated countryside. Delightfully unspoilt mountain villages dotted about the slopes will give you an insight into a way of life that has seen little change with the passage of time. The coastline here is softer than that of the neighbouring regions, and some of the seaside resorts are very picturesque, with attractive harbours, promenades and splendid sandy beaches. The famous prehistoric caves in the area are of great historical and cultural interest.

Tour 25

The Basque country is characterised in the north by the green landscapes of wooded hills and lush valleys. It has a rugged coastline with magnificent sandy beaches tucked in between spectacular cliffs. This itinerary includes some beautiful drives along the coast and stops in picturesque little resorts. A visit to Spain's busiest northern port provides a contrast to some of the typical small Basque mountain villages you will encounter in the interior of the country. The people and distinctive customs of the Basque country give the region an unmistakable character.

World of
Galicia

ITINERARY

LA CORUÑA	►	Betanzos (23km·14m)
BETANZOS	►	Lugo (73km·45m)
LUGO	►	Monforte (65km·40m)
MONFORTE	►	Orense (48km·30m)
ORENSE	►	Vigo (104km·65m)
VIGO	►	Pontevedra (34km·21m)
PONTEVEDRA	►	Isla de la Toja (35km·22m)
ISLA DE LA TOJA	►	Cambados (20km·12m)
CAMBADOS	►	Padrón (35km·22m)
PADRÓN	►	Santiago de Compostela (20km·12m)
SANTIAGO DE COMPOSTELA		
NOIA	►	Cabo Fisterra (93km·58m)
CABO FISTERRA	►	La Coruña (115km·71m)

3 DAYS • 702KM • 435 MILES

The capital of Galicia, La Coruña was the starting point for King Philip II's 'invincible' Armada sent against England in 1588. The old town is an area of narrow cobbled streets and little squares with notable churches. The Torre de Hércules, a Celtic/Roman lighthouse offers splendid views.

i *Dársena de la Marina*

▶ *From La Coruña take the NVI for 23km (14 miles) to Betanzos.*

La Coruña's harbour where up-to-date offices, traditional buildings and fishing boats rub shoulders.

FOR HISTORY BUFFS

Northeast of La Coruña is the town of Ferrol, birthplace of General Francisco Franco, who was born here in 1892 and ruled Spain for 37 years until his death in 1975. The town is one of Spain's major naval bases and is built around a beautiful bay, overlooked by the castles of San Felipe and La Palma.

❶ Betanzos, La Coruña

Betanzos is a small town of great charm, with medieval walls and steep narrow streets, lined with attractive houses and balconies. It has several notable churches. The 14th to 15th-century Iglesia de Santa María del Azogue has an elegant façade and a fine Flemish altarpiece. The Monasterio de San Francisco was built in the 14th century, in the shape of a cross, by the Conde de Andrade, lord of Betanzos. In the church is his tomb, a vast sepulchre resting on a boar and a bear. Another notable church is the parish church of Santiago, rebuilt in the 15th century by the tailors' guild. Note the fine carving of St James, known as the Slayer of the Moors, over the doorway. Inside are several chapels, one of which contains an impressive retable in Isabelline style.

FOR CHILDREN

There are a number of colourful fiestas in the region, which would appeal to children. They should particularly enjoy Fiestas de los Maios, which features mostly children and young people. This is celebrated all over Spain on 1 May, but is very attractive in Betanzos, which is also the scene of a popular pilgrimage on Easter Monday.

i *Ayuntamiento, Plaza del Generalísimo 1*

▶ *Continue on the NVI to Lugo. A new autovia to Lugo and beyond is being built and road numbers may change.*

2 Lugo, Lugo

Massive great slate walls surround the old Roman city of Lugo. Originally a Celtic settlement, it became a city of some importance under the Romans, who called it Lucus Augusti. Much of the old town was destroyed by fire, first under the Moors and then the Visigoths, and it was the scene of fierce battles during the Napoleonic Wars. The *murallas* (town walls) have a perimeter of over 2km (1¼ miles). They date back to the 2nd century AD and were reinforced in the 14th century. The Plaza de España is the town's attractive main square. It is lined with elegant buildings and is graced by a fountain in the centre, with a statue of Hispaña. The Ayuntamiento on

RECOMMENDED WALKS

You can follow in the footsteps of the old pilgrims along a section of the Way to Santiago. Cebreiro, Portomarín or Vilar de Donas could all be suitable starting points. However, you can seek guidance from the local tourist office.

the east side of the square has an impressive rococo façade.

On the western side is the cathedral. It was first erected in the 12th century, with alterations and additions continuing in the 15th and 18th centuries. Parts of the building show the Romanesque style, with traces of French influences related to the fact that Lugo was on the route of the French pilgrims going to Santiago. Much of the cathedral is Gothic. It has twin towers and an impressive 18th-century façade. Notable features inside are the rococo altarpiece in the Capilla Mayor, decorated choir-stalls and a lovely 18th-century Gothic cloister. In the south ambulatory is the wooden statue of the 'English' Virgin, which was transported here from St Paul's Cathedral,

London, during the 16th century. The museum has a collection of paintings and religious relics. Worth a visit is the 13th-century Iglesia de Santo Domingo, which features some fine Romanesque doorways and an impressive retable. The Museo Provincial displays some interesting ceramics, coins and regional handicrafts.

i *Plaza de España 27–29*

BACK TO NATURE

Near Lugo, in the Sierra de Ancares, is the Parque de Ancares (Ancares Park), which is rich in wildlife. Deer and wild boar are some of the animals you can see here.

Maize stored in a *horreos*

▶ *Take the NVI southeast and after about 6km (4 miles) turn right on to the C546 and go south to Monforte, 65km (40 miles).*

❸ Monforte, Lugo

The picturesque little village of Monforte is partly encircled by old ramparts and overlooked by a castle with a huge tower, which once belonged to the Counts of Lemos, hence the village's full name of Monforte de Lemos. Of major interest in the village is the Colegio de la Compañía (Jesuit College), whose church contains a beautiful 17th-century retable by Francisco Moure and three paintings by El Greco. Note, too, the fine 16th-century Renaissance doorways of the former Benedictine Monasterio de San Vicente del Pino.

▶ *Take the N120 southwest to Orense (Ourense).*

❹ Orense, Orense

Orense was founded by the Romans because of its thermal springs, around which the ancient town developed and

RECOMMENDED WALKS

Imagine yourself as a Roman sentry when you follow their route along the path round the top of the 3rd-century walls of Lugo. A walk along the ramparts also offers magnificent views of the surrounding countryside.

SPECIAL TO...

In Galicia you will see many stone buildings constructed on tall granite supports, with a saddle roof and a cross on top. These *horreos* are mainly used to store maize and were built to protect the crops from humidity and vermin. Between May and July the wild horses are rounded up in the mountains and brought to special corrals (*curros*) to be branded and have their manes and tails cut. This forms part of a rodeo-type festival known as La Rapa das Bestas (the marking of wild horses), held in various towns in the region.

from which it got its name, Aquae Urentes. In the 6th and 7th centuries it was the seat of Suevian kings. The town suffered damage during the Moorish

invasion in 716, but was built up again in the 10th century. Modern Orense is a busy commercial centre, but the old section of the town is delightful. The Palacio del Obispo (Bishop's Palace) stands on the corner of the Plaza Mayor and is noted for its attractive courtyard. This is now the Museo Arqueológico, where you can view items from prehis-

toric and Roman times, and religious relics.

The Catedral de San Martín was first built between the 12th and 13th centuries and renovated in the 16th and 17th centuries after damage caused by wars and earthquakes. It is noted for its triple-arched portal, Pórtico del Paraíso (Paradise), which is richly decorated and preserves some of its original colouring. Note the large 16th-century Gothic retable and the carved choirstalls. An interesting item is the crucifix in the Capilla del Crucificado (Chapel of the Crucified Christ), said to have been found on the coast of western Galicia and brought here in 1330. The Museo Episcopal (Episcopal Museum), located in the chapter house, has an interesting display of 13th-century enamels, statues and altars.

The 13th-century Romanesque Iglesia de la Trinidad, located in the southern section of the town, features two large round towers and a fine Gothic doorway. The Puente Viejo (old bridge), which spans the River Miño, is quite an

impressive structure, dating back to the 13th century. The little chapel in the nearby Campo de los Remedios contains a statue of the Virgen de los Remedios, to whom pilgrimages are made.

i *Curros Enriquez 1*

▶ *Take the N120 west to Vigo.*

5 **Vigo,** Pontevedra

Vigo is a major naval and fishing port, and one of Galicia's largest towns. It has Roman origins. However, its real growth began in the 16th century, when trading links were established with America. During the 15th and 16th centuries it was constantly under threat of attack by English ships which sought to divest the Spanish fleets of their precious cargoes from overseas. In 1702 a returning Spanish fleet was virtually destroyed by English and Dutch seamen. Treasures of immense value were seized and the Spanish fleet never recovered from the attack.

Vigo is a pleasant town with old and new sections. The old part, the fishermen's quarters, called the Berbes, can be fun and there is plenty of lively action in the Pescadería (fish market) when business is on. A stroll along the Paseo de Alfonso XIII promenade offers a good view of the harbour. In the new town there are some attractive buildings around the Plaza de Compostela. There is a sweeping view of the town and bay from the Castro (castle) on top of the hill.

i *Estación* (station)

Vigo's statue celebrating the wild horses of Galicia

Ages. In the Museo Provincial you can see Celtiberian exhibits and paintings.

ℹ️ *General Mola 1*

▶ *Take the C550 west for 35km (22 miles) to Isla de la Toja.*

7 Isla de la Toja, Pontevedra
This island has long had a reputation as the most exclusive summer resort in Galicia. It is linked to the mainland by a bridge. The neighbouring village of O Grove, back on the mainland, has an attractive little fishing harbour, known for its excellent shellfish.

▶ *Retrace the route for 5km (3 miles) from O Grove, then continue on the C550 west then north to Cambados.*

8 Cambados, Pontevedra
Cambados is a pleasant little village by the sea. The manor house of El Pazo de Fefinanes, which stands on the grandiose square of the Plaza de Fefinanes, is a typical example of the Pazo style of architecture, a style unique to Galicia and popular with the nobility of the region in the 17th and 18th centuries. The 17th century church in the square is built in a similar style to the manor.

▶ *Continue on the C550 toward Padrón. Turn left on to the N550 just south of the town.*

9 Padrón, La Coruña
Padrón is the place where the legendary vessel carrying the Apostle St James landed. He is said to have preached Christianity in Spain for seven years before returning to Judaea. In the parish church by the bridge is the mooring stone of the boat. The 11th-century Colegiata de Santa María contains some impressive tombs of bishops.

▶ *Take the N550 north to Santiago de Compostela.*

...ranite is the building stone of the ...cky west of Spain: here, elaborate ...anite turrets top a circular tower ... Pontevedra

▶ *Head northeast toward Redondela. Turn left at the N550 and travel north to Pontevedra.*

BACK TO NATURE

The archipelago called the Islas Cies is a paradise for birdwatchers. The islands are reached by ferry from Vigo and have been declared a nature reserve. They are important breeding grounds for many marine birds, and here you can see colonies of herring gulls and guillemots. Great numbers of ducks also converge here in winter.

6 Pontevedra, Pontevedra
This small provincial capital lies on the wide curve of the banks of the River Pontevedra. It has a bustling new town, and an old section that has changed little with time. The old port was known as Pontis Veteris (the old bridge) and parts of the old encirclement walls can still be seen.

The 18th-century Iglesia de la Peregrina (Pilgrimage), in the old quarter, is built in an unusual Italian-inspired baroque style. The Gothic Iglesia de Santa María la Mayor, built by the mariners' guild, has a lovely garden setting and is noted for its impressive baroque façade. The ruins of the 14th-century Iglesia de Domingo now house the Museo Arqueológico, which has a collection of items from Roman times as well as the Middle

10 Santiago, La Coruña

Santiago de Compostela, to give it its full name, is Spain's most famous pilgrimage centre, and the cathedral is the town's crowning glory. According to legend, the remains of the Apostle St James were found in 813 on the site of the present cathedral by the bishop of Iria Flavia, who was guided by a star. The name of Compostela is derived from Campus Stellae (Field of the Star). St James was made patron saint of Spain and by the mid-10th century masses of pilgrims were travelling from all over Europe, through France and along the north of Spain, to visit his shrine. The route they took became known as the Camino de Santiago (The Way to Santiago).

The cathedral, which stands on the Plaza del Obradoiro (or Plaza de España), dominates the whole town. It was built between 1060 and 1211, and is considered to be one of the finest achievements of Romanesque architecture. It is combined with a magnificent baroque façade from the 16th and 17th centuries. The richly carved decorations that adorn the west entrance are the work of the sculptor, Fernando Casas y Novoa. A statue of St James stands high on the front gable between two imposing towers. Within the west front entrance is the magnificent Pórtico de la Gloria (Door of Glory), a masterpiece of 12th-century Romanesque work by Mateo. The interior is simple, the main focus being the Capilla Mayor. Above the high altar is a silver shrine with a richly decorated statue of St James, and below is the crypt, which contains the tombs of the Apostle and his two disciples, St Theodore and St Athanasius.

Other notable features are the beautiful wrought-iron grilles, the large Plateresque cloister and the finely carved Puerta de las Platerías (Goldsmith's Door). The museum and treasury contain some interesting religious items.

When in the cathedral ask about the Botafumeiro. This is a gigantic incense-burner that is normally kept in the library and brought out on feast days and special occasions. It is hung from the transept dome and is swung from side to side by eight priets with ropes, higher and higher. This ceremony goes back to the time when large numbers of unwashed pilgrims descended on the cathedral to worship at the shrine of St James and some form of fumigation was necessary.

On the cathedral square are the elegant Renaissance Hostal de los Reyes Católicos, now a parador but originally founded by Fernando and Isabella as a hostal for poor pilgrims, the handsome Palacio del Obispo (Bishop's Palace) and the 18th-century Ayuntamiento. Other places of interest in Santiago include the seminary of San Martín Pinario, which features an elegant doorway and the twin-towered Convento de San Francisco. The 18th-century university is noted for its handsome classical façade.

[i] *Rua del Villar 43*

▷ *Take the C543 west to Noia.*

FOR CHILDREN

Children can enjoy a visit to the Paseo de la Herradura park in Santiago, which has swings and roundabouts and various other amusements. The park also offers wonderful views over the town.

---

11 Noia, La Coruña

Noia (Noya) is a pleasant little village situated in a large bay, with a few churches and handsome mansions. A notable building is the Casa de los Churrachaos, formerly the home of the local feudal lords.

▷ *Take the C550 northwest to Cée. Turn left on to the road to Cabo Fisterra.*

The stupendous Cathedral at Santiago de Compostela dominates the old quarter of the city

12 Cabo Fisterra, La Coruña

A most fitting end to this tour is a stop at Cabo Fisterra – 'end of the world' – to enjoy the dramatic setting of the lighthouse, poised on top of a great rock jutting out to sea. This is the most westerly point of Spain and was once the 'edge of the unknown'.

▷ *Return to La Coruña on the C552, 115km (71 miles).*

SCENIC ROUTES

Galicia offers very attractive landscapes of green hills and valleys, with striking coastal scenery. One of the most beautiful parts of the tour is the drive from Santiago to Cabo Fisterra on the C550, where the coast of the Rías Bajas offers magnificent views of cliffs and inlets, wooded hills and sandy beaches.

The Green Belt
of Asturias

Oviedo, the major industrial centre of Asturias, developed in the 8th century as the capital city of the kingdom. In the old part of the town, visit the Gothic Basílica del Salvador (Cathedral) north of the Plaza Mayor. Its south tower rises 82m (270 feet) and offers a splendid view and the Capilla del Rey Casto is the pantheon of the Asturian kings. On Mount Naranco see the two Romanesque churches, successors to King Ramiro's 9th century summer palace.

2 DAYS • 470KM • 292 MILES

ITINERARY

OVIEDO	►	León (121km-75m)
LEÓN	►	**Mansilla de las Mulas** (17km-11m)
MANSILLA DE LAS MULAS	►	**Potes** (127km-79m)
POTES	►	**Lebeña** (10km-6m)
LEBEÑA	►	**Covadonga** (77km-48m)
COVADONGA	►	**Cangas de Onis** (11km-7m)
CANGAS DE ONIS	►	**Gijon** (78km-48m)
GIJON	►	**Oviedo** (29km-18m)

the old. It was the capital of the kingdom of León for a period between the 10th and 13th centuries, and fortification walls were built around the city by the Asturian kings. The year 1230 saw the unification of the kingdoms of León and Castile and a loss of status for León. In the Middle Ages it was one of the main staging points for pilgrims travelling to Santiago de Compostela.

The old quarters lead off from the Plaza Mayor, which is surrounded by attractive portals. The cathedral lies to the north of the square. It was built between the 13th and 14th centuries and is a remarkable work of Gothic architecture. The west façade is outstanding, with two great steeples and a central turreted gable, with a

large rose window and three ornately carved doorways. The cathedral is renowned for its superb stained-glass windows, the earliest of which date back to the 13th century and are to be seen in the central choir chapel and the rose windows in the west and north fronts. The Capilla Mayor has an impressive 15th-century Gothic altarpiece with a magnificent painting of the Entombment. The cloister is in the Plateresque style and has notable frescoes.

The Colegiata de San Isidoro dates back to the 12th century and forms part of the ancient ramparts. It features a huge Romanesque tower and

Left: maize drying. *Below:* a granary worker wearing the traditional special clogs

---

i | Plaza de Alfonso, 11 El Casto 6

▶ From Oviedo take the N630 to León, 121km (75 miles).

❶ León, León
León lies at the confluence of two rivers, the Torío and Bernesga, and is known for its beautiful cathedral of Santa María de la Regla. As the centre of a thriving mineral industry the town presents a sharp contrast between the new and

SCENIC ROUTES

This itinerary takes in the famous Picos de Europa, and most of the route passes through magnificent scenery. Between Oviedo and León (N630) the route becomes very attractive after Mieres, with superb views over the beautiful Cordillera Cantábrica (Cantábrian Mountains). The drive from Cistierna to Riaño on the N621 offers magnificent views and continues to Gijón through some of the most spectacular scenery of Asturias, with an outstanding stretch, known as the Cares Route, between Panes and Cangas de Onís.

From the little village of Potes you can explore the Picos de Europa

two impressive doorways. In the Capilla Mayor is a fine 16th-century altarpiece and the remains of St Isidore, to whom the church was dedicated.

A number of handsome buildings are located around the central Plazuela de San Marcelo, including the Ayuntamiento, a splendid building with twin towers.

i Plaza de Regla 3

▶ Take the N601 south to Mansilla de las Mulas, 17km (11 miles).

2 Mansilla de las Mulas, León
Make a brief stop to look around this little village, which is surrounded by walls and has an attractive main square lined with arcades.

▶ Take the N625, then the N621, northeast through Riaño to Potes.

3 Potes, Asturias
Potes lies in a valley below the sharp peaks of the Picos de Europa. This little mountain village has great charm, with old wooden houses and a large 15th-century tower, which is now the town hall. It is an excellent centre for excursions into the mountains.

The Monasterio de Santo Toribio de Liébana, 3km (2 miles) west was founded by Franciscans, and became important in the following century when a piece of the True Cross was brought here from Jerusalem. This can be seen in a small chamber beyond the cloister. There is a fine view of Potes and the surrounding mountains from the end of the road.

From Potes make sure you visit Fuente Dé, situated 21km (13 miles) to the west. A road along the River Deva leads through forests and mountains to the Fuente Dé parador. Near by is the terminal of a cable-car that takes you up some 800m

Stork's nest on the tower of the Colegiata de San Isidoro in León

(2,625 feet) through magnificent scenery to the top of the rock. There are superb panoramic views from the lookout point here, called the Mirador del Cable, extending over the valley of the River Deva, the village of Potes and the central range of the Picos de Europa.

▶ Continue on the N621 north to Lebeña, which is reached by bearing right off this road.

RECOMMENDED WALKS

The Picos de Europa provide countless hikes and walks in beautiful surroundings. A drive south of Arenas de Cabrales brings you to Puente Poncebos, from which you can take a magnificent walk along the Cares Gorge. A pathway cut out from the rock takes you along the gorge, offering fantastic scenery and dizzy views of the swirling waters of the River Cares far below. You need a good head for heights. There are also some fine areas for walking in the beautiful oak forest, Bosque de Muniellos, or around the Lagos de Somiedo.

---

4 **Lebeña,** Asturias
The small Mozarab Iglesia de
Santa María de Lebeña lies at
the foot of steep cliffs, among
elegant poplars. It was built in
the 10th century and has been
well preserved. Note the fine
vaulting and horseshoe-shaped
arches, which bear finely carved
Corinthian capitals.

▶ *Rejoin and continue north on
the N621. At Panes take the
C6312 west and at Soto de
Cangas branch left to
Covadonga.*

5 **Covadonga,** Asturias
The sanctuary of Covadonga is
tucked away in a remote valley.
The setting is superb and the
place exudes an aura of mysti-
cism. The kingdom of Asturias
was founded in this region after
the defeat of Muslim forces in
722 by a Gothic nobleman
called Pelayo, who led the
Asturians to a resounding
victory against the Moors.

The sanctuary is dedicated
to the patron saint of Asturias, la
Virgen de las Batallas (Virgin of
the Battles). Pilgrimages are
made here on 8 September to
venerate her image, which
stands over the altar in the
Santa Cueva (Holy Cave).
Behind are the tombs of Pelayo,

who died in 737, his wife
Gaudiosa, and King Alfonso I.
The Basílica was erected at the
end of the 19th century in neo-
Romanesque style and features
two tall spires. The Tesoro de la
Virgen (Virgin's Treasury)
contains some fine treasures,
including a brilliant diamond-
studded crown.

ℹ️ *El Repelao*

▶ *Rejoin the C6312 and turn
west to Cangas de Onís.*

6 **Cangas de Onís,** Asturias
Once the Reconquest of Spain
had been started by the
Christians at the Battle of
Covadonga in 722, the court was
established at Cangas de Onís
and Asturias became known as a
symbol of the Christian resistance against the Moors. Some
elegant old mansions can still be
seen from those glorious times.
Of major interest is the 8th-
century Capilla de Santa Cruz,
which stands on a Celtic burial
mound. Look out for the old
Puente Romano (Roman
bridge) which spans the gorge
of the River Sella.

▶ *Take the C637 northwest. On
reaching the N632 turn left
to Gijón, 78km (48 miles).*

An ancient bridge across the River
Sella at Cangas de Onis

7 **Gijón,** Asturias
Before arriving at Gijón you
might like to branch off at
Villaviciosa and take a short
detour along a lovely route to
the charming little fishing
harbour of Tazones.

Gijón is one of the most
important towns in Asturias,
with a busy port. It is situated
between two wide bays with the
old town built on an isthmus,
while the harbour stretches
away to the west.

First Roman and then
Visigoth, the town was known
as Gigia. It was under Moorish
domination for a period in the
8th century, after which it was
for a time residence of the kings
of Asturias. Charles V built the
harbour in 1522, and it provided
shelter for the ships of the
Spanish Armada. The harbour
was rebuilt in 1766 and has
since been enlarged several
times. The town was severely
damaged during fighting in the
Spanish Civil War. Much of it
was then rebuilt and has been
enlarged more recently, with the
result that Gijón is essentially a
modern town.

Gijón was the birthplace of
Gaspar Melchor de Jovellanos

BACK TO NATURE

The Parque Nacional de
Covadonga (Covadonga
National Park) is a vast region
of great natural beauty, known
for its magnificent forests of
beech, oak and other trees. It is
watered by the rivers Cares
and Deje and contains the two
glacier lakes, Enol and Ercina. It
is home to the wild cat,
pole-cat, fox, wolf, badgers and
chamois, which inhabit the
higher slopes. Among the
many different types of birds,
you can see various species of
eagles, owls and magpies, while
the rivers are full of fish
including salmon and trout,
which are preyed upon by
secretive otters.

(1744–1811), renowned in Spain as a writer, statesman and economist. In 1794 he founded the Instituto Jovellanos as an institute for education in the natural sciences. This is located to the northeast of the town and now serves as the Provincial College of Industry and Nautical Science. His birthplace, Casa de Jovellanos (in the old part of town), has been restored and is now a museum with paintings by Asturian artists. Other places of interest in Gijon are the baroque Palacio del Conde de Revillagigedo (15th- to 16th-century), with two imposing towers, and the 16th-century Colegiata de San Juan.

The port is very busy and has large docks that handle commercial business and passenger lines. The harbour has been considerably enlarged and extends to the west for several kilometres. Gijón is also a popular seaside resort. Its long sandy beach, Playa de San Lorenzo, is usually packed in summer.

The old fishermen's quarter, known as the Cimadevilla, is built up the slopes of the Santa Catalina hill. Here you will find an area of tiny, narrow streets, old houses, bars and lots of activity. There are fine views of the harbour and the mountains of the Picos de Europa from the top of the hill.

ℹ️ *Marqués de San Esteban 1*

▶ *Return to Oviedo southwest on the N630.*

SPECIAL TO...

Those who like strong cheese will enjoy *picón*, a blue cheese produced in Arenas de Cabrales by a slow ripening process which takes place in caves. This cheese goes down well with a glass of cider, which is a speciality of Asturias. The area to the east of Gijón is an apple-growing region that produces cider (*sidra* in Spanish). In the middle of July there is a cider festival in Nava. Traditionally, the cider is poured into the glass from a pitcher held above the head.

Scenes from the life of Christ on the altar of Oviedo cathedral

Landscapes of
Cantabria

SANTANDER

ITINERARY		
SANTANDER	▶	**Santillana del Mar** (27km-17m)
SANTILLANA DEL MAR	▶	**Cuevas de Altamira** (2km-1m)
CUEVAS DE ALTAMIRA	▶	**Comillas** (17km-11m)
COMILLAS	▶	**Cabuérniga** (33km-21m)
CABUÉRNIGA	▶	**Carmona** (11km-7m)
CARMONA	▶	**Reinosa** (52km-32m)
REINOSA	▶	**Retortillo** (6km-4m)
RETORTILLO	▶	**Cervatos** (7km-4m)
CERVATOS	▶	**Castro Urdiales** (141km-88m)
CASTRO URDIALES	▶	**Laredo** (25km-16m)
LAREDO	▶	**Santoña** (21km-13m)
SANTOÑA	▶	**Santander** (48km-30m)

2/3 DAYS • 390KM • 244 MILES

While Santander's history goes back to the Romans, much of it was rebuilt after being devastated by a tornado in 1941. The 13th century Gothic cathedral, just off the Avenida de Alfonso XIII, has been rebuilt three times. The royal palace of La Magdalena was presented to Alfonso XII at the beginning of the 20th century, when Santander was a favourite summer resort of the Spanish kings. The Palace is now the International University.

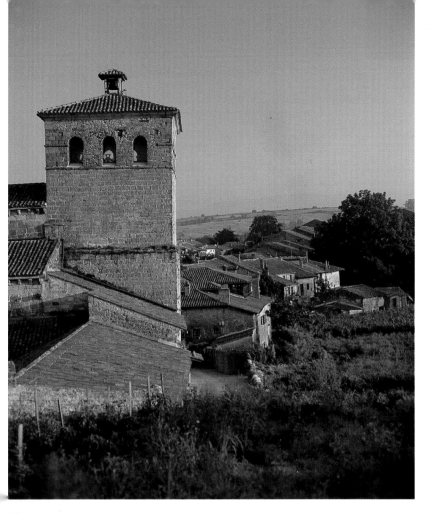

i *Estacion Marítima s/n*

▶ *From Santander take the N611 southwest. Turn right on to the C6316 to Santillana del Mar.*

❶ Santillana del Mar,
Santander

Santillana del Mar is an architectural delight, with beautiful mansions and churches, together with picturesque balconied houses and typical red-tiled roofs. Its little squares and old façades appear like stage settings from the past. Coats of arms on many façades relate to seamen of former times who returned from important voyages of discovery.

A focal point is the Plaza de Ramón Pelayo, which is lined with elegant buildings of the 14th to 16th centuries. The Romanesque Colegiata, one of the loveliest buildings, dates back to the 12th century with fine sculptures in the nave and aisle. The cloister contains a Renaissance alterpiece.

i *Plaza Mayor*

▶ *From Santillana take the road for 2km (1 mile) to the car park of the Cuevas de Altamira (Caves of Altamira).*

SPECIAL TO...

The festival of La Folia at San Vicente de la Barquera (west of Comillas) on the Sunday after Easter involves decorated boats, music and celebrations.

Evening sunlight gilds the church and houses of Santillana del Mar

❷ Cuevas de Altamira,
Santander

The prehistoric wall paintings discovered in the Altamira Caves in the latter part of the 19th century are among the most significant in the world. For conservation reasons the number of visitors is severely restricted. You should apply at least one year in advance to: Centro de Investigacíon de Altamira, Santillana del Mar, by letter or fax, 42-840157, specifying the number of people in the group. However, no special permission is needed to visit the small Museum of the Altamira Caves and another cave near by, with interesting stalactite and stalagmite formations.

The Altamira caves have a depth of 270m (885 feet) and are most impressive, containing paintings of animals that were hunted by palaeolithic man some 14,000 to 9,000 years BC. The paintings still retain their colours and reveal the unmistakable shapes of bison, deer and wild boars. More prehistoric animal paintings can be seen in the caves of El Castillo and La Pasiega in Puente Viesgo, south of Torrelavega on the N623.

▶ *Rejoin the C6316 and continue west to Comillas.*

3 Comillas, Santander
The little town of Comillas rises up a hill overlooking the sea. The resort has some elegant buildings and a pleasant beach. Of special note is the neoclassical Palacio del Marqués de Comillas, which stands in attractive gardens. In these is also a building known as 'El Capricho' (meaning 'the whim') designed by Antonio Gaudí, architect of the Templo de la Sagrada Familia and other buildings in Barcelona.

▶ *Take C6316 west to join the N634 and head south-east. Turn south at Cabezón de la Sal on C625 to Cabuérniga, 33km (21 miles).*

4 Cabuérniga, Santander
Take a look round this little mountain town, capital of the

RECOMMENDED WALKS

There are plenty of places for walking in the Cordillera Cantábrica. The village of Fontibre (northwest of Reinosa) is a good base for a number of walks, with marked trails you can take in various directions. The Valle de Campo is a beautiful area of poplar trees and lush vegetation, where you will find the source of the Ebro, one of Spain's most important rivers.

SCENIC ROUTES

The road from Cabuérniga down to Reinosa travels through the beautiful Cordillera Cantábrica mountains on the C625, over the passes of Puerto de Tajahierro and Palombera with magnificent views to Reinosa. The N611 from Cervatos up to Torrelavega follows a winding mountain road with many bends before passing through the dramatic Hoces de Bárcena gorge. The drive from Torrelavega on the N634 becomes very attractive again after Solares.

valley, with its quaint old houses and large wooden balconies.

▶ *Take the C6314 northwest for 11km (7 miles), to Carmona.*

5 Carmona, Santander
Carmona is another small village, typical of the area, where the pattern of life has seen little change from the old days. The detour is worthwhile, not only for a glimpse of this picturesque little place, but also for its beautiful surroundings.

▶ *Return to Cabuérniga and continue south to Reinosa.*

6 Reinosa, Santander
Set high up in the valley of the River Ebro is the little mountain town of Reinosa which has some charming streets and is a popular summer resort

▶ *Continue south on N611. Shortly, turn left to Bolmir, East of Bolmir turn right to Retortillo, 6km (4 miles).*

7 Retortillo, Santander
Stop here to see the Roman ruins of Juliobriga, just outside the village. You can get a good idea of the layout of this fortified village from the bell tower of the ruined church.

▶ *Return by the same route to the N611. Turn left and drive south to Cervatos, just off the road.*

8 Cervatos, Santander
The major feature of interest in this small village is the 12th-century Romanesque Colegiata, notable for the carvings that adorn the frieze above the door. Look for the figures of the three monkeys shown covering their ears, eyes and mouth, signifying prudence and wisdom in the beliefs of eastern cultures.

▶ *Take the N611 north. At Torrelavega take the N634 east to Castro Urdiales.*

9 Castro Urdiales, Santander
This attractive little fishing port has long been a popular summer resort. It was once a

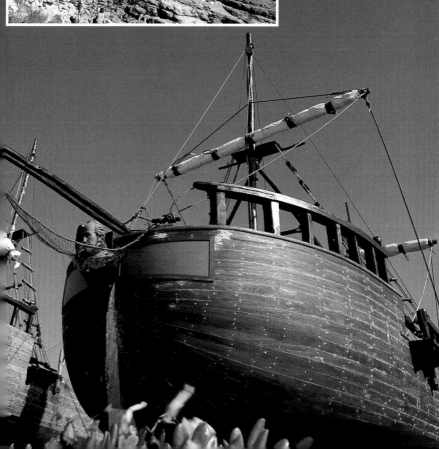

Roman port. The Gothic Iglesia de Nuestra Señora de la Asunción features an impressive Puerta del Perdón. Visit also the Castillo of Santa Ana (now a lighthouse), the medieval fortress and the Roman bridge.

ⓘ *Plaza del Ayuntamiento*

▷ *Take the coastal road N634 west to Laredo.*

🔟 Laredo, Santander
The little town of Laredo lies to the east of the wide bay of Santoña. With its pleasant villas and splendid beach it is a popular seaside resort. The old part of the town is picturesque, with some handsome old buildings and the ruins of two former monasteries.

ⓘ *Alameda de Miramar*

▷ *Continue west on the coastal road and turn right at Cicero for 5km (3 miles) to Santoña.*

⓫ Santoña, Santander
To the west of the bay is the port of Santoña on a peninsula beneath a steep rock. The town was fortified in earlier times – Napoleon is said to have had plans to conquer it. The Romanesque Colegiata was built between the 12th and 13th centuries. About 2km (1¼ miles) away is the splendid beach of Berria.

▷ *Take the C629 southwest to Gama and rejoin the N634, continue west. At Solares take the N635 back to Santander.*

Journey's end for these old fishing boats. *Left:* the Virgin del Mar ocean beach close to Santander

Exploring the
Basque Country

2 DAYS • 359KM • 222 MILES San Sebastián (Donostia in Basque) is the provincial capital of Guipúzcoa. The elegant buildings along the promenade are a reminder of the 19th century, when San Sebastián became Spain's most fashionable resort. The Alameda del Boulevard is a lively area of cafés, restaurants and shops. To the west is the busy fishing harbour.

ITINERARY

SAN SEBASTIÁN	▶ **Zarautz (26km-16m)**
ZARAUTZ	▶ **Guetaria (4km-2m)**
GUETARIA	▶ **Zumaia (6km-4m)**
ZUMAIA	▶ **Ondárroa (23km-14m)**
ONDÁRROA	▶ **Lekeitio (12km-7m)**
LEKEITIO	▶ **Guernika-Lumo**
	(23km-14m)
GUERNIKA-LUMO	▶ **Bilbao (35km-22m)**
BILBAO	▶ **Vitoria-Gasteiz**
	(66km-41m)
VITORIA-GASTEIZ	▶ **Salvatierra (25km-16m)**
SALVATIERRA	▶ **Tolosa (61km-38m)**
TOLOSA	▶ **Fuenterrabía (52km-32m)**
FUENTERRABÍA	▶ **San Sebastián**
	(25km-16m)

i *Paseo de los Fueros 1-bajo*

▷ *From San Sebastián take the N1 south. Turn right on to the N634 to Zarautz, 26km (16 miles).*

❶ Zarautz, Guipúzcoa

You may like to make a quick stop en route in the picturesque little fishing port of Orio, which lies along the bank of an estuary.

The old harbour at Zarautz (Zarauz in Basque) is backed by the tall Monte de Santa Barbara. It has a splendid beach and is a popular summer resort. Places of major interest are the Gothic/baroque Iglesia de Santa María, the Iglesia de San

SCENIC ROUTES

The Cornisa Cantábrica (Cantabrian Corniche) is a magnificent stretch between Zarautz, Guetaria and Zumaia on the N634. A zigzagging road follows the coast, offering magnificent views. From Zumaia the drive continues along the coast, on the C6212, with beautiful views, to Lekeitio. The N1 offers some scenic parts after Alsasua, with excellent views over the Puerto de Etxgarate, and there is more beautiful scenery between Tolosa and San Sebastián.

The lovely horseshoe-shaped beach at fashionable San Sebastián is popular with the Spanish

Francisco and the hermitages of San Pelayo and San Pedro. The Torre Lucea and the 15th-century Palacio del Marqués de Narros are also impressive. Zarautz was once an important shipyard. It was here that the *Victoria* was built, between 1519 and 1522, to carry Juan Sebastián Elcano, companion of Magellan, around the world.

i *Navarra*

▷ *Continue on the N634 for 4km (2 miles) to Guetaria.*

2 Guetaria, Guipúzocoa
There is some magnificent scenery as you approach Guetaria and a fine view down over the pretty little fishing village which stands on a promontory. The Gothic parish church of San Salvador overlooks the harbour, and has underground tunnels linking the two. Over the breakwater is the little fortified Isla San Anton (known as the 'Ratón de Guetaria', mouse of Guetaria, for reasons unknown), which rises up steeply to a lighthouse. It offers a rewarding view of the area. The Ayuntamiento contains frescoes describing the voyage around the world of the navigator, Juan Sebastián Elcano, who was born here.

▶ *Continue west for 6km (4 miles) to Zumaia (Zumaya).*

3 Zumaia, Guipúzcoa
Nestling at the foot of the Monte Santa Clara hill is Zumaia, another delightful little resort with a charming harbour and attractive houses. The Villa Zuloaga, formerly a monastery, is now a museum founded by the great painter Ignacio Zuloaga, and has a fine collection of paintings by Zuloaga, El Greco, Goya and many of Spain's most famous painters.

▶ *Follow the coast road, the N634, west. At Deva, turn right on to the C6212 to Ondárroa.*

4 Ondárroa, Vizcaya
You are now in the neighbouring province of Vizcaya. The resort of Ondárroa is set in a bay protected by low hills. The town is a combination of attractive old cottages and more modern blocks. It has a sandy beach and a pleasant harbour with lively fishermen's quarters. A Roman bridge, the Puente Romano, spans the river.

▶ *Continue on the coast road C6212, northwest for 12km (7 miles) to Lekeitio (Lekueitio)*

5 Lekeitio, Vizcaya
Lekeitio is another popular seaside resort of attractive houses and a good beach, which separates the resort area from the fishing port. The 16th-century Iglesia de Santa María is a fine example of Vizcayan Gothic architecture. Narrow cobbled streets lead down to the old part of town. The palaces of Abaróa and Uribarren are particularly elegant buildings.

▶ *Take the C6212 west for 23km (14 miles) to Guernica-Lumo.*

6 Guernika-Lumo, Vizcaya
The famous painting, *Guernica*, by Pablo Picasso is a reminder of the terrible event that took place here in 1937 during the Spanish Civil War, when German aircraft bombed the town, killing a large number of people. The town was devastated, but has been rebuilt in the traditional style. Originally displayed in the Museum of Modern Art in New York, Picasso's painting was returned to Spain and now hangs in the Centro de Arte Reina Sofía, in Madrid, together with all the preliminary sketches.

The Casa de Juntas (Assembly Hall) contains an interesting library and archives. The Sala de Juntas (Council Chamber) is the venue of the

General Assembly of officials of the provinces of Biscay. It also serves as a chapel, which is known by the rather grand title of 'la Iglesia Juradera de Santa María de la Antigua'. Near by is a monument commemorating the 1937 attack on the town.

Some 5km (3 miles) north the Cuevas de Santimamine wall paintings, believed to date back some 13,000 years, were discovered in 1917.

[i] *Ajuntament, Plaça Fuero 3*

▶ *Take the C6315 south and join the N634 west to Bilbao (Bilbo).*

FOR CHILDREN

A special attraction for children is to be found near Galdácano, a few kilometres southeast of Bilbao, where the Parque de Atracciones de Vizcaya offers a variety of amusements.
Horse-riding excursions into the countryside are available in a number of areas, and cater for adults and children. One centre is at Arantzazu (south of Oñati, off the C6213). Make enquiries at the local tourist office who are always pleased to help in any way they can.

The rivers of the Basque country end in picturesque harbours like this one at Ondárroa

noted for its modern west front, large bell tower and Gothic cloister. The Ayuntamiento (late 19th-century) has an imposing tower and a Moorish-style ceremonial hall. The Museo Arqueológico, Etnográfico e Historico Vasco has a collection of tombs, arms and carvings.

In the new town is the Museo de Bellas Artes with works by famous Dutch and Spanish painters of the 15th and 16th centuries. The Museu Moderno contains works by contemporary Spanish painters.

ℹ️ *Teatro Arrigo*

▶ *Return east along the N634 and take the N240 south-east for 66km (41 miles) to Vitoria.*

8 Vitoria-Gasteiz, Alava
Vitoria is the capital of Alava, and of the Basque Country, as well as being the seat of a bishop. A focal point of the old town is the Plaza de la Virgen Blanca, which is surrounded by houses and balconies typical of Vitoria. In the centre is an

7 Bilbao, Vizcaya
Bilbao is the capital of the Basque province of Vizcaya and its largest port. It is essentially a busy industrial town, which may be off-putting to the visitor at first glance, but it does have its attractions and is well worth a visit. Along the right bank of the river is the Paseo del Arenal, a pleasant esplanade that leads to the old quarters, known as Las Siete Calles (Seven Streets).

The Plaza Nueva is a charming square built in the neoclassical style and the Gothic Catedral de Santiago (14th–16th century) near by is

RECOMMENDED WALKS

Many areas all over the region offer splendid walks, and information is available from the local tourist offices.
In Bilbao a short walk is a climb up the hill from behind the church of San Nicolás de Bari, which brings you to the Gothic-style Begoña Basilica. It was built in 1588 and is the place of worship of Begoña, the patron saint of Bilbao. A colourful romería is held here on 15 August.

SPECIAL TO...

The national sport of the Basque country is *pelota* (also known as jai-alai). There are variations, but basically it is a type of ballgame played between four men in a court called a *frontón*, using scoop rackets and a small, hard ball which travels at tremendous speed. The sport is supposed to be the fastest in the world. Each town and village has a court and a team.
The Basque country has its own folklore, including the unusual *aurresku*, a war-like dance, and the *ezpata dantza*, a sword dance, accompanied by flutes and a drum.

imposing monument commemorating Wellington's victory over the French at the battle of Vitoria in 1813. Overlooking the square is the 14th-century Iglesia de San Miguel. A stone image of the Virgen Blanca (White Virgin), patron saint of the city, can be seen in a niche on the outside portal. Inside is a fine 17th-century altarpiece by Juan de Velázquez and Gregorio Hernández. The Catedral de Santa María was built between the 14th and 15th centuries in the shape of a Latin cross and is noted for its richly decorated triple-arched tympanums. An impressive Assumption can be seen in one of the side chapels. Look out also for a bullfighting scene carved on one of the pillar's capitals.

In the Plaza Santo Domingo near by is the Museo de Arqueología (Archaeological Museum), which displays objects from the Celtiberian and Roman times, among other items. The 14th-century parish church of San Pedro features a fine doorway and impressive sculpted tombs of the Alava family. From the middle of the 15th century, Vitoria was a centre for craftsmen who worked predominantly in the wool and iron trades. The Portalon, built in wood and

BACK TO NATURE

There is an area of great natural beauty in the province of Alava, north of Vitoria, around three artificial lakes. Embalse de Urrunaga (Lake Santa Engracia) is situated along the road from Bilbao to Vitoria. On the slopes of the mountain are the Cuevas de Mairelegorreta, which are well worth a visit. Embalse de Albiña (Lake Albina), east of the N240, lies at the entrance to the Aramayona valley. Further south is Embalse de Ullívari (Lake Ullívari), which stores water in the Gamboa canyon. The lake offers water sports and fishing.

brick, is a remaining example of one of the many trading houses of the medieval and Renaissance times. Other attractive areas are the Plaza del Machete and the Cuchillería (street of cutlery), where you will find the 16th-century Casa del Cordón, noted for a fine Gothic ceiling, and the Bedaña Palace, a 16th-century mansion with a magnificent façade. The new cathedral of María Immaculada, which was consecrated in 1969, has been built in a rather unusual neo-Gothic style.

The industrial town of Tolosa is set amongst the Basque hills

☞ *Parque de la Florida s/n*

▶ *Take the NI to Salvatierra.*

⑨ Salvatierra, Alava
The little town of Salvatierra was founded by Alfonso X in 1256. It still preserves its medieval streets and parts of the old defensive walls. Its two main churches, those of San Juan and Santa María, have a somewhat fortress-like appearance.

▶ Follow the NI east and then north to Tolosa.

⑩ Tolosa, Guipúzcoa
Tolosa was capital of the province of Guipúzcoa for a period in the middle of the 19th century and is now a thriving industrial town (known for the *boinas*, or Basque beret). There are Roman antiquities and ancient buildings of the Templars.

ⓘ *Centro de Iniciativas Turísticas, Calle San Juan*

▶ Continue on the NI north, bypassing the centre of San Sebastián, and then east. Turn off north for Fuenterrabía.

⑪ Fuenterrabía, Guipúzcoa
The little town of Fuenterrabía was a stronghold over a long period of time and consequently the scene of many battles. It is now a popular seaside resort. The remains of its ancient walls are preserved as a national monument and the 12th-century Palacio del Rey Carlos V (now a parador) was

built as a defence against pirate raids. There are good views from here. Other buildings worth a look are the 16th-century Iglesia de Santa María (mainly Gothic with Renaissance influences), and the 17th-century Ayuntamiento. A short drive up to the ridge of Jaizquíbel leads to the Santuario de Nuestra Señora de Guadalupe and offers fine views.

▶ *Rejoin the NI back to San Sebastián, 25km (16 miles).*

PRACTICAL INFORMATION

FACTS AND FIGURES

Bordered by: France, Andorra and Portugal.

IDD code: 34. To call the UK dial 07* 44 (*wait for second dialling tone).

Currency: Spanish peseta (Ptas1 = 100 centimos).

Local time: GMT + 1 (summer GMT + 2).

Emergency services: Madrid and Barcelona Police 091; Fire 080; Ambulance 092; in other towns call the operator.

Business hours:
Banks: Monday to Friday 9am–2pm. Saturday 9am–1pm.
Shops: Monday to Saturday 9am–1pm, 4.30pm–7.30pm.
Post Offices: generally open Monday to Saturday 9am–1pm. Post boxes are yellow and some have different sections for different destinations. Stamps can be bought at tobacconists.

Credit and charge cards: these are widely accepted.

Travellers' cheques: either in sterling or local currency are probably the most sensible way to take your money abroad. Note the numbers and keep the note separate from the cheques.

Tourist information:
UK Spanish National Tourist Office, Metro House, 57–8 St James's Street, London, SW1A 1LD. Tel: 0171 499 0901.
USA National Tourist Office of Spain, 665 Fifth Avenue, New York, NY 10022. Tel: (212) 759 8822.

Camping card: not compulsory, but recommended.

MOTORING IN SPAIN

ACCIDENTS
There are no firm rules of procedure after an accident. There is an assistance service for victims of traffic accidents which is run by the Central Traffic Department day and night on every main road in Spain.

You are advised to obtain a Bail Bond from your insurer with your Green Card. (See also **warning triangle**.)

BAIL BONDS
An accident in Spain can result in the impounding of car and property, and a Bail Bond is advisable. It provides a written guarantee that a cash deposit, usually of up to £1,500 will be paid to the Spanish court as surety for bail and for any fine which may be imposed. However, the Bond is not insurance cover as such, insofar as the insurers must be reimbursed. Bail Bonds are usually available from vehicle insurers. Alternatively, a Bail Bond is supplied free of charge with AA Five Star Europe.

BREAKDOWNS
If your car breaks down try to move it to the side of the road, or to a position where it will obstruct the traffic flow as little as possible. Switch on your hazard warning lights and place a warning triangle at the appropriate distance on the road behind. Bear in mind road conditions and, if near or on a bend, the triangle should be placed where it is clearly visible to following traffic.
(See also **warning triangle**.)

CARAVANS
Brakes
Check that the caravan braking mechanism is correctly adjusted. If it has a breakaway safety mechanism, the cable between the car and caravan must be firmly anchored so that the trailer brakes act immediately if the two part company.

Caravan and luggage trailers
Take a list of contents, especially if any valuable or unusual equipment is being carried, as this may be required by customs officers on arrival. A

towed vehicle should be readily identifiable by a plate in an accessible position showing the name of the make of the vehicle and the production and serial number.

Lights
Make sure that all the lights of the caravan or trailer are working – rear lights, stop lights, numberplate lights, rear fog guard lamps and flashers (check that the flasher rate is correct: 60–120 times a minute).

Speed limits
(see general notes on speed limits).

Tyres
Both tyres on the caravan should be of the same size and type. Before leaving home, you should inspect them carefully: if you think they are likely to be more than three-quarters worn before you get back, replace them before you leave. If you notice uneven wear, scuffed treads, or damaged walls, get expert advice on whether the tyres are suitable for further use. Find out the recommended tyre pressures from the caravan manufacturer.

CAR HIRE AND FLY/DRIVE
If you are not taking your own car, you can make arrangements to hire before departure. Many package holidays include car hire as an option. The main car hire companies are represented in Spain.

CHILDREN
Children under the age of 12 are not permitted to travel as front-seat passengers unless using a suitable restraint system.
Note under no circumstances should a rear-facing restraint be used in a seat with an airbag.

CRASH (SAFETY) HELMETS
Crash helmets are compulsory for motorcyclists.

DIMENSIONS AND WEIGHT RESTRICTIONS
Private cars and towed trailers or caravans are restricted to the following dimensions: height – 4m; width to 2.5m; length – 12m. The maximum permitted overall length of private vehicle/trailer or caravan combination is 12m. Trailers with an unladen weight in excess of 750kg must have an independent braking system.

DOCUMENTS
Licences issued by European Union countries are acceptable (for UK and Republic of Ireland driver's licences should be of the pink EU-type). Visitors from other countries should have an international driving licence, which should be obtainable from the motoring organisations in their home countries. The minimum age at which visitors from UK or Republic of Ireland may use a temporarily imported motorcycle (over 75cc) or car is 18 years. The holder of an older all green UK licence (in Northern Ireland any licence issued before 1 Aprilil 1991) should consider exchanging it for a new style licence if time allows to avoid any local difficulties. Alternatively these older licences may be accompanied by an International Driving Permit (IDP).
Note The licence of a Spanish driver who needs glasses to drive is endorsed accordingly. Such drivers must carry a spare pair of glasses in their vehicle. It is strongly recommended that visiting motorists should do the same to avoid any misunderstanding with the local authorities.

You also require the vehicle's registration document, plus a letter of authorisation from the owner, if not accompanying the vehicle, and the current insurance certificate (a green card, obtainable from your insurance company, is recommended). You are required to display a nationality plate or sticker on the vehicle.

DRINKING AND DRIVING
The laws in Europe regarding drinking and driving are strict and the penalties severe. The best advice is, as at home, if you drink don't drive:

DRIVING CONDITIONS
Driving in on the right. Tolls are charged on most of the motorways. The surfaces of the main roads vary, but on the whole are good. Secondary roads are often rough, winding and may be encumbered by slow horse-drawn traffic. In the Basque area, local versions of place names appear on signposts together with the national version. In winter snowfalls frequently close many of the roads across the Pyrenees.

FUEL
You will find comparable grades of petrol in Spain, with familiar brand names along the main routes. It is wise to keep the tank topped up, particularly in remote areas.

Remember when calculating mileage per litre (gallon) that the extra weight of a caravan or roof rack increases the petrol consumption. It is best to use a locking filler cap.

INSURANCE
Fully comprehensive insurance, which covers you for some of the expenses incurred after a breakdown or an accident, is advisable. See also **bail bond**.

LIGHTS
Full headlights are prohibited in built-up areas. Motorcyclists must use dipped headlights during the day. A replacement set of bulbs is required.

MOTORING CLUB
The Real Automóvil Club de España (RACE), which has its headquarters at Calle José Abascal 10, 28003 Madrid tel: (91) 4473200, is associated with local clubs in a number of provincial towns. The office hours of the RACE in Madrid are 8.30am–5.30pm

Monday–Thursday and
8.30am–2.30pm Friday during
the summer (15 June–15
September) and for the rest of
the year 8.30am–5.30pm
Monday–Friday.

POLICE
There are three different police
organisations in Spain dealing
with different aspects of public
order.

Policía Municipal whose
main responsibility are the local police.
They are identifiable by their
blue uniforms and white
checked bands on their
vehicles. Policía Nacional, who
wear grey uniforms and berets,
deal with law and order and
national security. Crimes should
be reported to the police station
(comisaría). Guardia Civil, who
are responsible for border posts,
policing country areas and the
coast and highway patrols, wear
olive green uniforms.

There are also special
Basque police in the Basque
country, recognisable by their
red berets.

ROADS
The surfaces of the main roads
vary, but on the whole are good.
The roads are winding in many
places, and at times it is not
advisable to exceed 30-35mph.
Secondary roads are often
rough and winding. In the
Basque and Catalan areas some
place names appear on signposts in both the local and the
national versions.

Spain has a good network
of motorways and dual carriageways. About half of these are
toll roads (autopista) and the
rest are free (autovías).

Emergency telephones are
located every 2km on all
Spanish motorways and dual
carriageways.

ROUTE DIRECTIONS
The following abbreviations
are used as prefixes to identify
Spanish roads.
A for Autopista and Autovías
C for CoMarchal
N for Nacional

SPEED LIMITS
Car
Built-up areas 50kph (31mph)
Other roads †90kph (55mph) or
††100kph (62mph)
Motorways 120kph (74mph)

Car/caravan/trailer
Built-up areas 50kph (31mph)
Other roads †70kph (43mph) or
††80kph (49mph)
Motorways 80kph (49mph)
†on ordinary roads
††on roads with more than one
lane in each direction, a special
lane for slow-moving vehicles
or wide lanes.

TOLLS
Tolls are payable on many
motorways (autopista) in Spain.
Tickets are issued on entry,
payment varies according to the
distance travelled and the class
of vehicle.

WARNING TRIANGLE
In the event of accident or
breakdown, the use of two
warning triangles is compulsory
for vehicles weighing more
than 3,500kg (3 tons, 8cwt,
100lb) and passenger vehicles
with more than nine seats
(including the driver's). The
triangles must be placed on the
road in front of and behind the
vehicle at a distance of 30m
(33 yards) and be visible from
at least 100m (110 yards). It is
strongly recommended that
other vehicles carry a warning
triangle for use in an emergency to avoid any misunder-
standings with the local
authorities.

Two-wheeled vehicles do
not require a warning triangle.

CAMPING AND CARA-
VANNING SITES
The majority of camping sites
in Spain are along the coasts
and there are not many sites
inland. Sites are officially classi-
fied according to the facilities
and services provided and their
classification should be
displayed at the site entrance
and on any literature.

It is not generally possible

The view from a look-out point
near Ronda (see Tour 9)

to book in advance at popular
resorts along the coast between
late spring and mid October,.
The best advice is to arrive
before midday, when the new
charge begins.

Opening dates through the
year vary considerably from site
to site. Late spring is a good
time to visit, when sites are less
congested and the heat is not
so intense. Sites usually do not
have equipment or tents for
hire, but some have bungalow
accommodation.

Off-site camping
Off-site camping is generally
prohibited. Permission to camp
off an official camp site must be
obtained from the landowner
or local police. It is forbidden
to free camp near beaches,
rivers, towns or established
camp sites.

Camp fires are absolutely
forbidden.

Sites

Wherever possible the sites listed are on the tour route, but this is not always possible owing to the paucity of sites in inland areas. Sites shown in this list with an asterisk are within a reasonable driving distance of the tour for an overnight stay, but are not actually on the route itself.

TOUR 1
SOLSONA Lleida
Solsonès (tel: 973 482861)
Camping card compulsory.
Open all year.

BELLVER DE CERDANYA
Lleida
Solana del Segre (tel: 973 510310)
On the River Segre.
Open all year except 15 September to 11 October.

PUIGCERDÀ Girona
Stel ctra Puigcerdà-Llivia (tel: 972 882361)
Open 20 June to September.

RIPOLL Girona
Solana del Ter (tel: 972 701062)
Open May to October.

*TARADELL Barcelona
Vall Cami de la Vallmissand
(tel: 93 8126336)
In the mountains near the Guilleries-Montseny.
Open all year.

CABRERA DE MAR
Barcelona
Costa de Oro (tel: 93 7591234)
Off the N11 at Km650, on the seaward side between road and railway embankment.
Open 15 May to 11 September

TOUR 2
CALELLA DE LA COSTA
Barcelona
Botanic Bona Vista (tel: 93 7692488)
Turn off the N11 at Km665.
Open all year.

PINEDA DE MAR Barcelona
Camell Los Naranjos 12 (tel: 93 7671520)

Turn off N11 at Km670; take av de los Naranjos towards sea.
Open March to September.

BLANES Girona
Blanes (tel: 972 331591)
On left of the Paseo Villa de Madrid coast road towards town.
Open 15 April to September.

PALAFRUGELL Girona
Kim's Llafranc (tel: 972 301156
Turn right off the Palafrugell-Tamariu road and follow a wide tarred road for about 1km, past the El Paranso Hotel, towards Llafranc. The site is 0.4km from sea.
Open May to September.

*SANT PERE PESCADOR
Girona
Amfora Mas Sopas (tel: 972 520540)
From Empuries turn right onto a minor road. After 5km, you will find the site, right on the beach.
Open 8 May to 8 September.

TOUR 3
VILADECANS Barcelona
Toro Bravo Autovia de
Castelldefels, Km11 (tel: 93
6373462)
Leave C246 at Km11 and
continue towards sea for 1km.
Open all year.

SITGES Barcelona
Roca (tel: 93 8940043)
Turn off C246 in the direction
of Sant Pere de Ribes/San
Pedro de Ribas. Almost at once,
(about 15m) turn right to the
site.
Open April to September.

TAMARIT Tarragona
Caledonia (tel: 977 694009)
Open all year.

AMETLLA DE MAR, L'
Tarragona
Nautic c Libertad (tel: 977
456110)
Turn right off N340 at Km20.1,
take TV3025 and continue to
the railway station via a flyover
and level crossing, turn right
then take third road on left.
Access road has a 10 per cent
gradient.
Open 15 March to 15 October.

ALCANAR Tarragona
Mare Nostrum (tel: 977
737179)
Turn towards the sea off the
N340 at Km58.3.
Open all year.

SANTA OLIVA Tarragona
Santa Oliva Jaume Balmes
122 (tel: 977 661252)
At 3Km on Vendrell-Santa
Oliva road.
Open all year.

TOUR 4
VALENCIA Valencia
Saler (Tel: 96 1830023)
From the coast road at El Saler,
turn left at southeast end of
village then turn right.
Open all year.

DAIMUS Valencia
Aventura ctra Platja Daimus
(tel: 96 2818330)
On beach.
Open March to September.

OLIVA Valencia
Azul Partida Rabdells (tel: 96
2854106)
Open April to October.

ALTEA Alicante
Cap Blanch Playa del Albir 25
(tel: 96 5845946)
Open all year.

BENIDORM Alicante
Armanello av de la
Comunidad Valencia (tel: 96
5853100)
Off N332 at Km123.1, north of
town.
Open all year.

TOUR 5
BAÑOS DE FORTUNA
Murcia
Fuente (tel: 968 685454)
Take the C3223 from Fortuna à
Pinoso to Balncario de Fortuna.
Site is signposted from this road.
Open June to 15 September.

AGUILAS Murcia
Calarreona ctra de Aguilas a
Vera (tel: 968 413704)
Near Km4 on N332.
Open 15 June to 3 September.

ALCAZARES, LOS Murcia
Cartagonova (tel: 968 575100)
On CN332.
Open July to September.

**GUARDAMAR DEL
SEGURA** Alicante
Mare Nostrum (tel: 96
5728073)
Turn towards the sea off the
N332 Alicante-Cartagena road
at about Km38.5.
Open 15 April to September

TOUR 7
GALLARDOS, LOS Almeria
Gallardos (tel: 950 528324)
Site is 500m from Km525 on
CN340.
Open all year.

ROQUETAS-DE-MAR
Almeria
Roquetas Los Parrales (tel: 95
343809)
West of Almeria turn off the
N340 at Km428.6. Site is 1.7km
from N340.
Open all year.

TOUR 8
TORRE DEL MAR Málaga
Torre del Mar (tel: 95 2540224)
Southwest of town; via N340.
Open all year.

TARAMAY Granada
Paraiso (tel: 958 632370)
Open all year.

CARCHUNA Granada
Don Cactus (tel: 958 623109)
On beach off N340.
Open all year.

GRANADA Granada
Sierra Nevada ctra de Jaen
107 (tel: 958 150062)
Within motel complex.
Open March to 3 October.

TOUR 9
FUENGIROLA Málaga
Calazul Mijas Costa (tel: 95
2493219)
Exit from C340 at Km200.
Open all year..

ESTEPONA Málaga
Parque Tropical (tel: 95
2793618)
Access via N340 at Km162.
Open all year.

SAN ROQUE Cádiz
Motel San Roque (tel: 956
780100)
Open all year.

RONDA Málaga
El Sur ctra de Algeciras
(tel: 095 2875939)
Open all year.

TOUR 10
CARLOTA, LA Cordoba
Carlos III (tel: 957 300697)
'La Carlota' exit from NIV.
Open all year.

***GRANADA** Granada
Sierra Nevada ctra de Jaen
107 (tel: 958 150062)
Within motel complex.
Open March to 3 October.

ALCALA DE GUADAIRA
Sevilla
Los Naranjos (tel: 954
5630354)
Southwest of Sevilla.
Open all year.

SEVILLA Sevilla
Sevilla (tel: 954 514379)
About 2km from airfield, 100m
from NIV at Km533.8.
Open 15 April to 15
September.

TOUR 11
*ALJARAQUE Huelva
Las Vegas (tel: 959 318141)
From Huelva cross the bridge
over the River Odiel and
continue for 8km towards
Punta Umbria. Site is sign-
posted.
Open all year.

*PUNTA UMBRIA Huelva
Derena Mar (tel: 959 312004)
Open all year.

*MAZAGÓN Huelva
Mazagón cuesta de la Barca
s/n (tel: 959 376208)
On coast road south of Huelva.
Open all year.

*SEVILLA Sevilla
Sevilla (tel: 954 514379)
About 2km from airfield, 100m
from NIV at Km533.8.
Open 15 April to 15
September.

TOUR 12
*SEVILLA Sevilla
Sevilla (tel: 954 514379)
About 2km from airfield, 100m
from NIV at Km533.8.
Open 15 April to 15
September.

*ALCALA DE GUADAIRA
Sevilla
Los Naranjos (tel: 954
5630354)
Southwest of Sevilla.
Open all year.

VEJER DE LA FRONTERA
Cádiz
Vejer ctra National (N340) (tel:
956 450098)
Open 15 June to 15 September.

CONIL DE LA FRONTERA
Cádiz
Cala del Aceite Roche Viejo
(tel: 956 440972)
South of N340 (Cadiz–Tarifa);
on coast.
Open all year.

**PUERTO DE SANTA
MARÍA, EL** Cádiz
**Playa Las Dunas de San
Anton** ps Maritimo de la
Puntilla (tel: 9566 872210)
Open all year.

TOUR 13
CALATAYUD Zaragoza
Calatayud ctra Madrid-
Barcelona (tel: 976 880592)
Open 15 March to 15 October.

NUEVALOS Zaragoza
Lago Park ctra Alhama de
Aragón-Nuevalos (tel: 976
849038)
Northeast towards Alhama de
Aragón. Off C202.
Open April to September.

TOUR 14
HUESCA Huesca
San Jorge Ricardo del Arco
(tel: 974 227416)
From town centre, about
1.5km along M123 towards
Zaragoza and follow signs.
Open April to 15 October.

*TIERMAS Zaragoza
Mar del Pirineo (tel: 948
887009)
West of Berdún on the N240.
Open Easter and May to
September.

JACA Huesca
At **GUASA**
Peña Oroel ctra Jaca-
Sabiñanigo (tel: 974 360215)
At Km13.8 off the C134 Jaca-
Sabiñanigo road.
Open 15 June to 15 September.

BIESCAS Huesca
Edelweiss ctra de Ordesa a
Francia (tel: 974 485084)
Turn right off C138 at Km97.
Open 15 June to 15 September.

*LABUERDA Huesca
Peña Montañesa ctra Ainsa-
Bielsa (tel: 974 500730)
Open all year.

TOUR 15
*NÁJERA La Rioja
Ruedo Paseo San Julian 24
(tel: 941 360102)
West of Logroño. Turn off the
N120 in Nájera and then

continue along the river banks,
just before stone bridge across
the River Majerilla, turn left.
Open April to October.

ESTELLA Navarra
Lizarra Ordoiz (tel: 948
551733)
Open July to August.

MENDIGORRIA Navarra
El Molino ctra N111 (tel: 948
340604)
Open all year.

ORICAIN Navarra
Ezcaba ctra Francia-Irun km7
(tel: 948 331665)
North of Pamplona. Turn off
N121 at Km7.3 towards
Berriosuso. Turn right and drive
uphill after crossing the bridge
over the River Ulzama.
Open all year.

TOUR 16
GETAFE Madrid
Alpha (tel: 91 6958069)
Open all year.

TOLEDO Toledo
Greco (tel: 925 220090)
On the southwest outskirts of
town. Approaching from the
town centre take the C401 and
drive southwest for about 2km.
Turn right at Km28 and drive
300m towards Puebla de
Montalban.
Open all year.

ARANJUEZ Madrid
Soto del Castillo ctra de
Andalucia 1 (tel: 91 8911395)
Turn off NIV at Km46. In the
village 200m beyond Firestone
petrol station turn sharply
northeast and continue for 1km.
Open April to September.

MADRID Madrid
Arco Iris (tel: 91 6160387)
From M40 (Madrid ring road)
take exit 36 to Boadilla del
Monte and continue towards
Villaviciosa to Km12.
Open all year.

TOUR 17
CUENCA Cuenca
Cuenca ctra Ciudad Bucautada
Km 8 (tel: 969 231656)

Open 15 March to 15 September.

MADRID Madrid
Arco Iris (tel: 91 6160387)
From M40 (Madrid ring road) take exit 36 to Boadilla del Monte and continue towards Villaviciosa to Km12.
Open all year.

**TOUR 18
MALPARTIDA DE PLASENCIA** Cáceres
Parque Natural de Monfrague ctra Trujillo (tel: 927 459220)
Open all year.

ALDEANUEVA DE LA VERA Cáceres
Yuste (tel: 927 560910)
300m south of C501 at Km47.1.
Open April to September.

MADRID Madrid
Arco Iris (tel: 91 6160387)
From M40 (Madrid ring road) take exit 36 to Boadilla del Monte and continue towards Villaviciosa to Km12.
Open all year.

**TOUR 19
SEGOVIA** Segovia
Acueducto (tel: 921 425000)
Southeast of city next to N601 at Km112.
Open April to September.

*ARANDA DE DUERO
Burgos
Costajàn (tel: 947 502070)
Just beyond town at Km162.
Open all year.

GARGANTILLA DE LOZOYA Madrid
Monte Holiday (tel: 91 8695065)
Turn off N1 (Burgos-Madrid) at Km69 towards Cotos and continue for 10km.
Open all year.

MADRID Madrid
Arco Iris (tel: 91 6160387)
From M40 (Madrid ring road) take exit 36 to Boadilla del Monte and continue towards Villaviciosa to Km12.
Open all year.

**TOUR 20
MÉRIDA** Badajoz
Lago de Proserpina Apdo 121 (tel: 924 313236)
Open April to 15 September.

* MALPARTIDA DE PLASENCIA Cáceres
Parque Natural de Monfrague ctra Trujillo (tel: 927 459220)
North of Cáceres on N630.
Open all year.

**TOUR 21
TORDESILLAS** Valladolid
Astral Camino de Pollos 8 (tel: 983 770953)
Open April to September.

SIMANCAS Valladolid
Plantió (tel: 983 590082)
On outskirts of town. Turn off N620 at Km132.2 and continue for 500m on narrow asphalt road and a long single track stone bridge over River Pisverga.
Open 15 June to 22 September.

CUBILLAS DE SANTA MARTA Valladolid
Cubillas (tel: 983 58500)
Entrance off the N620.
Open all year.

ARANDA DE DUERO
Burgos
Costajàn (tel: 947 502070)
Just beyond town at Km162.
Open all year.

SANTA MARTA DE TORMES Salamanca
Regio ctra Salamanca/Madrid Km4 (tel: 923 138888)
South of town, just off the N501. Behind Hotel Jardin-Regio.
Open all year.

**TOUR 22
BERGONDO** La Coruña
Santa Marta (tel: 981 791628)
Open April to September.

*LEIRO Orense
Leiro (tel: 988 488036)
Open all year, except November.

PORTONOVO Pontevedra
Paxariñas (tel: 986 723055)

Camping card compulsory.
Open all year.

SAN VICENTE DO MAR
Pontevedra
Siglo XXI (tel: 986 738100)
Open June to September.

SANTIAGO DE COMPOSTELA La Coruña
As Cancelas r do 25 de Xulls 35 (tel: 981 580266)
Open all year.

**TOUR 23
*VALENCIA DE DON JUAN** Léon
Pico Verde C/Santas Marchtas 18 (tel: 987 750525)
South of Léon, turn east off N630 at Km32.2 for 4km.
Open 15 June to 13 September.

*LLANES Asturias
Barcenas Antigua CN 634 (tel: 98 5402887)
Turn right at Arriondas and follow N634 coast road for 10km.
Open June to September.

*PERLORA-CANDAS
Asturias
Perlora (tel: 98 5870048)
Turn off N632 7km west of Gijon towards Luanco and continue for 5km.
Open all year.

**TOUR 24
SANTILLANA DEL MAR**
Cantabria
Santillana (tel: 942 818250)
Open all year.

CÓBRECES Cantabria
Cóbreces Playa de Cóbreces (tel: 942 725120)
50m from beach.
Open 15 June to 15 September.

COMILLAS Cantabria
Comillas (tel: 942 720074)
Open June to September.

LAREDO Cantabria
Carlos V pl de Carlos V (tel: 942 605593)
Turn off N634 (Santander–Bilbao) at Km171.6 into an avenue and drive towards the sea. Turn left before reaching

SPECIMEN BOOKING LETTER FOR RESERVATIONS

Spanish

Muy señor mio,
Desearia me reservara espacio por ....dias, a partir del ....hasta el ....
Nuestro grupo comprende ....personas todo comprendido, ...adultos y ....niños (....de años de edad).
Necesitarimos un espacio por ....tienda(s) y/o espacio para apacar nuestro choche/caravana/remolque.
Deseariamos alquilar una tienda de campana/caravan/bungalow.
Le ruego nos comunique los precios y nos informe sobre el depósito que debemos remitirle.

English translation

Dear Sir
I would like to stay at your site for ..... days, arriving on .... (date and month) and departing on ......(date and month).
We are a party of .... people, including .... adults and .... children (aged ....) and shall require a pitch for .... tent(s), and/or parking space for our car/caravan/caravan trailer.
We should like to hire a tent/caravan/bungalow.
Please quote full charges when replying and advise on the deposit required, which will be forwarded without delay.

the beach and drive round the roundabout in Plaza Carlos V to site.
Open May to September.

TOUR 25
ZARAUZ (ZARAUTZ)
Guipúzcoa
Talai Mendi (tel: 943 830042)
On the outskirts of town. At the Firestone filling station at Km17.5 on the N634 turn towards the sea on a narrow asphalt road and continue for 350m.
Open July to 10 September.

MOTRICO (MOTRIKU)
Guipúzcoa
Aitzeta (tel: 943 603356)
0.5km northeast on C6212 turn at KmSS56.1.
Open all year.

SAN SEBASTIAN
(DONOSTIA) Guipúzcoa
At **IGUELDO**
Garoa Camping Igueldo (tel: 943 214502)
Follow the signs to Monte Igueldo from town or beach, for about 4.5km to Igeldo.
Open all year.

ORIO Guipúzcoa
CM Playa de Orio (tel: 943 834801)
Turn off the N634, the San Sebastian-Bilbao road, at about Km12.5 in village of Orio. Shortly before the bridge over the River Orio take a road towards the sea and continue for 1.5km to site.
Open all year except November and December.

UNFAMILIAR ROAD SIGNS

ADUANA
Customs

ALTO! PARE
Stop!

CALZADA DETERIORADA
Bad road

CEDA EL PASO
Give way

CUIDADO
Caution

CURVA PELIGROSA
Dangerous bend

DESPACIO
Slow

DESVIACION/DESVIO
Diversion

DIRECCION UNICA
One way

ENTRADA
Entry

ESTACIONAMIENTO DE AUTOMOVILES
Car park

ESTACIONAMIENTO PROHIBIDO
No parking

OBRAS
Road works

PASO PROHIBIDO
No entry

PEATONES
Pedestrians

PELIGRO
Danger

SALIDA
Exit

INDEX

A

Aqüeducto de les Ferreres 21
Agreda 93, 94
Aguas, River 43
Aguero 78
Aguilas 33
Ainsa 90
Alava (province) 155–6
Albarracín 79, 81, 83–4
Alburquerque 124–5
Alcalá de Henares 105
Alcañiz 84
Alcoy o Alcoi 28–9
Alcúdia 37, 38
Aledo 32
Alhama de Murcia 32
Alicante 30, 31
Alicante (province) 31–2
Almería 42, 43
Almería (province) 43–5
Almuñécar 49–50
Alora 53
Alquézar 90
Altamira, Cuevas de 149–50
Andalucia 40–1
Anguiano 95
Ansó 87
Antequera 52, 53
Aracena 67–8
Aragon 78
Aranda de Duero 131
Aranjuez 99, 102–3
Arcos de la Frontera 73
Arenys de Mar 15
Arenas de Cabrales 147
Arganda 108
Arguedas 93
Arroyo de la Luz 125
Artajona 92
Asturias 132, 145–7
Ávila 110–12
Ávila (province) 110–12
Ayerbe 87

B

Badajoz 124
Badajoz (province) 124–5
Baena 62–3
Baeza 45, 47
Balearic Islands 6
Banyoles 18
Barbastro 90
Barcelona 8, 14, 19
Barcelona (province) 9–11

Basque country 132
Baza 45
Béjar 112
Belmonte 107
Benalmádena-Costa 55
Benalmádena-Pueblo 55
Benidorm 28
Berdún 87
Besalú 18, 18
Betanzos 135
Biescas 89
Bilbao 155
Blanes 15, 17
Bourg-Madame 11
Buitrago del Lozoya 119
Burgos 129–31
Burgos (province) 129–31

C

Cabo de Trafalgar 75
Cabo Fisterra 140
Cabra 61, 63, 64
Cabuérniga 150
Cáceres 120, 125
Cáceres (province) 112, 121–3
Cadaqués 18
Cadi Moixero, National Park 11
Cádiz 73, 75–6
Cádiz (province) 57–9, 73–7
Calafell 21
Calahorra 95
Calamocha 81, 82
Calatayud 81
Calella de Palafrugell 16, 17
Calpe 27
Cambados 139
Cambrils de Mar 21
Camprodón 12
Canfanc 89
Cangas de Onís 146, 146
Cantabria 132
Cap Formentor 37
Cardona 10, 11
Cares Gorge 145
Carmona (Santander) 150
Carmona (Sevilla) 61
Cartagena 33
Cartuja de Miraflores 130
Casares 55, 56–7
Castella de Palafuegell 16, 17

Castellar de la Frontera 59
Castellón 22
Castillo de Loarre 87
Castro del Río 62
Castro Urdiales 150–1
Catalunya 6
Cazorla 41, 45–6
Cervatos 150
Chiclana de la Frontera 75
Chinchón 103
Chipiona 76
Ciempozuelos 103
Cifuentes 106
Coín 59
Colmenar Viejo 116
Comillas 150
Consuegra 101
Cordillera Cantábrica 132
Córdoba 40, 62,
Córdoba (province) 62–4
Cornisa Cantábrica 153
Cortegana 67, 68
Cortijada de los Molinos del Río Aguas 43
Costa Blanca 6, 24–9
Costa Brava 6, 14–18
Costa de la Luz 40
Costa del Sol 40
Costa Dorada 6
Coto Doñana 67
Coto Nacional de los Quintos de Mora 101
Covadonga 146
Coves d'Artá 38
Coves del Drac 39
Coves del Hams 39
Cuenca 106, 108
Cuenca (province) 106–8
Cueva de la Pileta 57
Cuevas de Altamira 149–50
Cuevas de Santimamine 154
Cullera 26

D

Daroca 81, 82
Deià 7, 36
Denia 27

E

Écija 61
El Barco de Ávila 112

El Escorial 110–11
El Palmar 25
El Pardo 115
El Paular 116
El Porto, lagoon of 70
El Puente del Arzobispo 113
El Puerto de Santa María 73, 76
El Rocío 70
El Vendrell 21
Elche o Elx 31
Empúries 17
Estella 95
Estepa 64

F

Felanitx 39
Ferrol 135
Figueres 18
Fuendetodos 82
Fuengirola 56
Fuente Dé 145
Fuentevaqueros 53
Fuenterrabía 157

G

Galicia 132
Gandía 26–7
Getafe 103
Gibraleón 69
Gibraltar, Rock of 57
Gijón 146–7
Girona/Gerona 16, 17
Girona/Gerona (province) 15–18
Granada 40, 50, 51–2
Granada (province) 50–2
Grazalema 59
Grutas de las Maravilles 68
Guadalajara 106
Guadalajara (province) 106
Guadalest 28–9
Guadalquivir 61
Guadalupe 123
Guadix 47
Guernika-Lumo 154
Guetaria 154
Guipúzcoa (province) 153–4

H

Hornachuelos 61

Huelva 67, 69
Huelva (province) 68–71
Huércal-Overa 45
Huesca 86
Huesca (province) 87–90

I

Illescas 99
Isla de la Toja 139
Islas Cies 139
Itálica 67, 67

J

Jaca 88, 89
Jaen 46–7
Jardí Botànic de Cap Roig
16
Jerez de la Frontera 76, 77
Jimena de la Frontera 55,
59
Jota (dance) 78, 87

L

L'Albufera 25, 26
La Bisbal d'Empordà 17
La Bota 70
La Ciudad Encantada 106,
107
La Coruña 134, 135
La Granja 115, 116
La Línea 57
La Mancha 98–103
La Manga del Mar Menor
33
La Palma del Condado
71
La Rioja 78, 95
La Rioja (province) 78, 95
La Seu d'Urgell 11
La Unión 33
Laguna de Gallocanta 82
Laguna de la Fuente de
Piedra 53
Lagunas de Córdoba 64
Laredo 151
Las Alpujarras 51
Le Reitio 154
Lebena 146
León 143–5
León (province) 143–4
Lerma 130, 131
Levant 6
Lria 29
Lafranc 16, 17
Leida 22–3
Leida/Lérida (province)
11, 22–3
Livia 11
Logroño 95

Loja 52
Lorca 32, 33
Lucena 63
Lugo 136
Lugo (province) 136–7

M

Madrid 96, 99, 104, 109,
113, 114, 115
Madrid (province) 102–3,
105, 108, 110–11, 113,
115–16, 119
Magaluf 35
Málaga 48, 53, 54
Málaga (province) 48, 53,
55–57
Mallorca 7, 34–39
Manacor 38
Mansilla de las Mulas
145
Manzanarer el Real 116
Marbella 56
Matalascañas 67
Mazarrón 33
Medina Sidonia 73
Mérida 122, 123–4
Mijas 55, 55
Minas de Ríotinto 68
Miraflores de la Sierra
116
Moguer 67
Mojácar 43–5, 44
Monasterio de Piedra
81–2
Monasterio de Poblet
23
Monasterio de Santo
Toribio de
Liébana 145
Monasterio de Yuste 112
Monasterio de La Rábida
70, 71
Monestir de Lluc 36–7
Monestir de Monserrat,
see Montserrat
Monestir Santes Creus
23
Monforte 137
Montblanc 23
Montes de Toledo 101
Montes Universales 78,
81, 84
Montserrat 9–11
Mota del Cuervo 108
Motril 50
Murcia 32
Murcia (province) 32–3

N

Navalcarnero 113

Navarra 78
Nerja 49, 49
Niebla 70–1
Noia 140
Numancia 95

O

O Grove 139
Ojén 56
Olite 93
Olot 12
Ondárroa 154, 155
Orense 137–8
Orense (province) 137–8
Orihuela 32
Orihuela del Tremedal 81,
82
Orio 153
Osuna 64, 65
Oviedo 142, 147

P

Padrón 139
Palafrugell 16, 17
Palamós 16
Palencia 128–9
Palencia (province) 128–9
Palma de Mallorca 34
Palmeral de Europa 31
Palos de la Frontera 70
Pals 16
Pamplona 91, 92
Panticosa 89
Parc Natural del Delta de
L'Ebro 23
Parque Nacional de
Covadonga 116
Parque Nacional de
Ordesa 89–90
Parque Natural de Cabo
de Gata–Nijar 43
Parque Natural de Cazorla
46
Parque Natural de
Gzazalema 59
Parque Natural de
Monfragüe 121
Pedraza 118–19
pelota 155
Peñafiel 131
Penedès 20
Peñíscola 22
Peñón de Ifach 27
Petra 38
Picos de Europa 143, 144,
145
Piedrahita 112
Pinto 103
Plasencia 112

Plumbaria 28
Pollença 37
Pontevedra 139
Pontevedra (province)
138–9
Port d'Andratx 35
Port de Pollença 37
Port de Sóller 36
Portlligat 18
Porto Cristo 38
Potes 144, 145
Priego de Córdoba 61,
63
Puerto de Mazarrón 33
Puerto de Piqueres 93
Puerto de Somosierra
119
Puerto José Banús 56
Puigcerdà 11
Punta Umbria 70

Q

Quinto de Mora Game
Reserve 101

R

Reinosa 150
Retortillo 150
Riaza 119
Ribes de Freser 12
Ripoll 12
Rock of Gibraltar 46
Roncesvalles 92, 93
Ronda 58, 59
Rota 76
Royal Andalucian School of
Equestrian Art 77

S

Sabiñanigo 89
Sagunto 25
Salamanca 126, 127, 131
Salamanca (province) 127
Sallent de Gállego 89
Salvatierra 156
San Juan de la Peña 88
San Roque 55, 57
San Sebastián (Donostia)
152, 153
Sanlúcar de Barrameda
76
Sant Feliu de Guixols 15,
17
Sant Joan de les Abadesses
12
Santa Fé 53
Santa Fé del Montseny 13
Santander 148, 151
Santander (province) 127

Index & Acknowledgements

Santanyi 39
Santiago de Compostela 132, 140, 141
Santillana del Mar 149
Santiponce 67
Santoña 151
Santuario de la Fuensanta 32
sardana 18
Segóbriga, ruins of 108
Segovia 96, 115, 116–118
Segovia (province) 116–19
Sepúlveda 119
Serra de Tramuntana 35
Serranía de Cuenca 96, 107
Serrania de Ronda 55
Sevilla 40, 60, 61, 66, 72
Sevilla (province) 60–1, 67
Sierra de Albarracín 84
Sierra de Cazorla 46
Sierra de España 32, 33
Sierra de Gredos 96, 112
Sierra de Guadarrama 96, 112, 115, 119
Sierra Morena 40
Sierra Nevada 40, 51
Sierra Peña de Francia 127
Siguenza 106

Sitges 19, 20
Soller 36
Solynieve 51
Sorbas 43
Soria 94, 95
Soria (province) 94–5

T

Tabernas 43
Tafalla 93
Talavera de la Reina 113
Tamariu 16
Tarancón 108
Tarazona 93, 94
Tarifa 75
Tarragona 20, 21
Tarragona (province) 22–3
Teruel 84
Teruel (province) 82–5
Toledo 99–101
Toledo (province) 99–100
Tolosa 156–7
Tordesillas 131
Torla 89
Torredelvinagre 46
Torrelaguna 119
Torremolinos 55
Tortosa 22–3
Tossa de Mar 15

Totana 32
Trujillo 121
Tudela 93

U

Úbeda 46, 47
Ucles 108
Ujué 93
Utrera 73

V

Valdealgorfa 84
Valdemoro 103
Valencia 24
Valencia (province) 25–7, 29
Valencia de Alcántara 125
Valladolid 128
Valladolid (province) 128
Valldemossa 35
Valle de los Caidos 110
Valverde del Camino 67, 69
Vejer de la Frontera 73, 74
Vélez Blanco 45
Vélez de Benaudalla 50, 51
Vélez Rubio 45
Vélez-Málaga 49
Vic 13

Vigo 138
Vilanova i la Geltrú 20
Villanueva de Cañedo 127
Vitoria–Gasteiz 155–6

X

Xabia 27
Xátiva 29

Z

Zalamea la Real 67, 68
Zamora 127–8
Zamora (province) 127–8
Zaragoza 78, 80, 85
Zaragoza (province) 81–2
Zarautz 153
Zumaia 154

The Automobile Association
would like to thank the following libraries and photographers for their assistance
in the preparation of this book:

Michael Buselle Photolibrary 4, 25, 54, 79, 82/3, 83;
Pictures Colour Library 63b, 64/5, 122/3;
Spectrum Colour Library 21b, 24, 26, 38, 78, 96, 145, 151, 150/1, 154/5, 156/7;
The Travel Library 2, 44, 77, 117, 118/9, 133, 136/7, 149, 153.
The remaining pictures are held in the Association's own library (AA PHOTO LIBRARY) and were taken by:
P. Baker 7, 34, 35a, 35b, 36/7, 37, 39a, 39b, 152; J Edmunson 6, 27, 28/9, 30, 31a, 31b, 32, 33, 45, 47, 50b, 51, 52/3, 55, 56, 57, 58, 59, 62, 68b, 73a, 99,100, 101, 102, 103, 104, 105, 106, 106/7, 108, 113, 115, 116, 120, 121, 124, 125; P Enticknap 8, 9, 10a, 10b, 12/13, 14, 15, 16/17, 17, 18, 19, 20, 21a, 22/3, 48, 80, 81, 84/5, 85,86/7, 87, 88, 89, 90, 91, 923/3, 93, 94, 95, 110, 110/1, 126, 127a, 127b, 129, 130/1, 130, 132, 134, 135, 138, 139, 140/1, 142/3, 143, 144/5; 146, 147, 148; A Molyneux 40, 60, 61, 64; J Poulsen 49a, 53; D Robertson 41, 42, 43, 46/7, 49a, 50a, 63a, 66, 67, 68a, 69, 70, 71, 72, 73b, 74, 75; R Strange 97, 98, 109; J A Tims 114, W Voysey 161.
Front cover: Main picture: Tony Stone Images; Top picture: Zefa Pictures Ltd; Inside flap: Powerstock Photo Library. Back cover: (a) D Robertson; (b) R Strange; (c) S Day

Author's acknowledgements:
Mona King thanks the following for help: Turespaña, Madrid; TurMadrid, Madrid; The Spanish Tourist Office, London and Iberia Airlines of Spain.

Contributors
Copy editor: Helen Douglas-Cooper   **Indexer:** Marie Lorimer